America's Corporal

America's Corporal

James Tanner in War and Peace

JAMES MARTEN

The University of Georgia Press

Athens and London

The project is supported, in part,
by the Amanda and Greg Gregory Family Fund.

© 2014 by the University of Georgia Press
Athens, Georgia 30602
www.ugapress.org
All rights reserved
Set in Adobe Caslon Pro by
Graphic Composition, Inc., Bogart, Georgia
Manufactured by Thomson Shore
The paper in this book meets the guidelines for
permanence and durability of the Committee on
Production Guidelines for Book Longevity of the
Council on Library Resources.

Most University of Georgia Press titles are
available from popular e-book vendors.

Printed in the United States of America
14 15 16 17 18 P 5 4 3 2 1

Library of Congress Cataloging-in-Publication Data
Marten, James Alan.
America's corporal : James Tanner in war and peace / James Marten.
pages cm. — (Uncivil wars)
Includes bibliographical references.
ISBN-13: 978-0-8203-4320-4 (hardcover : alk. paper)
ISBN-10: 0-8203-4320-X (hardcover : alk. paper)
ISBN-13: 978-0-8203-4321-1 (pbk. : alk. paper)
ISBN-10: 0-8203-4321-8 (pbk. : alk. paper)
1. Tanner, James, 1844–1927. 2. United States. Army. New York Infantry Regiment, 87th (1861–1862) 3. Soldiers—New York (State)—Schoharie County—Biography. 4. Disabled veterans—United States—Biography. 5. Amputees—United States—Biography. 6. Veterans—United States—Biography. 7. New York (State)—History—Civil War, 1861–1865—Biography. 8. United States—History—Civil War, 1861–1865—Biography. 9. Cobleskill (N.Y.)—Biography. I. Title.
E523.587th .M38 2014
362.4086'97092—dc23 [B]
2013043277

British Library Cataloging-in-Publication Data available

For Linda, as always.

CONTENTS

ACKNOWLEDGMENTS

Normally I can't wait for a book to leave my house, but not *America's Corporal*. I learned of Tanner while writing *Sing Not War: The Lives of Union and Confederate Veterans in Gilded Age America* (a long-gestating book whose completion I definitely celebrated!) and decided I wanted to get to know the Corporal better. A chance conversation with Steve Berry coincided with a sabbatical from Marquette University, and this little book came together quickly and seamlessly—almost too quickly. I quite unintentionally finished the first draft on the 150th anniversary of the Corporal's catastrophic wounding at Second Bull Run, and ever since I've been a little sad about the project's inevitable end.

My greatest thanks go to UnCivil Wars editors Steve Berry and Amy Murrell Taylor, whose enthusiasm, good ideas, and collaborative mind-set made the entire process a pleasure. Research assistance was provided by a number of Marquette University graduate students, including Robert "B.J." Marach and the RAs who worked on *Sing Not War*: Kyle Bode, Charissa Keup, Stanford Lester, Chris Luedke, and Monica Witkowski. Friends and colleagues who responded to queries or offered sources or illustrations include Dan Blinka, Jasmine Bumpers, Charlotte D. Gdula (of the Buffalo Bill Center of the West), Bert Hansen, Courtney E. Jacobs (of the University of North Texas Libraries), Brian Jordan, George Kane, and Darlis Miller. The staffs at the Brooklyn Historical Society and the Brooklyn Public Library were also helpful, while Jeff McClurken provided useful comments on a paper that explored part of Tanner's story. At the University of Georgia Press, Mick Gusinde-Duffy, John Joerschke, Beth Snead, and David E. Des Jardines provided enthusiasm and efficiency, while Barb Wojhoski did a fine job of copyediting.

Finally, I thank Sabrina Ramoth, who called me out of the blue one day last summer wondering if I could help her figure out why there was a personal letter from Corporal Tanner and a typescript of an article he had written among her grandmother's effects. I couldn't help her, I'm afraid, but she helped me; the letter makes a poignant appearance in the last few pages of the book.

Of course, any errors of commission or omission are mine alone.

Although she's probably tired of my sometimes too-frequent references to the Corporal, I nevertheless dedicate this book to my wife, Linda. I hope she knows that, in fact, they're all for her.

America's Corporal

Prologue

No Regrets

It was Good Friday, April 14, 1865, and almost everyone in the squalid, bustling capital city wanted to celebrate. Just five days before, Gen. Robert E. Lee had surrendered the Confederacy's largest army at Appomattox Court House in Virginia. The war was finally ending, the Union would be preserved, and Leonard Grover, owner and proprietor of Grover's New National Theater—locals usually just called it Grover's or the National—pulled out all the stops. A lighthearted fantasy called *Aladdin, or the Wonderful Lamp* would set just the right celebratory tone. But Grover also decorated his theater with evergreen wreaths, arranged for the reading of an "Original Patriotic Poem," asked one of the cast members of *Aladdin*, Effie Germon, to sing a new song called "When Sherman Marched Down to the Sea," and mounted a "Magnificent Pyrotechnic Display" and a "Panoramic View"—a stage-sized painting—of Charleston Harbor and Fort Sumter, where the war had started almost four years earlier. As a matter of custom, Grover invited President Lincoln and his wife to watch from the private box he had built for them. The Lincolns chose instead to attend the production of a rather worn play called *Our American Cousin* at Ford's Theater. But a tutor took their twelve-year-old son, Tad, to Grover's for the child-friendly spectacle.[1]

Among the hundreds of others attending the gala was a young government clerk, James Tanner. Tanner was a boy from upstate New York who had joined the army as a seventeen-year-old in the fall of 1861. After recovering from the loss of his lower legs at Second Bull Run less than a year later, Tanner had learned to walk on prosthetic limbs; mastered the craft of stenography, or shorthand; and taken a clerk's job in the War Department. Tanner would describe the remarkable events of this April evening and his role in them in a letter he began writing a few days later to a former classmate named Henry Walch.[2]

Tanner's narrative skipped the patriotic poems, songs, and even the play and jumped directly to the moment just after ten o'clock, when someone threw open a theater door and shouted that the president had been shot. The audience gasped and many surged toward the exits, but others scornfully argued that it was simply a ruse of pickpockets hoping to take advantage of a panicked crowd. Most of the audience uneasily returned to their seats, and the play went on. Soon, however, the manager stepped onto the stage and confirmed that the president had been critically wounded.

Tanner and his friend hoped to discover more about the assassination at nearby Willard's Hotel, a favorite hangout for politicians and officers—the poet Walt Whitman once referred with contempt to the hotel saloon being "full of shoulder-straps." After learning nothing, they took a horse-drawn car to Ford's Theater, coincidentally located across the street from Tanner's second-floor flat on Tenth Street, between Avenues E and F. They found the street jammed with civilians and soldiers who had streamed into the neighborhood from saloons and other theaters. Gen. C. C. Augur, the military commander of Washington, and several soldiers and policemen maintained order; Tanner described the growing multitude as "very quiet" but "very much excited." He squeezed through the crowd, crossed the street, and entered the building next to the house where the president had been taken.[3]

Tanner hobbled up the stairs to his room and out to a balcony overlooking the street, where he watched generals, politicians, and other dignitaries arrive and depart and could hear occasional grim reports about the president's condition. Inside the Petersen House, as it came to be called, the irascible, gray-bearded secretary of war, Edwin M. Stanton, had begun hearing testimony from witnesses, but taking down evidence in longhand was too slow. Another government clerk on the scene knew of Tanner's training, and soon Augur called Tanner into the house.

Tanner managed to get down the stairs, through the soldiers and civilians crammed into the street and sidewalk, and into the middle room of the three-room flat. He sat at a small table, surrounded by most of the president's cabinet, several generals, and the chief justices of the U.S. Supreme Court and of the District of Columbia. "Never in my life was I surrounded by half so impressive circumstances," wrote the farm boy who had turned twenty-one just a week earlier. Across from him loomed Secretary of War Stanton, who had taken charge of the scene and spent most of the night writing hurried dispatches to military and police units hunting

In his letter to Henry Walch, Tanner claimed to have stood next to General Meigs, the officer leaning against the door frame. *Frank Leslie's Illustrated Newspaper*, April 29, 1865, Prints and Photographs Division, Library of Congress.

for the assassins. A judge sat next to Tanner, questioning a stream of witnesses, including members of the audience and the star of the play, Henry Hawks, who identified the shooter as the actor John Wilkes Booth. Tanner's initial excitement made for a shaky hand and nearly illegible writing, but he eventually settled down and scribbled without pause for more than four hours. Despite the coming and going of people and the large numbers crowded into the room at any given time, "a terrible silence pervaded the whole throng; it was a terrible moment." From time to time Tanner heard Mrs. Lincoln sobbing in the next room and "early in the morning heard her moan, 'O, my God, and have I given my husband to die?'"[4]

Tanner finished his work and slipped into the death chamber at about 6:45 a.m., joining army chief of staff Henry Halleck; U.S. senator Charles Sumner; Secretary Stanton; Lincoln's son Robert; his personal pastor, Phineas Gurley; and a few others. He claimed in his letter to Walch that he had stood between and just behind Secretary Stanton and Gen. Montgomery Meigs. Only the sound of men crying broke the silence; Lincoln's breathing gradually eased and finally stopped. When Reverend Gurley "offered up a very impressive prayer," Tanner fumbled for his pencil, hoping to record the words for posterity, but the lead had broken. In future years, Tanner's recollection of Stanton's benediction for the evening— "Now he belongs to the ages"—would become part of the official memory of the event.[5]

Stanton ordered Tanner to "take charge" of the testimony. The young man immediately went to his room and made a copy, keeping the original. He wrote to his friend, "[These documents] will ever be cherished monuments to me of the awful night and the circumstances with which I found myself so unexpectedly surrounded, and which will not soon be forgotten." The young New Yorker closed his letter by affirming the accuracy of two sketches of the death scene and of the Petersen House (which included a view of his apartment) published in *Frank Leslie's Illustrated* and by proudly reporting that an article in a Washington newspaper had quoted from the testimony he had recorded.[6]

All of this was a lot for a young man from Schoharie County, New York, to take in, and a few days later he was still processing what he had seen. "I would not regret the time and money I have spent on Phonography," he told Walch, "if it never brought me more than it did that night, for that brought me the privilege of standing by the deathbed of the most remarkable man of modern times and one who will live in the annals of his country as long as she continues to have a history." Yet that night was just the beginning of a life that would at one time make Tanner's name much more recognizable to most Americans than the names of many of the men with whom he had shared the stuffy, strangely silent little apartment.[7]

And yet he did not appear in the various sketches of the deathbed published in illustrated magazines at the time nor in subsequent paintings. There are many reasons for his disappearance from Americans' historical memory, but equally important are the reasons he became famous in the first place and why it matters. James Tanner intersected with virtually every major event from the Civil War through the turn of the twentieth century. He was a soldier during America's deadliest war, a politician during an infamous period in American politics, and an entrepreneur during one of the most entrepreneurial eras in history. Although he may not have been a "representative" man of the Gilded Age—his experiences were, in some ways, too unique to represent fairly a typical life—he certainly embodied many characteristics of the period. His brush with fame on that dark Good Friday was just the beginning of a lifetime of prominence.

Tanner frankly relished fame. He purposefully thrust himself into history, remaking himself whenever circumstances allowed or required. He stepped into the war and the world by joining the army before virtually anyone else from his tiny hometown; later, he would reframe his rather mundane military service to match more closely the country's image of a savior of the Union. His grievous injury must have crushed the teenager's hopes for the future, but ultimately that tragedy seems to have inspired him not only to learn how to walk again but also to learn new skills. Acquiring a taste for politics and government work, he moved to a new city to take advantage of political and cultural opportunities unavailable in upstate New York. He expertly navigated the political currents of his time to achieve notoriety and financial security. And despite the pain and difficulty posed by any kind of movement, he traveled the country for years, keeping himself in the public eye and weighing in on most of the issues of the day. The "Jimmie" who went off to war grew to be the "Jim" who read law and became a government clerk, then the "James" who became a leading advocate for veterans' interests, and finally "the Corporal" who became one of the best-known public speakers of the 1880s and 1890s.

We can never fully know a person from another age. But *America's Corporal* rescues from obscurity a man who, with intent and luck, threaded himself and his war deeply into the fabric of Gilded Age society, politics, and culture.

CHAPTER ONE

The War Hit Me and Hit Me Hard

Jimmie Tanner's Civil War

As a Union veteran, Tanner was part of the most recognizable single group of American men during the last third of the nineteenth century: 41 percent of all northern white men born between 1822 and 1845 served in the Union army, while an astounding 81 percent of all men born in 1843—just a year before Tanner's birthday—took up arms for the Union. In many ways, Tanner's military experience was typical: most of his time was spent drilling, marching, waiting. But when something finally did happen, it changed his life forever.[1]

Young in War

Four years before James R. Tanner recorded history in shorthand a few feet from the dying Abraham Lincoln, he had been a seventeen-year-old farmer and country schoolmaster in Schoharie County, a rural area west of Albany. Born on April 4, 1844, in 1860 he lived in the town of Seward with his father, Josiah, his mother, Elizabeth, and three siblings, twenty-four-year-old John, and twenty-year-old Julia and Job (apparently twins). In New York a "town" encompassed farmland as well as villages and hamlets; virtually all the residents of Seward actually lived on farms, with a few dozen families clustered in tiny hamlets.[2]

Later in life, Tanner identified much more with the *village* of Cobleskill; although his address growing up was actually Richmondville (a town sliced away from the *town* of Cobleskill shortly after Tanner's birth), the family farm was just a few miles from Cobleskill. Perhaps 360 people lived in the village, and the only businesses or institutions of note were a series of mills clustered along Cobleskill Creek, three churches, a general store, a hardware store, a two-room schoolhouse, and a large brick hotel called The National. Like Cobleskill, the other hamlets and villages in Schoharie

County sustained a few small lumber and flour mills and factories. Railroads would not reach the area until after the Civil War, when the economy began to flourish and the population began to grow. But prior to the war the place was better known as the site of frequent clashes between settlers and Native Americans in the early part of the eighteenth century and of tension between American patriots and pro-British Tories (and their Indian allies) during the American Revolution, as well as for a natural cave that would become a major tourist attraction in the 1870s.[3]

In a cheery, chatty memoir published by a local newspaper just a few months before his death, Tanner recalled first seeing the little town at the age of eight, when he and his mother walked over to Cobleskill to help with the hops harvest. He recalled the sunny early-autumn day and the warm spirit of cooperation and celebration that infused the neighbors and townspeople, who worked all day and then danced and drank all night.[4]

As an adult, "Jimmie," as he was called by many locals until he was a grown man, virtually never wrote about his family, and very little is known about them. A history of Schoharie published in 1882, when Tanner had already gained statewide fame, included short biographies of "Some of Its Prominent Men and Pioneers," but the only Tanner mentioned was James. Reporters and admirers would later tend to follow the same story line when describing Tanner's mostly generic childhood. "His early life was spent on the farm," went a typical account, "working in the fields in summer, and attending the district school in winter, besides 'doing the chores' about the farm which fall to the lot of every country boy."[5]

But there was something different about him. It is impossible to identify the source of the impetus—there is no reason to think his parents were particularly well educated—but census records reveal that, unlike most rural boys their age, both Jim and Job had attended school within the last year. And by the time the 1860 census was taken, Jim was a sixteen-year-old country schoolteacher. Other young men probably did the same (although no doubt few teenagers); before the Civil War local school boards in New York and most other states had the authority to issue teaching certificates to anyone they deemed qualified. His discharge certificate from the army reported his "occupation when enlisted" as "School Teacher," and he no doubt taught in one of the dozens of tiny one-room schools scattered throughout the county. The facilities were Spartan—wood-frame buildings painted white or red, long, backless benches rather than desks, perhaps a rough blackboard and a globe—and the curriculum straightforward and often taught out of borrowed books. Tanner's teaching career would be short-lived. As it did for millions of young Americans in 1861, the Civil War interrupted plans, inspired patriotism, and sparked a sense of adventure that would end tragically for perhaps a million dead, maimed, and wounded men.[6]

Tanner wrote frustratingly little about his one or two terms as a country schoolteacher, but there seems to have been evidence that even as a teenager he was a little more ambitious, a little more interested in things beyond the fields of his childhood. Yet sixteen-year-old Jimmie did not enlist during the first, enthusiastic response to President Lincoln's call following the surrender of Fort Sumter in April for seventy-five thousand volunteers to put down the "rebellion," as he called it. By mid-July over forty-six thousand New Yorkers had joined, mostly in two-year regiments. Later in the summer, after the Union defeat at First Bull Run, Lincoln authorized a vast increase in the Union army, calling for up to one million volunteers to serve for three years. Recruiting offices opened all over the state—apparently one in nearby Seward was open by fall—and over seventy-five thousand men were enrolled from New York during the second half of 1861.[7]

Tanner badly wanted to join these men, but his father's opposition meant that Tanner could not get the permission he needed to sign up as an underage soldier. Tanner once spoke of his enlistment in a speech at a veterans' meeting, in which he referred to himself as a "big, green country boy." Josiah had "brought [him] up to glory in [his] native land, and he believed that its liberties should be preserved at any cost." Despite the hundreds of times in his life in which he talked about this enlistment and service and the ways in which the war had changed his life, Tanner rarely spoke about why he so desperately wanted to go to war beyond this sort of generically patriotic ideal. Although Josiah and Jimmie both "wanted the country saved," the father didn't want *his* boy to go to war." After endless, unresolved arguments, Jimmie simply announced while working in the field beside his father one day that he intended to enlist. On the next rainy day, he slipped away from the farm, walked to nearby Seward, and was "duly mustered in." After communicating somehow with his father— perhaps he wrote a letter or asked a brother to act as intermediary—he received Josiah's approval and returned home for a short leave. Ironically, although many years later he wrote of his relief at having "the consolation of going to the front with his consent and blessing," it was literally the only time he ever referred to his father in writing.[8]

Drawing of the seventeen-year-old Tanner at the time of his enlistment. James Tanner, "Before Red Cross Days; or, Second Bull Run and the End of the War for Me," *American Red Cross Magazine* 11 (October 1916): 344.

Hundreds of thousands of young Americans could tell of similar decisions, of parental misgivings and reluctant acceptance, of journeys never before imagined. Tanner claimed to have never seen a train before he climbed aboard the one that took him to the army. It carried him to the camp of the Eighty-Seventh New York, where he joined Company C. Most Civil War companies and even regiments consisted of men from specific communities, which made Tanner's choice of unit somewhat of a mystery. The ten companies in the thousand-man Eighty-Seventh came largely from New York City, Brooklyn (then a separate city), and other parts of the New York metropolitan area, over 150 miles away. Parts of two companies came from Dresden in the Finger Lakes district of New York and from Whitehall, well north of Albany near Lake George, while Tanner's company came together in Brooklyn and Williamsburg. He never explained how he ended up in a regiment formed so far away, although it is possible that he simply refused to wait for the chance to join up with a hometown unit. Many years later, the *New York Times* reported that antiwar sentiment was widespread in Schoharie, and even that Tanner "was subjected to many jibes when it became known that he thought of enlisting." A local history confirms that Democratic, even pro-southern, ideas prevailed in the county, which eventually had to resort to high enlistment bounties to encourage men to enlist. In any event, it took a while for the patriotism of the other young men in the county to catch up with Tanner's. The 134th New York, recruited mainly in Schoharie County, would not take the field until several months after Tanner was wounded. At least three other local boys, Benjamin Harvey of Richmondville and Silas Shumway and Nicholas Hilton, both from Seward, ended up in the Eighty-Seventh; Silas and Nicholas also served in Company C with Tanner.[9]

As a result, unlike most other Schoharie men, Tanner and his two friends or acquaintances marched to war alongside strangers, unbound from the sense of community that united most Civil War–era regiments. The Eighty-Seventh was officially mustered into federal service in New York City, where it was sent for a few weeks of training. Just after reaching New York, Tanner came down with the measles, which kept him hospitalized from late November to early January. Tanner's illness was typical for Civil War armies. Although mid-twentieth-century children regularly survived bouts of measles, mumps, and other illnesses—by the twenty-first century, most children in the United States were vaccinated against these "childhood diseases"—they could be disabling and even deadly to Civil War–era soldiers. Many men developed secondary infections such as bronchitis and pneumonia, while some lost their hearing. Measles could render entire regiments at least temporarily out of action. During the first year of the war, when there were only about 280,000 men in the army, doctors treated over half a million cases of sickness. In fact, both Union and Confederate soldiers were more or less under siege by germs and diseases of various kinds throughout the war. Poor diets (hardtack or crackers, beans, fried pork, and only rarely vegetables or fruits) and even worse hygiene combined with physical exhaustion and hot, humid weather (most campaigns were fought in the South, after all) to ensure that few soldiers were ever completely healthy. Diarrhea or dysentery attacked 70 percent of Union soldiers at one time or another, while over half came down with malaria, and a quarter reported some sort of respiratory or digestive ailment. Obviously, most men had more than one of these common complaints.[10]

Tanner made a slow recovery but eventually rejoined his regiment, which was assigned to the Army of the Potomac, under the command of Gen. George B. McClellan. "Among the gallant array whose names have won deathless renown on the sanguinary fields of our great Civil War," wrote one of Tanner's many admirers, "none is more widely esteemed, or is more deserving of his fame, than that hero of the rank and file known [to] all men as 'Corporal Tanner.'" That was an extraordinary exaggeration. Although Tanner would never lie about his rather mundane military service, his many speeches and writings about the war would imply that his experiences had been much more dramatic than they really were; in fact, there is no evidence that the youngster ever fired his gun in battle. Indeed, Jim and his comrades in the Eighty-Seventh had little chance to earn glory on the battlefield. The highlight of their service probably occurred on the day that, after drilling for a month or two at Palace Garden in Manhattan, they made a stirring march through Brooklyn, home to most of the men in the regiment, up Fulton Street to City Hall, where the mayor presented them with an American flag and a white regimental flag featuring the city's coat of arms. This was probably Tanner's first exposure to the city where he would later spend twenty years of his life. The regiment then occupied defense works near Washington, D.C., for a couple of months.

In late spring 1862, the still-inexperienced recruits moved south with the 120,000 men of the Army of the Potomac in a bold campaign to capture the Confederate capital of Richmond. Although McClellan had irked his commander in chief throughout the early months of 1862 by refusing to deploy his magnificent army against the Confederates, he finally made a move in late spring. His plan was to move his army swiftly down the Potomac River and Chesapeake Bay to the southeastern tip of Virginia—the peninsula formed by the James and York Rivers as they flowed into Chesapeake Bay. From there he would march his army the seventy-five or so miles up the peninsula, take Richmond, and end the war.

In the meantime, despite his youth—he would turn eighteen while campaigning on the Virginia Peninsula—Tanner was promoted to corporal. A series of letters written by Silas Shumway, who had also made corporal, provide a sense of what Tanner's army life might have been like during the spring and summer of 1862. Silas filled his letters with homely details: reports of travel, sickness, and the weather, and news of the handful of other men from home who were in the regiment. He reported that they were encamped less than a hundred yards from the U.S. Capitol and that they could see Rebel fortifications across the Potomac River from one of their outposts near Alexandria, Virginia. His appointment as corporal relieved him from guard duty and gave him a monthly salary of fifteen dollars instead of the thirteen dollars privates were paid, but it also required him to stand in the front rank when in the line of battle. His letters described the regiment's lack of action during the Peninsula Campaign, but also reported the novelty of seeing a hot-air balloon ascend over Union lines to spy on the Confederates and of talking to the African American slaves who were all over the place (indeed, in one letter he remarked, "There are very few white women here now, but plenty of beautiful girls, partly white"). Although the enemy did not pose much of a threat to the Eighty-Seventh, exposure to the elements; the low, swampy terrain; and the frequent rains resulted in diseases that by May had begun claiming victims among his friends.[11]

That was pretty much the extent of the danger facing most members of the regiment. Despite the brilliance McClellan displayed in the campaign's first phase, his innate caution and chronic overestimation of Confederate manpower resurfaced, slowing his every decision and movement. He wasted a month laying siege to Yorktown, which was occupied by a Confederate force much smaller than his own. He pushed the Confederates back at Williamsburg and held off a Rebel attack at Fair Oaks. Yet after fending off several savage attacks by the Confederate army under their new commander, Gen. Robert E. Lee, during the week of fighting known as the Seven Days Battles, McClellan began a slow retreat back down the peninsula.

Well over sixteen thousand Union soldiers were killed, wounded, or captured during the long campaign, and the Confederates suffered more than twenty thousand casualties. For the most part, however, the Eighty-Seventh New York marched, stood guard, and prepared for actions they did not enter. They were present but not deeply engaged at some of the biggest battles of the campaign, including the siege of Yorktown, Malvern Hill, and Fair Oaks, where part of the regiment—but not Tanner's Company C—did engage the Confederates and suffered fourteen killed and forty-four wounded. Nine more men from the Eighty-Seventh were killed and seven wounded during other phases of the campaign.[12]

For his part, Tanner recalled sleeping cold in a muddy furrow his first night in Virginia, but he did not record any fighting. In a brief recollection of army life, Tanner remembered the feeling of the men before they had "seen the elephant," as some called the experience of combat: "We were all young in war then, and did not know the terrible scenes that awaited us."

In that instance, he was talking less about the captivating danger of combat and more about its results; when the Eighty-Seventh entered a deserted fortification, he was struck by the dozens of dead Confederates he saw, most of whom had been shot in the head. Tanner did come under fire on at least one occasion while picking blackberries to ease his constant hunger. A Confederate shell shattered the tree he was standing beside, showering him with splinters and bark. But that was apparently the greatest danger in which he found himself during the three months he spent on the peninsula.[13]

Both Legs Off

By June the Army of the Potomac had begun a slow withdrawal. At the same time, the Army of Virginia, under Union general John Pope, had begun gathering in northern Virginia to face a Confederate force under Gen. Thomas "Stonewall" Jackson, whom Lee had ordered north from Richmond. Fearing for the safety of the capital, President Lincoln ordered many of McClellan's men to reinforce Pope. By early August the Eighty-Seventh had joined Pope, the Army of the Potomac had all but abandoned the peninsula, and the bulk of Lee's Army of Northern Virginia had also headed north. Once again, the Eighty-Seventh found itself on the sideline for much of the fighting, which began in the middle of the month with skirmishes at a number of sites along the Rappahannock River. The fighting intensified to nearly daily engagements during the last week in August, as Pope and Jackson maneuvered and tried to determine what the other one was doing.

Toward the end of the month, the Eighty-Seventh was split up, with most of the regiment assigned to guard bridges and train depots extending southwest from Manassas Junction, including Bristow Station and Catlett's Station. It may have been during these two days just before the main battle started that Tanner and Silas Shumway shared an adventure when, after hearing from escaped slaves that there were Confederates in the nearby woods, they "went out and took three prisoners."[14]

Corporal Tanner took charge of a squad assigned to protect a bridge just south of Catlett's Station. If the enemy approached, they were to retreat back toward Manassas, firing their guns to warn the rest of the regiment of the Rebels' approach. The night passed uneventfully for the isolated squad of Yankees, but when they marched back toward Manassas the next day, they discovered that Confederates had swooped down on the outnumbered Eighty-Seventh, destroying millions of dollars' worth of supplies, killing several men, and capturing scores, if not hundreds, of others, including their commanding officer. The exact number of men captured is impossible to verify, but the regiment was, in effect, destroyed. After Second Bull Run, it would be absorbed by the Fortieth New York, which would take heavy casualties in the battle. As Tanner wrote many years later, "the regiment was scattered; great demoralization existed," and many members of regiment ended up missing or simply lost—"stragglers," in military terms. The official roster of the Eighty-Seventh suggested its collapse. Of its 1,014 men, 124 had deserted, 57 were captured, and 218 simply disappeared from the rolls, with the rather vague "no subsequent record" the only explanation. Combined with the 35 who died of disease and the 41 discharged for illness, well before the regiment had finished its first year in the field nearly half the men and many officers had melted away—with most never having fought in a major battle.[15]

Having failed to locate any of their officers, the men with Tanner and a dozen or more others found a sergeant, who led them to brigade headquarters. The commanding general complimented them on their "fidelity and stick-to-it-iveness" and told them to go into line with the 105th Pennsylvania, another regiment in the brigade. Two years later, when Tanner applied for a government pension, the commander of the 105th, Col. C. A. Craig, confirmed Tanner's account and commended him for his "good conduct and bravery."[16]

Although there was little evidence to support their claims, a few of Tanner's political opponents would later try to make an issue of the regiment's poor performance, suggesting, in the 1887 words of the editor of the *Grand Army Gazette and National Guardsman*, that the Corporal had been a "coffee cooler and straggler" and was wounded by a stray shell falling far from the battle line. Tanner was very sensitive about this issue and his regiment's mediocre war record and sought out members of the 105th Pennsylvania to support his version of events. He received several letters from men who clearly remembered the tragic wounding of a young boy. The men recalled the specifics of the regiment's movements throughout the days leading up to the battle, the small detachment of New Yorkers joining their regiment, and even the moments leading up to Tanner's wounding. Because of Tanner's youth, the unusual nature of his injuries, and the fact that he was apparently the only man hit on that part of the line, they had very specific memories of the day in general and of Tanner's injury in particular. It was a story they had told other veterans from time to time, and one had even written about it in his journal. One witness, a sergeant major, was outraged that anyone thought Tanner had been a shirker: "He must be a low-lived son of corruption and prompted by the evil one that would assert that you were not in line of duty when wounded."[17]

That debate would not occur, of course, until a quarter century after the war. The incident that would stick in those old soldiers' memories and provide the climax of Jimmie Tanner's war occurred on the second day of the Second Battle of Bull Run, fought on roughly the same ground as the war's first battle just over a year earlier. It began on August 29, when the heavy fighting between Jackson's and Pope's men ended in a stalemate. The next day Pope attacked again, unaware that the Confederates had been reinforced by the rest of the Army of Northern Virginia during the night. A Confederate counterattack crumpled the left wing of the Union army. At the same time, on the Union's far right, the soldiers of the 105th Pennsylvania and their new comrades from New York moved to a hillside near the front and prepared to support an artillery unit holding a position just over the hill. They came under fire when a Confederate battery spotted a few Yankees gathering peaches from a grove of trees at the crest of the hill. Officers ordered the men to fix bayonets and lie down. Tanner stretched out and crossed his legs at the ankles. A later newspaper article claimed he had learned the habit of crossing his legs while apprenticing as a tailor—the only reference to his being a tailor in the thousands of newspaper articles written about Tanner—but Tanner claimed that he had formed the habit as a little boy. A few minutes later a shell burst above him, and a whirring fragment struck his legs just above the ankles, virtually tearing off one foot and mangling the other.[18]

Tanner became just one of the thousands of Union soldiers wounded at Second Bull Run. Their "suffering," one eyewitness would claim, had "probably not been equaled ... during this war." The problem was the almost complete lack of appropriate medical care available to the wounded Yankees. A little more than a year earlier, the Union had gone to war with a few dozen ill-trained surgeons, no military hospital system, no way of delivering medicines, and no ambulances. Little had changed since then.[19]

"I was the first man wounded on that part of the line," Tanner recalled, "and it created quite a sensation in that immediate vicinity." Tanner's biographer gathered several eyewitnesses' accounts of the young corporal's

wounding. One of the men lying next to the young corporal, Isaac Lawrence, recalled that "the butt end of the shell came down, struck Tanner's
left ankle, and passing through that member, lodged in his right ankle, sev-
ering the left and shattering the right. Both feet hung by shreds of flesh."
Several comrades later recalled that the "plucky" youngster made some sort
of remark like "never mind, boys," or the more elaborate—and harder to
believe—"Yes, and if you don't get me out of here pretty quick my head
will be off."[20]

Tanner recalled that he had no idea how severely he had been wounded
until a nearby sergeant cried, "Good Lord! Look at that boy. He has both
legs off!" Tanner recalled, "My mind was never clearer in my life. It was, as
I say, a great shock; but about the only sensation I felt was one of numb-
ness—there seemed to be no immediate pain to speak of." Several soldiers
threw together a stretcher made of rifles and a blanket and rolled the boy
onto it, apparently face down. He was shocked to see his "feet dangling by
the skin as they hung off of the other end. Some kind-hearted soul gently
lifted them and laid them on the edge of the blanket." One of the men
handed him the fragment that had ripped into his legs; he held it for a
moment but dropped it. The soldiers rushed Tanner back to a field hospital
located in a farmyard about half a mile behind the lines.[21]

Tanner had been wounded just as the hard-pressed Union right had
begun to retreat. The day was lost, Pope would be removed from command, and Lee would lead his army into Maryland, where on September 17
McClellan and the Army of the Potomac would fight him to a standstill at
Antietam. Lee and his army would be back in Virginia by the end of the
month.

But none of that mattered to Tanner. Even as the Union line began to
crumble, the surgeon in charge of the chaotic field hospital took one look
at Tanner's shredded lower legs and decided to finish the job started by the
shrapnel. Someone began cutting away the young corporal's blood-soaked
trousers as the doctor opened a bottle of chloroform, held it to the boy's
nose, and told him to breathe deeply. Although popular images of Civil
War–era surgery has often suggested that men faced amputations by swal-
lowing a shot of whiskey and clamping their teeth down on a stick, most
surgeries were performed under anesthesia. In the field, as in Tanner's case,
the usual method was chloroform. Doctors had to work fast to control the
bleeding and to ensure that patients did not remain under the influence of
anesthesia too long (no one had studied the side effects of this new drug),

so they administered very small doses and kept patients unconscious for just a few minutes. Tanner's doctor took off the shredded right leg first. As he started work on the left leg, a shell exploded overhead; the entire group flattened, but no one was hurt. The next thing Tanner heard was someone saying, "He's coming to." The doctor, "without waiting to wipe [the blood from] his instruments . . . threw them into his saddle bag, threw the saddle bag over his horse, flung himself into the saddle and galloped away."[22]

Late in his life, Tanner told a gathering of veterans in New York, "The war hit me and hit me hard." But his remark was in the context of the long life he had lived since surviving his battlefield ordeal. In the rush of the moment, however, Tanner had assumed the worst. Even sixty years later, he recalled his panic as he became aware of his condition and of the army collapsing around him:

> I had recovered enough from the effects of the chloroform to realize some-what the situation from the rushing past us of men and the remarks of my comrades. Twilight had fallen and I had no doubt that it was not only the close of the day but the close of my life. . . . I rallied enough to argue with my comrades that it was a hopeless task to which they had set themselves and would simply result in all of us being taken prisoners. . . . But a great horror arose in my mind at the possibility of their being compelled to lay me down in the field or by the roadside to die alone; and I begged them to see if they could get me where there was anybody else, and then to leave me and seek safety for themselves.[23]

Tanner recalled his fear of dying, but he must have feared living nearly as much. Despite his limited combat experience, he had obviously seen muti-lated soldiers while spending months in a military hospital and marching and waiting on the edges of two of the biggest battles of the war. As Megan Kate Nelson has noted, Civil War soldiers were appalled by the destruction wrought on humans by the era's up-to-date military technology. Even a brief glimpse at a typical battlefield would have provided hellish scenes of dismemberment and gore. Tanner's description many years after the war of the head-shot bodies of the Confederates in the captured fortification had been a bit detached and generic. However, as a still-green eighteen-year-old, he must have been sickened at the torn jaws, spilled brains, and blown-out eyes he left unmentioned. Now that he had been terribly violated by a Confederate shell, he must have been terrified not only of death but also of a future life as a severely crippled man.[24]

The same group of men who had carried Tanner to the field hospital now sought a safe place for their comrade. Eventually they found a farmhouse crowded with critically wounded Yankees, where, Tanner later estimated, 170 men were lying on the floors or in the dirt and grass in the yard.[25]

At that point his friends took turns shaking the young corporal's hand and dashed off to join the retreat. Everyone seemed to think, as did Tanner, that they would never see one another again. At one point in the ordeal, Silas Shumway stopped to say good-bye. According to a letter he wrote just a few days later, Tanner had told him, "I feel badly enough, but how will our poor folks feel when they hear of this?" Tanner's best friend in the regiment, Corp. Jonathan Sproul, who had been "Jonathan to [his] David"—a biblical reference meaning that Sproul had been protective and generous, rather a big brother to the young Tanner—was last to lean over the stretcher. Tanner recalled, "[As he] clasped my hand he could not speak for an instant. The tears from his eyes splashed on my face; and then, with a quick grasp of the hand, he sobbed out: 'Goodbye, old boy, 'til I come over.'"[26]

In later years, after Tanner was famous, newspapers would occasionally report on the men who had carried Tanner from the field or witnessed the event. More than forty years later, the death of William Shute, "a veteran of the civil war, who saved the life of Corporal Tanner," was reported in an Oklahoma newspaper. In 1906, a Minneapolis paper published a short article about a man who had recorded the wounding of the young corporal in his diary but did not realize who it was until Tanner was a public figure and actually stayed in a local veteran's home after delivering a lecture in Quincy, Illinois. When showing the document to Tanner, the men came across the entry on Second Bull Run that told the striking tale of the young victim of a Rebel shell. Years later Tanner would reward with jobs at least two of the men who had helped him that day; Isaac Lawrence survived the war and became a clerk in the Brooklyn city government when Tanner was collector of taxes, while Shute was given a job in the Pension Bureau later in the decade.[27]

But all that would take place in the impossible-to-imagine future. Within fifteen minutes of the departure of the last healthy Yankee, Tanner and the other wounded men were prisoners of the Confederates.

CHAPTER TWO

Living with Disability
Jim Tanner Reinvents Himself

There have always been disabled people in the United States, of course, and during the nineteenth century industrialization and the development of railroads led to a dramatic increase in the number of men disabled in work-related accidents. But the Civil War would lead not only to over six hundred thousand deaths but to the disabling of hundreds of thousands of other men by sickness, injuries, and a combination of poor diet, exposure to harsh weather, and grinding toil. Disabled soldiers would become a powerful symbol of the costs of war. Some would wear their empty pinned sleeves as badges of honor. Some, worn down by their injuries, resorted to begging, while others simply faded back into their families and communities. Jim Tanner belonged to this massive group of men ruined by war, but he was also one of many who fought back. His successful battle to overcome his grievous injuries certainly reveals a set of strengths particular to him, but it also reflects something about the values and opportunities of the era.

The fame and fortune that would eventually come to Jim Tanner were impossible to imagine as he lay in a filthy field hospital in Virginia, hovering between life and death, experiencing the worst of the limited medical knowledge of the time. The war changed Tanner, as it changed every man who experienced its sharp end. It turned him into a different person physically, tottering on artificial legs and suffering constant pain. But the physical limitations wrought by the war would also lead him to embark on a determined, often painful course of self-improvement and self-reliance.

A Nervy Little Cuss

For many years Tanner had no idea who had cut off his legs a few inches below the knee. He knew the names of the five men who had carried him from the field, but as he stated on more than one occasion, he did not know the name of the surgeon who had slashed his mangled feet off above the ankle, tossed his bloody instruments into a saddlebag, and galloped away from the advancing Rebels. Twenty-eight years after the war, however, after Tanner gave a public lecture in the small Michigan city of Hillsdale, a member of the audience asked, "Where and how did you lose your legs?" As he had on countless occasions, Tanner described the scene but also mentioned the mystery of the surgeon's identity. "I performed the operation," a man in the audience abruptly declared. He was a much-loved local doctor named Robert A. Everett who had lived in the town since before the war. When Everett asked if he could take a look at the stumps, the Corporal let the doctor unstrap his prosthetics. After a "thorough examination," Dr. Everett declared that he remembered the case clearly. At the time he was the twenty-two-year-old assistant surgeon of the Fifth Michigan. He had sliced off Tanner's feet "very much in haste," then, leaving him "under the influence of chloroform[,] rolled up [his] surgical instruments and got out of the way of the enemy." Not surprisingly, he had not recorded Tanner's name, company, or regiment; in his postbattle report, he had simply labeled the patient "unknown." Tanner and Everett became friends and later visited the site of the field hospital together.[1]

It is almost inconceivable to modern readers that a twenty-two-year-old—just four years older than Tanner—would be put in Everett's position, but such was the state of medical education and military medicine in the 1860s. Everett was, in fact, better trained and more experienced than many. He had received a two-year MD degree from the state university and practiced medicine with his father for two years before joining the army; he had also been in combat prior to Second Bull Run, as the Fifth had seen hard fighting during the Seven Days Battles. Like Everett, most doctors were trained by other physicians or by taking a few semesters of classes at one of the medical schools that had begun appearing earlier in the century. There were no such things as internships or residencies, and although some newly certified doctors may have dissected a dead body, most would merely have observed a professor cutting up a cadaver in a lecture hall.[2]

The doctors charged with caring for the sick and wounded were obviously not trained as combat surgeons, and the U.S. Army Medical Department was woefully unprepared for the scale of the carnage at battles like Second Bull Run, where over twenty-two thousand Yankees and Rebels were killed or wounded. Another doctor in his early twenties described a scene on a different part of the battlefield remarkably like the one that

Tanner encountered, where retreating Union soldiers had also left behind badly hurt comrades:

> The army left, and left me practically stranded. . . . I found in the little church in Centreville one hundred wounded men who needed attention. . . . All of these men were severely wounded, for the slightly wounded marched away with the army. Upon a few mattresses, and with almost no other conveniences or comforts, the men were laid in rows on the floor. Most of them had in fact not even a mattress, but only a little straw under them, and this in a very little time . . . became soiled and had to be diminished daily. The bed-sores which followed were something frightful, often larger than an entire hand; and when we add to this the secondary hemorrhages, which often soaked the floor before they could be arrested, one can have an idea of the sufferings of these poor fellows, and of the task of those who were caring for them.[3]

That was also the situation facing Tanner at twilight on August 30, 1862, when he and dozens of other severely wounded Union soldiers lay in and around a ravaged farmhouse praying vainly for medical attention. Tanner recalled just one image from that first night of horror. A single Union surgeon had been left behind to do what he could for the abandoned Yankees; Tanner became conscious at some point in the evening and overheard the doctor tell a fellow sufferer that his stomach wound was mortal and that he would die before morning. After sighing deeply, the man asked the surgeon to pass along detailed instructions to his wife about how to deal with his property and other financial matters. He paused, and the surgeon asked, "Is that all, my friend?" The man replied, haltingly, "No, that is *not* all! I am leaving two little boys behind. Oh, my God!" He pulled himself together and asked the surgeon to "say to his wife . . . to rear those boys so that if . . . the country should need their services they would give them, even unto their lives, as cheerfully as . . . their father gave his life." The next morning the man was dead. Many years later, Tanner called the dying soldier's desperate words "one of the finest orations on patriotism which my ear has ever drunk in."[4]

Tanner would no doubt have been listed in "critical condition" in a modern hospital, but he stood a better chance of surviving than the anguished young father from Michigan. On or off the battlefield, amputation was the only major surgery that left patients much chance of survival. Surgeons performed about thirty thousand amputations on Union soldiers—over a fourth lost all or part of an arm, while about a third lost all or part of a leg—and just under three-fourths survived, with the best results on men whose amputations occurred farthest from the trunk (in other words, Tanner's chances of surviving his amputations were much better than if surgeons had taken his leg at the hip).[5]

Although statistics suggest that Tanner's prognosis was actually fairly positive, he first had to survive ten days of indifferent care by his Confederate captors. He was wounded on a Saturday; on Tuesday he was carried out to a spot under an apple tree behind the house. His hazy memory of the first few days indicated that the only attention given him was an occasional drink of water. Burning up with fever, Tanner was constantly thirsty. When a thunderstorm boiled up in the late summer heat, he lay with his mouth wide open, desperately seeking relief. Later in the day, a Confederate soldier loaned him a canteen full of fresh water and said, "Here, Yank; God knows if this will do you any good, you are welcome to it." Despite his gentleness with the dying soldier, the Union surgeon who had been left behind turned out to be less than useless. He was drunk most of the time and barely paid attention to the men he was supposed to be nursing.[6]

Eventually Tanner and five other amputees—"the six of us had had seven legs amputated," he wrote, in a story that he told time and again throughout his life—were placed in a small tent with a wooden floor. They were virtually ignored as they lay, nearly naked, with only a dirty rubber blanket below and a somewhat gratuitous (considering the heat) blanket above for bedding. Flies were everywhere. The drunken doctor made one appearance in the tent and promptly stepped on one of Tanner's stumps; "for the first time," Tanner remembered, "in all that horrible experience I screamed with agony." Other wounded men crawled around and near the farmyard, retrieving food from the abandoned haversacks that still littered the area. In another story Tanner told often, a severely wounded man—a shell fragment had pierced his side—painfully pulled himself along the ground by clutching at clumps of grass, collecting fallen apples. He crawled to the opening of the amputees' tent and handed the apples in one at a time as Tanner distributed them to his tent mates. It was one of the last things that the unnamed soldier did; he was dead by nightfall.[7]

After a week and a half, Tanner and the other wounded were finally sent to Fairfax Seminary Hospital, a U.S. Army facility less than a day's ride away. First, they had to sign a parole promising not to fight again until they were officially "exchanged" for paroled Confederates. Although it was a moot point for Tanner, when the Confederate officer recording his name and unit said, "Poor boy, you'll never do us any more harm," Tanner replied with the spunk and optimism that would characterize his attitude during the painful months and years that would follow: "I presume that's so, Johnny, but don't forget that while the flesh is weak the spirit is mighty willing." The wounded Yankees were piled into ambulances that lurched over rough roads, fields, and rocky creek beds; the men bounced and bumped against each other and cried out in pain, until the driver passed around a bottle of whiskey. "Truth compels me," wrote Tanner, who would intermittently make temperance a minor part of his public persona, "to confess that we lay there and drank that whiskey until we were in a drunken stupor." It was the only way they could endure the daylong trip.[8]

Silas Shumway checked in on Tanner right after his transfer to the hospital. "His wound was in bad condition," he reported in a letter home. A few weeks later, when he wrote that Jim was about to be discharged and sent home to New York, Silas wished that "conditions were such that [he] could go with him and spend a couple of weeks with [his family]." Although he hoped to be home "before many months," Silas would never return to Schoharie County. He was killed in action in May 1863.[9]

It was far from sure that Jim would make it home either. Relieved finally to be in a proper hospital, Tanner was ignored until he demanded attention. The doctor immediately began his examination, stopping to curse from time to time when he found maggots infesting the boy's stumps and bedsores on his back that in some places had ground down to the spine itself. "I have heard profanity in my time," Tanner wrote, "but I have never heard anything to excel that in which Doctor Smith indulged when he fully grasped the condition I was in." At one point in the extraordinarily painful process of cleaning and wrapping the wounds, the doctor asked why Tanner remained quiet. "I don't belong to the yelling kind," he replied. Later, when the doctor warned the eighteen-year-old that the condition of his back was actually much more dangerous than his legs and that he might have no more than a one-in-one-hundred chance of surviving, Tanner said, "Well, all that I can say, Doctor, is—wade in on that one chance and I will back you up to the best of my ability." It was at that point, Tanner wrote later, that "the long, hard struggle began." Tanner learned much later that at dinner that night the doctor had told the rest of the staff about the "nervy little cuss" at the far end of the ward.[10]

Tanner had survived indescribable pain and hardship in the days since his injury, but the most dangerous moment came when the doctor quietly told him that the bedsores on his back had become infected with gangrene and that, unless it was treated, he would certainly die. The surgeon obviously had no choice but to act quickly. "Hospital gangrene," as Tanner's condition was called, was perhaps the most feared disease among patients in Civil War hospitals. The fast-moving infection could consume a half inch of flesh in half an hour, growing from a small, dark spot on an arm or a leg into what one historian of Civil War medicine calls "an evil-looking, exquisitely painful, putrid-smelling mass of decaying flesh." The death rate was 50 percent; worse still, it was highly contagious and could infect an entire ward in a matter of days. The only treatment for gangrene at the time was cauterization with nitric or hydrochloric acid. The manual that many military surgeons would have consulted recommended "mopping the affected surface freely with strong nitric acid," which would have caused intense burning and pain and turned the skin yellow. The chemical was so strong that, if used without adequate ventilation, the fumes could cause respiratory damage. An article published just a few years after the war urged doctors "to apply strong fluid caustics boldly," perhaps even injecting them into tissue surrounding the wound to ensure that "every germ of the disease . . . be destroyed." Tanner "had some realization of what this meant and the agony it would involve," but he had "made up [his] mind to battle to the limit and do [his] part in every way, shape, and manner," so he gave the doctor permission to proceed.[11]

The next few moments were among the worst of his life. "It seemed afterward that . . . hell would have no terrors for me after the siege I went through there." Although sometimes doctors administered anesthesia during procedures like this, Tanner was awake through all of it. Lying "prone upon my face . . . I bit the pillow and suppressed all the groans I could while they seared and seared and seared."[12]

Tanner passed the next few days in that weird state when time seems to crawl, yet passes, as he wrote, "unheeded." He lay on his stomach, sometimes looking out the window. Around the third day of his stay at Fairfax, his brother John suddenly appeared. After hearing of his brother's wounding (perhaps from a relative of Silas Shumway), John had gone immediately to Washington to search for his brother in the city's many hospitals. He finally came across a man who knew of a double amputee at Fairfax, which led him to Tanner's bedside.[13]

The Tanner brothers' temporary home during those weeks was located in an abandoned Episcopal seminary (it survived the war and is now Virginia Theological Seminary). If Jim had been at all able to explore his surroundings, he would have found a reasonably well-run facility, eventually able to treat 1,700 men at a time. According to Jane Stuart Woolsey, a nurse who came to work in the hospital just after Tanner left, the stately brick buildings and tree-studded grounds retained their peacetime beauty, although the surrounding countryside had been stripped of trees by the Union and Confederate armies that had campaigned in the region during the first year of the war. Two hundred patients occupied the main building, but most of the wounded and sick, including Tanner, were housed in a series of wooden barracks down the hill from the main building, not far from the cemetery that would eventually hold five hundred Union soldiers. The wards had plenty of windows and rested on footings that allowed air to pass under the building; ventilation, experts believed, would help prevent disease. Oddly, however, the barracks were located near the horse stables and latrines, which supported huge colonies of flies and no doubt made the air almost unbreathable at times. Fairfax was just one of what would become a vast system of military hospitals; by war's end there would be over two hundred, with more than 120,000 beds.[14]

Tanner did not provide more details about the state of his wounds during this point in his recovery. He may have received painkillers in the form of morphine—sometimes applied directly to the wound before the bandages were applied but taken orally afterward. His stumps would have been smeared with a poultice, or cream, made from flaxseed to prevent inflammation, covered in lint (scraped from flannel and other cloth by nurses in the hospital or by women and children back home), and then wrapped in several yards of linen bandages. Hanging out of the ends of the bandages would have been at least several—and perhaps as many as twenty—silk strings. Each was attached to a ligature, or knot, used to tie off arteries. When the arteries had rotted away and no longer carried blood, the ligatures could be pulled off. Although it apparently did not happen to Tanner, a constant worry was that the ligatures would come loose, causing dangerous bleeding and forcing surgeons to reopen the wound and repeat the procedure.[15]

Once Tanner survived the cauterizing of his near-deadly bedsores, most of the treatment consisted of keeping his wounds clean and building up his strength. Without a scientific approach to hygiene and countless other facets of medical care that modern Americans take for granted, hospital stays were not only longer than we would consider normal; they were also more dangerous, as infection, diseases, and other complications could occur at any time. Neither Tanner's reminiscences nor Woolsey's recollections mention any sort of physical therapy and certainly no occupational therapy. Antibiotics were still unknown, so infections had to be left to run their course. Many American doctors still believed that the best therapy for almost any condition was to relieve patients of excess fluids by "bleeding" them with a number of small incisions, purging them by administering drugs that caused vomiting or diarrhea, or raising blisters on various parts of the patient's body. This so-called heroic therapy was popular from the late eighteenth until well into the nineteenth century and was still being employed by some doctors in the 1870s and 1880s. Of course, although nineteenth-century doctors would not have known it, these treatments would have caused dangerous levels of dehydration, while purgatives such as calomel contained toxic substances such as mercury, which caused extreme salivation and loosened teeth.[16]

Tanner seemed to improve enough after the cauterization to have avoided such treatments, so mostly he waited. He likely witnessed major procedures performed on other patients; like the caustic treatment of his back, many operations in army facilities took place in full view of nearby patients. At a Union hospital in Tennessee, for instance, a young officer who had survived the amputation of a foot was surrounded by other amputees. He witnessed two bleed to death when their wounds hemorrhaged and watched another die after the flesh on his remaining leg began to wither, leaving several inches of bone protruding from the decaying stump.[17]

The doctors in charge of Fairfax believed that diet played an important role in a patient's recovery from wounds or disease, although some of the decisions they made about what to feed the men in their care seem questionable today. Indeed, Woolsey wrote that the chief surgeon "believed in food as a curative agent" and "ordered it in large quantities for men who had suffered severe operations." Doctors prescribed different meals depending on the condition of the patients. Men consumed various kinds of gruel (cereal boiled in milk or water), eggs (raw or soft-boiled), dried beef and crackers, chicken and potatoes, even stewed oysters and custard. What seems particularly odd to modern Americans is the amount of alcohol they were prescribed. Virtually everyone received brandy for days or weeks at a time, in a "milk-punch," mixed with eggnog, or even straight up. A milder alcoholic concoction was "wine-whey," made of milk and white wine. The central place of alcohol in Civil War–era medicine is reflected in the fact that, when young Dr. Keen headed out to the hospital in Centre-ville in August 1862, he took with him 4,800 bottles of whiskey, brandy, and sherry, and 2,600 blankets. Assuming that each patient was supposed to receive one blanket, then it would mean that each patient was also expected to consume well over a bottle and a half of an alcoholic beverage in a matter of days![18]

John Tanner acted as a kind of auxiliary nurse to his brother, shopping for food that might tempt James's poor appetite and fashioning a device so that he could lie on his back without putting pressure on his infected wound. Eventually they moved into a semiprivate room, where John could sleep in the next cot. James became accustomed to hearing the "Dead March" played on a fife and drum most afternoons at four when the men who had died during the previous twenty-four hours would be buried after a simple military funeral. He even enjoyed a visit from the men who had carried him off the field, who could hardly believe he was still alive. Tanner's memoir does not necessarily support Woolsey's contention that the wounded men she nursed a few months after Tanner left the hospital "were marvels of good and even gay humor." Rather, he seemed to remember being bored and rather impatient, badgering his doctors about when they would release him. They told him he could go when he felt ready.[19]

The eighteen-year-old apparently thought he was ready sooner than the medical staff. Against his doctor's wishes, Tanner finally ventured out into the world as a man—a boy, really—with stumps for feet on October 15, 1862, less than two months after the shell fragment had ended his military career. Because his injuries were apparently still very tender, attendants carefully laced a makeshift uniform onto his body. Tanner still had his old army cap, with its red diamond insignia denoting the division in which he served: the Third Division of the Third Corps of the Army of the Potomac. Putting it on made him feel "almost thoroughly dressed." The trip home took about two weeks: first to Washington in an open carriage; then by overnight train to New York (he lay on a makeshift bed built by a group of soldiers with their overcoats and blankets), with a quick stop in Philadelphia, where the ladies of the famous Cooper Refreshment Shop brought snacks and drinks to him on the train; a weeklong stay in a friend's house in Albany; and then the last fifty miles over two days back to Scoharie. By November, he was home at last, as he described it, "In the arms of my mother, and back on the old farm, from which I had gone out in such high hope less than fourteen months before, and where now I must lie for many months and look out over the fields I had played over and worked on, but over which I could roam no more." As he recalled, at least, once his desperate fight for survival had ended, once he was confronted at the age of eighteen with a life of hardship and dependence, he committed himself to finding some way of creating a useful life despite his handicap.[20]

Living with Disability

Tanner's double amputation was something of a rarity, and everyone who met him instinctively felt sorry for the teenager. A local doctor happened to be on hand when the Tanners' carriage arrived at a town (now called Altamont) on the Albany–Schoharie Plank Road about twenty five miles east of Richmondville. Seeing "a boy minus both legs" being "gently carried" into the station's dining room, the doctor followed and, as Tanner rested on a table, changed his bandages. Many years later, the *Altamont Enterprise* published a memoir of a local resident who as a youngster witnessed the same scene. He described the patient as a "smiling boy," who sat with his back against a wall. "Between mouthfuls of food, the soldier joked and smiled and answered the questions fired at him." The little boy stood near the door, no doubt shocked to get such a close look at the havoc war could wreak on the human body, until the young soldier asked, "What's the matter, sonny?" The boy—probably only a few years younger than the eighteen-year-old Tanner—asked, "Corporal Tanner, will you ever walk again?" Tanner shot back with the confidence and prescience that only a memoir published ninety years after the event can provide: "You bet I will. I'm going home to Richmondville, 'till I'm all healed up, then get me some store legs and maybe—maybe someday I'll get back to Washington."[21]

If this story seems too pat to transcend the apocryphal—in fact, when it was originally published, it went on for several long paragraphs to chronicle all the accomplishments of Corporal Tanner as he beat the odds and, by God, did end up back in Washington—it does reveal the two salient facts about Tanner's postwar life: in a very real way, he would never again be completely independent, but he would also virtually never complain about it. As one historian has recently written, severely wounded soldiers from the Civil War era were remarkably taciturn when it came to explaining their suffering. They were part of a culture that did not reward men who betrayed too much emotion, especially when it came to long-term physical maladies. They might describe their injury or illness but refused to reflect deeply on how they endured it. Incredibly, two-thirds of Union soldiers who lost a limb actually returned to duty, usually in the Invalid Reserve Corps, where they served as guards, clerks, or in other noncombat roles. Such men, despite their severe wounds, "rarely discussed the emotional impact of wounds or prolonged illness," and Tanner followed suit.[22]

Yet the problems caused by his wounds were many. Over and above the difficulties of getting around on the crude prosthetics then available to him, Tanner faced constant pain for the remaining sixty-plus years of his life. Apparently the problem was that the stumps had never healed properly. There is no record of what amputation technique was used on the young corporal, although the surgeon told Tanner many years after the operation that "he did not believe there was ever a limb amputated quicker." In the haste and confusion and even panic that gripped the field hospital in the trees just behind the collapsing Union line, it is not surprising that the job was done rather poorly. The procedure likely performed on Tanner was listed in the *Hand-Book of Surgical Operations* published during the war as an "Amputation of the Leg at the 'Place of Election'"—about four inches below the knee. On four illustrated pages, the *Hand-Book* provided detailed instructions for making a circular incision in the skin and muscle, pulling the flesh away from the wound "like a cuff," marking and sawing off the fibula and tibia at a slight angle, and carefully cutting the skin to make a four- or five-inch flap; there were "double" and "single" flap methods, but it is impossible to tell which was carried out on Tanner's legs. Of course, in the heat and dust and fear of the moment, the young surgeon probably took a number of shortcuts. Interestingly, Tanner actually appears in a footnote as one of only five examples of successful double amputations of a certain type (out of over seven hundred) in the multivolume *Medical and Surgical History of the War of the Rebellion*, which was compiled from thousands of after-action reports from regimental surgeons and statistics gathered by hospital officials. The Medical Department also collected specimens of amputated limbs and took thousands of photographs of men displaying naked stumps of desecrated arms and legs. The *Medical and Surgical History* would be a standard reference for military surgeons until the First World War.[23]

In his 1874 application for a pension increase, Tanner indicated that the amputations had been "imperfectly performed, and in consequence thereof the bone of each leg cut through the end of the stumps rendering them very painful to walk upon." Writing in support of his application, a neighbor testified under oath that the Corporal was "greatly crippled and at times rendered nearly helpless and almost entirely dependent on the ministrations of others." Warm weather was particularly hard on Tanner's condition—apparently the humidity irritated the spots where his stumps met the wood and metal of his artificial legs—and a summary of his case indicated that on hot days he was "obliged to lay aside the artificial limbs and remain at home helpless as a child." On many occasions the neighbor had been asked to extend Tanner's apologies to his employers at the New York Custom House that he would be unable to come to work. In fact, any time his family was gone—by this time Tanner was married with small children—the neighbor was in the habit of stopping to see if Tanner needed help.[24]

After he became well known, newspapers often kept the public informed of the Corporal's medical problems. The *Brooklyn Eagle* reported on the "tumors" (actually "neuroma," growths caused by excess blood and nerve fibers that tended to develop around his stumps) that from time to time had to be drained. When he returned to New York in 1894 to undergo major surgery on both legs—surgeons took another two and a half inches of bone from each leg and removed part of the sciatic nerve—newspapers reported on the operation and on his recovery. The *Brooklyn Eagle* featured the stacked headline "On the Amputating Table: Corporal Tanner under the Knife for Two Hours: Dr. George R. Fowler Shortens His Legs." A week after the surgery, doctors banned visitors, fearing that the people crowding into the popular old soldier's room were causing too much excitement, leading to a "bad spell" on the previous Sunday. He was still recovering in early April, when the *Brooklyn Eagle* reported that he was waiting for his left stump to finish healing so he could be fitted for new artificial legs. As late as July, an *Eagle* correspondent in Washington, where Tanner then lived, reported that he had not yet recovered and was, in fact, considered to be in "critical" condition.[25]

Unfortunately, this was not an unusual problem for Civil War–era amputees. Like Tanner, most amputees had to endure frequent treatments and sometimes devastating side effects. In the short term, wounds often reopened or required additional surgery. In the long term, when hurried surgeons had left too little flesh between the bone and the skin, wearing prosthetics could be quite painful. An 1890 petition to Congress by disabled soldiers cataloged problems facing amputees other than the constant treatment of their stumps, including chronic heart problems and complications from the use of painkillers and other medicines.[26]

Many amputees took advantage of programs established by the federal and many state governments that distributed free artificial legs and arms to amputees, and Tanner appears on a list of men receiving prosthetics from the U.S. government in 1866. If men decided that constantly updating their prosthetics was not worth the trouble, or realized that the particular condition of their stumps did not support the use of a prosthetic, they could receive the equivalent value in cash. By the 1890s, veterans with missing limbs could get a replacement every three years or, if they were unable to use a prosthetic, fifty dollars per arm and seventy-five dollars per leg. Indeed, many men complained about the discomfort of artificial legs, especially, as well as their weight and the noise they made. Once Tanner told of a time when a friend kept glancing around for a bird tweeting nearby when all along it was the Corporal's squeaky artificial leg. Artificial legs required constant maintenance; one brand came with a pocket oilcan and a screwdriver.[27]

But ambitious inventors kept trying to make them better, obtaining 133 patents for artificial limbs and other prosthetic devices between 1861 and 1873. Entrepreneurs sought to make them not only more realistic looking with natural woods, dyes, and leather coverings but also more functional. They invented joints, ball bearings, springs, and rubber bands to substitute for joints, ligaments, and tendons, and other mechanical innovations to try to create a natural gait and to help men conceal their disability if they so desired. A self-serving "treatise" published by a manufacturer of prosthetic limbs indicated that the rise of increasingly dangerous industrial techniques and the wars of the mid-nineteenth century (in the Crimea, in America, and between France and Germany, all between the 1850s and the 1870s) had "augured the recurrence of accidents and the dismemberment of the human body" and made it possible for an entrepreneur and inventor to find a market for his prosthetics. Because improved surgical techniques allowed critically wounded or injured men to survive, it finally became possible for men with vision and good ideas for improving prosthetics beyond the time of "peg legs" and hooks to actually make money. In true Gilded Age fashion, the artificial-limb manufacturer declared that "the bent of human ambition is for the acquisition of money instead of a few plaudits from the world."[28]

Tanner never provided a complete description of his artificial legs—newspapers often referred to the Corporal's "cork" legs, although that lightweight product of the bark of the cork tree had originally only been used as a covering or lining—but an 1888 reference work on artificial limbs featured a model that likely resembled Tanner's. Made for survivors of

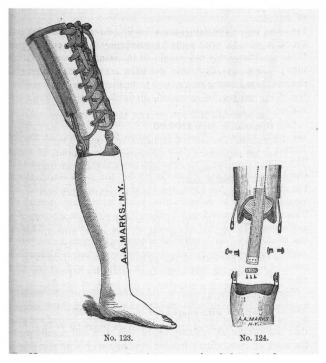

Tanner's artificial legs were likely very similar to this popular model. *A Treatise on Marks' Patent Artificial Limbs with Rubber Hands and Feet* (New York: A. A. Marks, 1888), 37.

below-the-knee amputations, the device sought to ensure that most of the wearer's weight was carried by the upper leg rather than the stump. An amputee would strap his thigh into a buckskin-covered leather brace held tightly in place by laces threaded through eight pairs of eyelets. At the knee, a pair of hinged metal braces connected the brace to the "tough kiln-dried willow wood" whose top was hollowed out and padded to receive the stump. The wood was strengthened and made to look more natural with a covering of parchment or buckskin. This particular model did not bend at the ankle, although some limbs featured ball-and-socket contraptions that allowed heels to rise and fall as the wearer walked. Each leg cost one hundred dollars, including the suspenders that provided additional leverage and security.[29]

It would have been hard enough to walk with one of these legs, when the user's good leg could carry most of the weight and provide balance. But wearing two must have been a little like walking on stilts. Tanner would not have been able to feel the ground, to judge its texture or sense sidewalk cracks and irregularities. He used at least one cane and sometimes two, and for much of his life he required the steadying hand of his wife, his children, a friend, or a paid steward.

Although Tanner rarely mentioned his condition or complained about his artificial legs, friends and observers did remark from time to time on the ways his circumstances tested the Corporal's physical stamina and moral perseverance. One admirer wrote that Tanner had "suffered untold torture, uncomplaining as an ancient philosopher." A long-time friend declared, "[I have] been with him by day and I have been with him by night. . . . I have seen him suffering the agonies of the damned; I have seen him and heard him cry out with pain that was torturing his body." An Albany newspaper reported that fellow guests at the Hudson Valley resort of Round Lake, where Tanner often spent his summers, were witness to the Corporal's "nights of moaning." One correspondent reported that most days Tanner could not go to sleep until 10 o'clock in the morning. "He is accustomed to sit up till, thoroughly tired out, he is obliged to lie down." But even then, he often "can only ache and toss, and now and then he is obliged to get up again and sit in his library for an hour or two and smoke himself still more tired." The *Brooklyn Eagle* published the same story and added, "It is to deaden this that the Commissioner of Pensions is never without a cigar in his mouth."[30]

Tanner's insomnia, which he acknowledged in letters to his good friend Capt. John "Jack" Crawford, may have been exactly what everyone said it was—simply a natural reaction to pain that apparently grew worse at night. However, it is possible that Tanner was experiencing some form of post-traumatic stress, a syndrome well known to modern doctors treating combat veterans or victims of other forms of violence or trauma. Civil War–era medical professionals called it "irritable heart" or "nostalgia" or "hysteria," but the symptoms they described seem to match Tanner's night-time visitations at least superficially: "nightmares, flashbacks, anxiety, agitation, irritability, nervousness, unexplained headaches, and nausea." Although Tanner did not specifically mention any of these symptoms, it is hard to imagine that he did not suffer some sort of long-term trauma.[31]

Sometimes rumors spread of Tanner's use of alcohol—he claimed from time to time that he never touched the stuff, although the evidence is inconclusive—only to be contradicted by friendly reporters who assured readers that Tanner's real problem was the pain that required doses of painkilling opiates, which, one paper declared, brought relief and allowed his "disposition" to "remain . . . genial and generous." When, early in the twentieth century, Tanner came out in favor of retaining the saloons found at federal soldiers' homes, at least one editor once again felt the need to defend him against accusations of abusing alcohol.[32]

Civil War soldiers, like soldiers in almost any era and place, could make their black humor out of any condition. This was reflected in a pun-filled poem supposedly written by an amputee that began

Good leg, thou wast a faithful friend,
And truly has thy duty done;
I thank thee most that, to the end
Thou didst not let this body down.

Tanner generally went no further than pithy or even humorous remarks about his condition. When he was unable to speak at a soldiers' reunion in Toledo, he apologized by writing, "It happened to me, once upon a time, when . . . I was opposing [Confederate general "Stonewall"] Jackson" that "I had a dispute with a rebel shell, and the shell got the best of me; and I am sorry to say that, even after so many years, its effects have confined me to my room for the past month." Just after the 1894 surgery, which removed even more of his legs, Tanner responded to the well wishes of a women's organization with the characteristic statement, "I'm a couple of inches shorter than yesterday, and, of course, it is agonizing, but nerve is good yet, and your sympathy is sweet to a sufferer." He jokingly complained that his practice of wearing rubbers over his shoes for traction "made his feet sweat and were bad on his corns" but also admitted that while out duck hunting he did have an advantage over his complaining comrades in that his feet did not suffer from the damp chill. One of his favorite stories appeared in numerous newspaper articles over the years. It happened while he was recovering in the Fairfax Seminary Hospital, when, one version went, "a woman with a bundle on her arm came up to the bed where he was lying unable to move, and treated him, not to a delicacy that he was anticipating, but to [a] tract on the evils of dancing," a fairly inappropriate gift to a teenager with no feet. A slightly longer version of the story ended with Tanner revealing the stumps "to the astonished pietist" and promising, "I swear to you, ma'am, that I will never dance again."[33]

Tanner was not above using his artificial feet to play practical jokes. An acquaintance once criticized him for using excessively hot water to bathe one of his racehorses—oddly, no other source mentions his owning horses—and asked Tanner how he would like it if someone forced him to put his feet in such warm water. When Tanner said it would not bother him a bit, the friend bet one hundred dollars that he could not keep his feet in hot water for five minutes. Tanner pocketed the money five minutes later and never told the man how he endured the scalding water.[34]

"Exceptional sufferers," as Frances M. Clarke calls them, provided models of humor and fortitude, raising their self-esteem and uplifting their fellow patriots. Even though their heroic narratives rescued positive outcomes from extraordinary suffering, they did not help explain how they would manage to live normal lives. Tanner was a perfect example, and his approach set the tone for how others referred to his handicap. Time and time again, anyone who had the chance referred in some lighthearted way to the absence of several inches of Tanner's leg. When he was appointed commissioner of pensions, for instance, the *Pittsburgh Dispatch* reported, "Tanner was probably the happiest man in Washington to-day. He literally danced about all day without legs." When a member of the Women's Relief Corps introduced Tanner at its national convention in 1896, she said that, despite the two major operations he had endured, the veterans "had sent him word that the shorter he grew the more they thought of him." At an appearance at a soldiers' reunion in Topeka, one newspaper reported, Tanner "buckled on his legs, and at command of his comrades again reported for duty." One newspaper published a joke in which a newlywed bride asks her husband, "Isn't this Corporal Tanner the man with the amputated legs?" The husband replies, "No darling, he is the man without the amputated legs." Finally, a newspaper published for veterans once referred to him as "a soldier without legs, but with plenty of brains." Those brains would have to carry him through a painful, challenging postwar world.[35]

Making His Way

Although Tanner never said so specifically, the drive and ambition that he displayed almost immediately after leaving the army seemed to be a reaction to common perceptions of former soldiers. Although most of the stories would be published in 1865 and 1866, two or three years after Tanner received his discharge, the sudden demobilization of the Union army led to newspaper reports of soldiers looting stores and fighting in the streets of New York and Washington, of a sharp spike in crime rates that civilians

blamed on demobilized soldiers, of veterans failing to obtain jobs or bringing "soldiers' habits" like drinking and gambling back to civilian life.[36]

Not Jim Tanner. One can assume that Tanner tired of having to rely on
others—the few accounts of the immediate aftermath of his wounding
often refer to being carried from one place to another and other forms
of charity and personal favors. Less than five months after losing his feet,
Tanner listed his occupation on a pension application as "student." His
course of study was phonography, which in the twentieth century tended to
be called shorthand but which, in the twenty-first century, is a nearly lost
craft. But the fact that he had sought to learn phonography nearly before
his ravaged legs had healed suggests something about the drive and imagination that propelled him through his long life.[37]

Although no evidence exists that Tanner ever used shorthand after he
left Washington late in 1865, that he learned it in the first place indicates
something about his character and his determination to get ahead despite
his disability. Like many other disabled soldiers, Tanner wanted to prove
that he was not helpless. A symbolic but very public demonstration of
that attitude emerged in a "Left-Handed Penmanship Contest" organized
just after the war by William O. Bourne, editor of *The Soldier's Friend*, a
newspaper for veterans. Bourne offered five-hundred-dollar prizes for the
four best examples of left-handed writing by amputees who were asked to
describe their personal experiences during the war. In addition to inspiring patriotism, Bourne intended the contest to be "an inducement to the
class of wounded and disabled soldiers . . . to make every effort to fit themselves for lucrative and honorable positions." Eventually the entries were
exhibited in Washington, where the hall was decorated with patriotic and
inspirational mottos like "The empty sleeve should not be the badge of
an empty purse" and "The empty sleeve, disabled but not disheartened."
Hundreds of people attended, and a number of prominent politicians and
generals visited the exhibit.[38]

Tanner did not participate, of course, but the same sense of self-
improvement and dedication that the competition celebrated also characterized the rhetoric of phonographic advocates, who promoted their craft
as a profession, not just an occupation, made up of persons of the highest character, reliability, and trustworthiness. At a time when many occupations were becoming professions—the fields of medicine, engineering,
teaching, and scientific research are just a few examples—phonography
was yet another opportunity for up-and-coming young men and women

to get ahead. This was especially true in the years after the Civil War, when most states began to mandate that reporters take official court records in phonography. "It is indispensable that the training of the shorthand reporter," insisted a stenographer of the day, "should be so thorough as to insure the highest efficiency and that his personal integrity should be above suspicion."[39]

Benn Pitman's 1856 *History of Shorthand*, written entirely in shorthand, although later editions also included the history in printed English, provided a history of the practice of "short writing" going back to ancient Rome. It referred to shorthand as a "philosophic alphabet" and assured readers that it was "rapidly gaining the position of a regular branch of study in educational establishments." Indeed, according to a quote from the superintendent of the Saint Louis public schools, "an education that does not embrace a knowledge of Phonography must be regarded as incomplete, and short of the wants of the age." Also reflecting the spirit of the age were the five pages listing various manuals, supplies (paper and gold pens), and other publications and items that could be ordered from Pitman's Phonographic Institute in Cincinnati. Benn was the brother of Isaac, who developed the Pitman method. Tanner kept at least one of his phonography texts, perhaps because he felt a certain affection for them as the source, after all, of his most memorable experience. It is preserved in a Texas archive complete with inscriptions apparently in Tanner's handwriting and a printed bookplate featuring the words "James Tanner" and "Brooklyn" and two large chevrons—the insignia of a corporal.[40]

Tanner almost certainly studied Isaac Pitman's *Exercises in Phonography*, which offered rather grandiose ideas about the value of shorthand to society: "An easy and distinct mode of communicating our thoughts and feelings to similarly constituted beings," Pitman wrote, "is one of the first and most pressing wants of social intercourse. . . . Facilitation of intercourse diminishes the number of dialects, and . . . we may perhaps look forward with some degree of hope to a time when 'the whole earth' shall again be 'of one language and of one speech.'" Pitman considered *his* version of shorthand nothing less than a way to knit together the world. "A philosophical language, when it has become a practical reality, can be none other than the universal language in which each individual has thought and felt from childhood." Tanner was not learning some minor trade but rather entering a profession with a philosophical underpinning and a progressive attitude that fit Gilded Age ambitions perfectly.[41]

This personalized bookplate from one of Tanner's stenography books creates a minor mystery. Tanner seems to be living in Brooklyn by the time he had it made and is identifying himself, obviously, as "Corporal Tanner"—hence the chevrons— which would have been consistent with his known biography. However, if "1864" refers to a year, it is unclear why it would appear on a bookplate printed at least five or six years later. Archives and Rare Books Collection, University of North Texas Libraries, Denton, Texas.

The man who founded the Syracuse business school attended by Tanner, Daniel T. Ames, took a less philosophical and more entrepreneurial approach. Ames promoted training in penmanship, stenography, calligraphy, and other related skills as a clear path to success. "No other one attainment," he wrote about professional-quality handwriting—this was before typewriters were in wide use in most offices—"assists an equal number of young ladies and gentlemen to positions of profit and advancement." The processes of learning and perfecting handwriting and phonography taught such key values as thoroughness, patience, efficiency, economy, precision, and the willingness to learn from one's mistakes. Moreover, although some people thought neat handwriting was simply a gift—either you had it or you did not—Ames argued that it was, in fact, a talent that could be nurtured, a specialization like any other business, art, or science.[42]

Tanner attended Ames National Business College for at least several months between the fall of 1863 and the spring of 1864. Although many of the students at Ames took correspondence courses, Tanner actually lived in Syracuse during his time in school. More than fifty years later, in a speech at a veterans' reunion, he stated that he was "always at home in Syracuse," asserting, "After my wounds healed my only education, save for the grammar schools, was in business college here, where I learned stenography." The school had opened in 1862. Five years later a business directory for Syracuse described the college as having three large classrooms devoted, respectively, to "practical business," phonography, and a telegraphic institute. Phonography was taught in one of the large lecture halls and several smaller practice rooms. Another large room was filled with mock-ups of banks and shops in which students could "practice the details of actual business as applied to the various kinds of trade and commerce." The third room was equipped with thirteen different stations for learning telegraphy. The college claimed that over five hundred students had attended courses in 1866–67. Tuition was apparently around one hundred dollars for the three-month course.[43]

Learning a trade at a business college was just one way in which Tanner sought to make something of himself. There is also evidence that he read books intended to help young men succeed in the dynamic economy of the Gilded Age. One of the books—a booklet, really—that Tanner owned was *Manners*, which translated into shorthand the advice given in an obscure how-to book that, like many others published in the nineteenth century, gave rising young men practical advice on getting ahead. Only the chapter titles appeared in normal English, but they indicated that the book addressed the kinds of concerns covered in most how-to-succeed-in-life manuals, featuring such topics as "Manners: Our Being's End and Aim," "Good Manners Founded on Human Rights," "Care of the Person," "Dress Habits and Manners," "Eating and Being," "Conversation," "The Graces of Speech," "Conversational Equity," "Writing and Correspondence," and "Scandal and Toleration."[44]

Dozens of advice books covering these and many other issues related to etiquette, ambition, and values were published in the years after the Civil War. One of the most prolific authors of self-help volumes, Samuel Smiles, provided a description of the keys to success in his book *Duty: With Illustrations of Courage, Patience, and Endurance*. Like most authors in the genre, Smiles—who also wrote books titled *Character* and *Thrift*—used mini-biographies of great men to show the importance of creating long-term goals, accepting delayed gratification, and displaying courage in the face of adversity. Borrowing liberally and selectively from the lives of great men from many occupations and across the generations, Smiles told stories that showed the fortune and respect that would follow from perseverance and skillful management. The values put forward by these authors were quite simple: "Young man," wrote H. A. Lewis in *Why Some Succeed While Others Fail*, "two ways are open before you in life. One points to degradation and want, the other, to usefulness and wealth."[45]

Whether or not Tanner ever read those words, their message resonated in his own ambitions. Americans deeply admired severely disabled veterans who were able to support themselves despite their crippling injuries. The most striking example of a disabled soldier succeeding despite—perhaps because of—a grievous disability was J. F. Chase, a Maine artilleryman who nearly died when a shell landed three feet from his artillery piece during the bombardment of Cemetery Ridge on Gettysburg's third day. The shell tore off his right arm and knocked his left eye out of its socket; the shrapnel left six wounds in his neck and torso. He woke up just before he was to be taken away for burial and, according to witnesses, gasped, "Did we win the battle?" After the war Chase received the Medal of Honor for distinguished bravery at Chancellorsville, worked as an inventor (receiving patents for an improved hoop skirt and a bustle, among other things), and gave lectures about his injuries and temperance. His promotional pamphlet advertised him as the "Battle Scarred John F. Chase" and featured a woodcut showing his stump and the thicket of scars on his chest and shoulder, as well as a poem written in his honor. Chase clearly made his disability work for him. He became famous as a temperance speaker, and his terribly scarred likeness appeared on temperance publications; he lectured visitors to the Gettysburg battlefield; and the famous etching of his wounds also appeared on brochures for the clothes wringer and the water still that he invented.[46]

Tanner was no John Chase, but his choices after the war reflected the self-reliance expected of veterans, and his quick reentry into gainful employment can be traced in the pages of the *Schoharie Republican*, his hometown newspaper. The *Republican* had followed Tanner since he went off to war and had published a series of letters from the eighteen-year-old army recruit. (Unfortunately, neither paper, microfilmed, nor electronic copies of the pertinent issues exist.) Nearly three weeks after Tanner was wounded, the *Republican* reported that Mrs. Tanner had stopped by the office to let them know of Tanner's injuries. The paper also noted when James and his brother passed through town on his way home: "Poor boy! O, the pains of war! We will not give expression to our thoughts as we saw him stretched, helpless in his carriage."[47]

From time to time over the next several years, the *Republican* noted Tanner's jobs with various government agencies in New York and Washington. In Albany, he served as assistant postmaster to the assembly while the legislature was in session in February 1864. This, like several of the jobs he and many other disabled veterans would hold in the years following the Civil War, required little work and was mainly a selective but very public way of rewarding unfortunate veterans for their sacrifices. Tanner went to Washington in the fall of 1864 to take the job that would lead to his witnessing the death of President Lincoln but returned to New York in late 1865. He split his time between Cobleskill and Albany and over the next several sessions of the assembly, occupying part-time sinecures as clerk to a legislative committee, assistant postmaster, assistant doorkeeper, and doorkeeper. He joined hundreds of disabled veterans employed by northern states and the federal government to do myriad nondemanding but more or less necessary positions. Tanner's duties would probably have consisted of filing, delivering messages, and other light work that his disabilities would not have impeded.[48]

Tanner's appointments to temporary state jobs—he would probably have worked only during those weeks when the legislature was in session—reflected the commitment by local, state, and federal governments, through formal policies and informal practices, to employ veterans, especially men too disabled to perform manual labor, in the countless small jobs in nineteenth-century governments. Congress passed resolutions and laws that gave disabled veterans and widows preference over others in applying for federal positions, and veterans' groups often sent representatives to urge heads of city agencies to hire veterans. Thousands of men thus managed to earn meager, if regular, livings as government employees.[49]

Words of Encouragement

Although Tanner deflected pity through humor and ambition, he did once describe the period just after the loss of his feet as "a time which I can truly designate as the blackest hour of my whole life. I seemed to be enveloped in Stygian darkness. I could figure out no ray of hope." Tanner's comments about his condition, however humorous or offhand, indicated just how difficult his life must have been. Condemned to walk stiffly and painfully on creaky prosthetics, Tanner would have reexperienced that nightmarish dusk at Second Bull Run with every step. Comments about his pain, his insomnia, his surgeries, his inability to travel alone became so commonplace in the countless articles written about him that it was doubtless easy for contemporaries to forget the world of pain in which the Corporal lived. His own stories highlighted his use of disability to make jokes or win bets, but also revealed deeper truths and limitations. For instance, it is hard not to understand Tanner's constant retelling of the tale of the woman handing out pamphlets on the evils of dancing as evidence that he was still dealing with the fact that he had never danced as an adult and never would.[50]

Tanner and the many thousands of other disabled soldiers who survived into the Gilded Age were living during a time in which, according to one historian, disability was "institutionalized." As the federal government took on more responsibilities, as medical technologies appeared, and as urbanization continued, policies and institutions emerged that sought to deal with the disabled in coherent, responsible ways. At the same time, however, Gilded Age Americans remained ambivalent about the disabled. Asylums for the mentally handicapped, for instance, often led to horrific treatments, while even the homes built to house disabled soldiers could result in decades of aimless living and alcoholism. Moreover, many cities passed so-called ugly laws that banned begging by anyone with visible disabilities; the San Francisco ordinance baldly stated that the law was an effort to remove from public view "any person who is diseased, maimed, mutilated, or in any way deformed so as to be an unsightly or disgusting object." Being disabled in Gilded Age America could clearly lead to indignity, misunderstanding, and even shame.[51]

Tanner, like all disabled Americans, bore a psychological burden caused in part by the simple fact that he could not function like a normal person. Observers sometimes remarked on Tanner's difficulties but rarely described how he navigated his world. Small hints of Tanner's difficulty in getting around emerge here and there in newspaper accounts. At a massive Republican meeting in 1885, for instance, Tanner "hobbled out of" his small carriage. A squad of young men, "knowing his deformity," helped him to negotiate some debris in the gutter and got him safely to the sidewalk. The fact that a newspaper felt free to refer to Tanner's condition as a "deformity" rather than a "disability" or some other more neutral term says something about the public's blithe indifference to the feelings of the disabled. Although Tanner virtually never spoke in public about the day-to-day challenges of his disability, he did admit on his 1874 application for an increase in his government pension that the pain of his injuries had rendered him "perfectly helpless for all purposes of manual labor" and made physical exercise possible only "at the expense of intense pain." The presence of "a regular attendant, someone within call night and day is a necessity," he wrote. Later he would mention receiving help from his wife or grown daughters, but the practical business of identifying and paying for other helpers was never again mentioned.[52]

Tanner deflected his disability with humor or by simply ignoring it, but it was more complicated than that. Those who had lost limbs, jaws, or eyes, or who suffered internal injuries or chronic fevers or dysentery, or who were simply worn down by exposure, terrible diet, and stress faced a crisis in masculinity. Their physical losses led to an incapacity to fully engage in life, to make decisions unbound by physical limitations, to align themselves with normal assumptions about physical appearance and traditional male roles. Any disability, even as it provided evidence of a man's previous bravery and service, immediately placed survivors on a spectrum of helplessness; even the loss of a finger or two reshaped men's abilities and affected their self-confidence; the loss of two feet put Tanner at the far end of the spectrum.[53]

On rare occasions he betrayed a continuing awareness of the depression that had nearly defeated him. A tiny piece in a New York newspaper published in 1887, a quarter century after his injury, quoted Tanner as saying that hearing of passengers being burned to death in railway accidents never failed to make him "shudder." In fact, railway travel was fairly dangerous in the late nineteenth and early twentieth centuries, with thousands of passengers and employees being hurt and killed every year (it did not help that wooden passenger cars were heated by coal-burning stoves). Several accidents occurred in the months just before or after Tanner's comments. He may have been referring to the Rio, Wisconsin, accident of the previous October, when seventeen passengers in a single car burned to death, or to an accident in March 1887 that killed thirty-three near Boston. "I travel a great deal," he said—according to available newspaper reports, in 1887 and 1888 Tanner traveled throughout New York and to Vermont, New Hampshire, Pennsylvania, Illinois, Indiana, Ohio, Wisconsin, Missouri, Oregon, and California—"and I can't jump an inch. But I shall never burn to death in a derailed car. I always place a good revolver under my pillow." His chilling point was that if he was pinned in a burning train wreck, he would kill himself before the flames could get to him.[54]

Another source of that "Stygian darkness" may have been his fear that he would become one of the damaged survivors of the war who were forced to fall back on family resources, or be consigned to a county poorhouse, or even beg on the streets. This was a major concern immediately after the war, when newspapers and other sources described the shattered veterans begging on street corners, still wearing ragged uniforms and leaning on makeshift crutches. A broadside encouraging Philadelphians to contribute to the building of a home for disabled veterans asked donors if they were "prepared to see them beg from door to door, or seek an asylum in the Almshouse, as common paupers."[55]

The possibility that poor soldiers could be forced to rely on charity struck many as unworthy of the United States and of the men themselves. "Are you to sit down at the street corners, as you have seen some of our number in the metropolis, and depend upon the charities of the people for a support?" thundered the *Soldier's Friend* as the Union army demobilized. "Are you to entertain the idea that, because you have suffered so much in your country's service, the world owes you a living, and you have a right to sit idle and demand it? No!" Yet even a few years after the war, the same paper suggested that the sight of one-armed veterans making a meager living by playing hand organs on the streets of New York was so common that, when a child asked about the source of the music being played down the block, an adult could say, "Only a soldier grinding an organ." One observer worried that doing too much for all but the most seriously injured veterans, due to civilians' "bad and demoralizing sentimentality," might create a "class" of men "with a right to be idle, or to beg, or to claim exemption from the ordinary rules of life."[56]

Tanner must have felt close to that chasm of poverty and shame. When the war ended, the twenty-one-year-old Tanner was earning a small salary as a government clerk and collecting a disability pension of eight dollars per month, enough to support himself but certainly not enough to feed and house a family. The day-to-day worry about earning a living and the possibility that he would never earn much more than that obviously weighed heavily on the twenty-year-old in 1864. Those worries would never dissipate completely—throughout his life he was very honest about his desire to make as much money as possible—but in 1864 he had met a woman who, he wrote years later, "came to me with words of gentle sympathy and encouragement that fired my brain with a determination to make a man's fight for a man's place in the world."[57]

Meroah White, usually called Mero, also born in 1844, belonged to a local family that traced its lineage back to the *Mayflower*. The Whites seemed to have been better off than the Tanners; Mero's father and grandfather had been teachers (it is tempting to speculate that Mero's father had met Tanner when the boy was teaching school in 1861) and minor local officeholders. There is no record of how the Whites felt about their daughter marrying a man with no feet and an eight-dollar pension. In fact, little research has been done about the relationships formed between the thousands of amputees and the women they married. It must have given Mero and other young women pause to consider sharing long decades with men who might not be able to dress themselves or whose wound would require daily bandaging, or who could not go for walks or carriage drives—much less earn a regular living. Nearly thirty years after their marriage, the White family genealogy featured a proud entry about Tanner, so if there had been concerns about twenty-two-year-old Mero plighting her troth to a crippled veteran with few prospects, they were never recorded.[58]

Whether or not her family entertained doubts about the young amputee with whom their daughter had fallen in love, James and Mero married in 1866, and their first child, a girl named Ada, was born in Cobleskill in 1868. It is indicative not only of Tanner's characteristically low-key description of his plight but also of his relationship with Mero that he provided the most elaborate description of the darkest period of his life not to elicit pity from readers but rather to show how she had given him the strength and encouragement to forge ahead. Mero became "the great compensatory fact of all my career," he wrote, and a steady source of encouragement lighting his way out of that darkness.[59]

A Man of Broad Views

When Tanner submitted his resignation from the War Department before his return to Schoharie, his supervisor wrote a brief note with this hopeful encouragement: "Having been severely wounded in the Military service of the country I hope that you will be successful in any legitimate enterprise you may engage in." Taking temporary jobs in Albany was just the beginning of Tanner's pursuit of "legitimate enterprise." By 1867, when Tanner once again reported his occupation as "student" in the directory of New York legislative employees, he had begun "reading law" back in Cobleskill. Cobleskill had changed since he was a boy. The Susquehanna Railroad had connected the village to the outside world, and although the population had yet to grow significantly, a number of businesses had opened, including two more hotels and a saloon, a threshing-machine factory and a repair shop for train engines, a doctor's office and a law office, a bank and an insurance agency, and several shops and stores. Tanner and Mero rented rooms in a house on Grand Street, which stretched away from the village center toward the tannery and the threshing-machine factory.[60]

His teacher and mentor in the law and, in many ways, life, was Judge William C. Lamont, whom Tanner may have known as a young boy. Lamont had become a lawyer in nearby Otsego County, but after serving in the state assembly for a term, he moved to Richmondville and later, after the railroad arrived, to Cobleskill. He also served for nearly a decade as a county judge. Tanner followed the long tradition of learning the legal trade by "reading law" under the tutelage of established lawyers. For several years students would work as office clerk and personal assistant, all the while studying the statute books and laws of the state in which they lived. Tanner was a member of perhaps the last generation of attorneys who, for the most part, received their training under this "apprenticeship" model of legal education rather than at a formal law school. Tanner wrote very little about his course of study, although it is likely that it resembled the legal education of Abraham Lincoln, who recalled that his training in a Springfield, Illinois, law office in the 1830s included reading Blackstone's *Commentaries*, Chitty's *Pleadings*, Greenleaf's *Evidence*, and Story's *Equity* and *Equity Pleading*. These thick tomes of cases and precedents were nearly ubiquitous in the libraries of lawyers throughout the country. New York State gave the state bar association a great deal of leeway in admitting members. After an indefinite period of study, the legal apprentice would be examined by a panel of judges who determined whether the applicant should be admitted to the bar and thus be allowed to practice law. Other than passing this nonstandard bar exam, the only requirements for a new lawyer were that he be at least twenty-one years of age and an American citizen and have good moral character. Over the next few decades, a number of law schools were established, and legal education became much more formal. Tanner joined the profession when the law was becoming one of the obvious pathways to success for a young man; the number of lawyers nearly doubled between 1850 and 1870, from 23,939 to 40,376.[61]

Tanner clearly admired Lamont and, in some ways, sought to emulate him. Tanner may have learned less about the law from the older man than he did about life. Indeed, the description of Lamont that Tanner wrote toward the end of his life could well have been a description of how Tanner would have liked to have seen himself in the fullness of age:

> His was a complex character. If you did not know him through and through, you did not know him at all, a man of broad views, a man with vision, of an ability no one would suspect him of through a casual acquaintance, a man,

who when he held views, did not hesitate to express them, free of speech, sometimes roughly so; his heart was on his sleeve. He made no profession of Christianity, joined no church, but lived Christianity; exemplified it in many ways and many acts. He delighted to do good.[62]

No other paragraph published about James Tanner better captured his own complex personality—at least as he sought to project it. Tanner was always proud of his humble beginnings and took great pleasure in being a "corporal" among generals and presidents and other notables who usually had started life with much greater resources than he had. He believed himself to be a straight talker—others thought he spoke too carelessly, but generally honestly—and, although Tanner often articulated fairly traditional religious values and associated himself with at least one Methodist church during his days in Brooklyn, he was hardly a model member of any church.[63]

Tanner loved working with Judge Lamont and devoted several pages in his memoir to relating a case in which Lamont, who still called him "Jimmie," used his deep understanding of human nature and talent for heart-tugging rhetoric to mediate a property dispute between a widowed mother and her grown son. One of Tanner's first cases, tried before a justice of the peace before he was a full-fledged lawyer, was a suit seeking damages from a man who had chopped off the tail of a valuable hunting dog. Tanner, who wrote, "In my whole life I have loved a dog," took the case enthusiastically and demanded one hundred dollars in damages. When the defendant complained that a missing tail could not interfere with a dog's hunting ability, Tanner declared that, without a tail to swish them away, "the lice and flies would have free access to [the dog's] head and kill him." That was enough for the judge, who awarded the plaintiff forty dollars.[64]

Although he took great satisfaction from his work with Lamont, Tanner always had his sights set on moving up and out of Schoharie County. By the time he started reading law and working in the legislature, he was a confirmed Republican in a county with, in the words of the *New York Times*, "rock-ribbed Democratic sentiment." Even his mentor Lamont was a Democrat. During elections Tanner "worked" the Republican side hard but enjoyed little success. When local men suggested that, as a disabled veteran, he could easily win the job of postmaster—which at the time was a purely political appointment made by the president of the United States (then and for many years afterward a Republican)—he told them that his "thoughts were far afield" and turned down their offer.[65]

By 1869 he was ready to stand for the bar exam. Although the fact that both examiners were Democrats gave the young Republican pause, the exam was not difficult. The two older men took him into a room and asked him one question: "A man enters your office and asks you to commence action" on an overdue debt worth $100. "What would be your first move?" Tanner replied immediately, "I would ask him for a ten dollar retainer"—in other words, he would ask for his fee up front, before doing any work on the case. One examiner said to the other, "I must say . . . that Jim seems to have a proper appreciation of one of the first principles of our noble profession," and the exam was over. The three men smoked cigars and then reported back to the judge that Tanner was the newest member of the New York bar.[66]

Within months he had moved his family to New York.

Brooklyn Bound

Tanner began his Cobleskill memoir with two lines from an old lullaby:

> Backward, turn backward, oh Time in your flight,
> Make me a child again, just for tonight!

The quote from Elizabeth Akers Allen's poem "Rock Me To Sleep" was meant to invoke a nostalgia appropriate for the task of remembering his childhood and early adulthood. And most of the poem was devoted to contrasting the present with the distant, comforting past, when a mother could erase all unease and sorrow by rocking her child to sleep. But the second stanza must have spoken to Tanner after his many decades in the public eye:

> Backward, flow backward, O tide of the years
> I am so weary of toil and of tears,
> Toil without recompense, tears all in vain,
> Take them, and give me my childhood again,
> I have grown weary of dust and decay,
> Weary of flinging my soul-wealth away;
> Weary of sowing for others to reap;
> Rock me to sleep, mother,—rock me to sleep![67]

Whatever latent bitterness or regret Tanner inadvertently revealed when he chose to begin his only reminiscence of young manhood with those words lay in the future, which must have been alive with possibilities in 1869, when Tanner left Schoharie County for good to take a job in the U.S. Custom House in New York City.[68]

And because in that place and time, government work and politics went hand in hand, Tanner immersed himself in local Republican politics. Over the next twenty years, he would truly become "Corporal Tanner" to Brooklyn and, eventually, the nation.

CHAPTER THREE

Brooklyn Days

Becoming Corporal Tanner

James Tanner took to the rough-and-tumble politics of Brooklyn like a native. He thrived in the rising economic might and political influence of his new home and embraced the veterans' culture that offered another kind of support and attention. With the same determination he had demonstrated in overcoming his physical disability, he built a reputation for honesty in one of the most politically corrupt cities in America, carved out niches in the movements that addressed veterans' needs and promoted sectional reconciliation, and began traveling the country as a public speaker and crusader for the Republican Party and the Grand Army of the Republic (GAR). The time and the place were perfectly suited to Tanner's ambitions.

Growing with the City

Although a cholera outbreak that year would kill over five hundred residents, Brooklyn was one of the great cities in the United States when the Tanners arrived in 1869. Called the "City of Churches" in the late nineteenth century, Brooklyn dominated Kings County, which occupied the western end of largely rural Long Island, across the East River from Manhattan, and was the third largest city in the United States. It would remain independent until 1898, when it became one of the five boroughs of modern New York City (the Bronx, Queens, Staten Island, and Manhattan are the others). Brooklyn was also just recovering from the Civil War, when an unsettled economy and the absence of thousands of husbands and fathers forced the Kings County government to extend nearly half a million dollars in aid to the poor and to house about 5,500 of the worst off in the county almshouse.[1]

By the late 1860s, the hard times were starting to fade, and the Tanners came to Brooklyn at the beginning of a period of dramatic growth. The population of Brooklyn would soar from 396,099 in 1870 to 566,663 in 1880. James, Mero, and the children would also witness a startling economic expansion during the twenty years they lived in Brooklyn. Construction finished on a massive dry-dock complex to maintain giant ocean-going vessels shortly after their arrival, and dockside warehouses filled with tobacco, hides, wool, coffee, molasses, sugar, and other products represented the city's role in the national and global economies. Brooklyn businesses refined sugar, distilled liquor, constructed machinery, baked bread, brewed beer, bound books, and refined petroleum. In 1865 there were about five hundred factories in Brooklyn; by 1880 that number had increased more than tenfold. There was also constant construction of streets, businesses, and homes, with nearly twenty thousand buildings going up between 1864 and 1874 alone.[2]

As in most American cities, Brooklyn's residents were deeply divided by money and geography. A third of them were immigrants from Ireland, Germany, and England. Middle-class and well-to-do Brooklynites lived in Brooklyn Heights and on "The Hill." They patronized the countless shops and stores along Fulton Street that Tanner had marched past with his regiment eight years earlier. But at least for the first decade or two after the Civil War, most residents lived in squalid neighborhoods filled with ramshackle tenements and shacks; on streets polluted with manure, garbage, and dead animals and barely lit at night; and with little access to clean water or sanitation services.

Although slums like these would resist change, the Tanners also witnessed the beginning of the construction of massive Prospect Park—still one of New York's great parks—which eventually covered more than five hundred acres, contained over five miles of lanes and eight miles of walking paths, a playground, several lakes, and fine views of Manhattan. The Prospect Park development was part of a massive expansion of cultural institutions and government services, including the Brooklyn Theater, the sanitary system, and the fire and police departments. Finally, shortly after Tanner's arrival, one of the most impressive engineering feats of its time, the Brooklyn Bridge, began to rise from opposite banks of the East River. It would be completed in 1883.[3]

Tanner never explicitly explained why he ended up in Brooklyn, although it is entirely possible that he had received the appointment before deciding to move. As a disabled veteran, experienced state government appointee, and enthusiastic Republican, he was a likely candidate for an appointment to the highly politicized customs office in New York. But the fact that his old regiment had been recruited largely in the city probably made him feel comfortable. His best friend in Company C, Jonathan Sproul, was a Brooklyn native, and although Jonathan had been killed a little over a year after their tearful farewell, his brother Wilson, another member of Company C, had survived the war. Both Sprouls had been among the men who carried Tanner off the battlefield a few years earlier. Brooklyn was, in fact, filled with Union veterans. The city had sent perhaps thirty thousand men to the Union army or state militia units, and Union veterans formed forty-five different Grand Army of the Republic posts in Brooklyn alone during the decades following the war.[4]

As their adopted home flourished, so did the Tanners. A second daughter, Antoinette, joined two-year-old Ada in 1870, while sons James and Earl were born in 1874 and 1876, respectively. By 1874 they resided on Ninth Street near Seventh Avenue, in the Prospect Hill neighborhood—now called Park Slope—three blocks from Prospect Park, where they joined an influx of middle- and upper-middle-class families from Manhattan taking advantage of the more affordable housing in the new, four-story brownstones sprouting up across the river. In 1886 prices for these houses ranged from $2,500 to a whopping $30,000. The prices for homes on Tanner's street ranged from $6,500 to $10,000 (roughly between $155,000 and $227,000 in modern terms). At the same time, the neighborhood saw the construction of four public schools, Methodist Hospital, and nearly two dozen churches (mainly Protestant, but with five new Catholic congregations). The Tanners would live in Prospect Hill until they left for Washington in 1889.[5]

Brooklyn was nothing like tiny Cobleskill—and just the place for a young, ambitious, and talented man. In fact, the changes that Brooklyn experienced during this time are an almost perfect metaphor for the changes in Tanner's life.

A Man of Mark

Within a decade of his arrival in Brooklyn, Tanner had become a major force in his work, in local politics, and in the Grand Army of the Republic. "His eloquence, his vim and tact soon made him a man of mark in the councils of his party," his biographer remarked. Like many young men in the mid-nineteenth century, Tanner came to the city seeking oppor-

Tanner in Brooklyn at the height of his fame. William E. Roscoe, *History of Schoharie County, New York, with Illustrations and Biographical Sketches of Some of Its Prominent Men and Pioneers* (Syracuse: D. Mason, 1882), 444.

tunity and success. The burgeoning retail establishments drew ambitious twenty-somethings like a magnet. These men "on the make," as a historian has recently called the clerks who flooded the city, "subscribed to an . . . ideology of self-making" that would provide "a promising platform from which to attain respectable character as well as power and prestige." Although Tanner worked as a public employee rather than as a salesman or an accountant, he certainly displayed the assumptions and dreams of this generation of white-collar workers.[6]

Tanner's launching pad to respectability was the custom house. The U.S. Customs Service controlled shipping, collected duties on imports, prevented smuggling, and enforced all other laws regulating exports and imports. Import duties were the federal government's primary source of revenue during this time, and the New York Custom House collected more revenue than any other branch—$108 million in 1877, the last year Tanner worked there. The vast number of people required to staff the customs bureaucracy, combined with the fact that all federal positions were filled by political appointees who managed huge amounts of money, made the customs service particularly ripe for scandal. Before, during, and after Tanner's time in the New York office, newspaper and congressional investigations repeatedly discovered instances of corruption. Investigators found that many senior agents took bribes to undervalue imported goods (thus reducing the duties paid on them) or to store them illegally in government warehouses. Some paid bribes simply to be appointed to one of these potentially lucrative jobs. One senior administrator made $20,000 a year in under-the-table payments, and it was estimated that fraud and incompetence in the New York office alone cost between $23 and $25 million a year. Smaller graft took the form of supervisors firing perfectly competent employees to make room for friends and relatives, taking kickbacks to protect jobs, and raising money from employees to fund political candidates.[7]

One of Tanner's colleagues—although they worked in different offices—was the novelist Herman Melville, author of *Moby-Dick*. Throughout his twenty years in the customs service, the apparently honest Melville, bitterly dependent on his job as a deputy inspector to support his family and his writing, feared that he would be fired. A friend's description of the desperate Melville indicates something of the atmosphere that prevailed in the office: "Proud, shy . . . he strives earnestly to perform his duties as to make the slightest . . . reprimand impossible from any superior. He quietly declines offers of money for special services, quietly returning money which has been thrust into his pockets . . . steadfastly doing his duty" in the face of temptation by "corrupting merchants and their clerks and runners, who think that all men can be bought."[8]

It is impossible to know if Tanner resisted corruption so studiously, but he was never publicly implicated in any wrongdoing, although he was a chief clerk by 1871 and rose to the position of deputy collector under the direction of former Union general and future president Chester A. Arthur. However, in late 1877, about the time that Arthur came under fire from President Rutherford B. Hayes, who wanted to begin implementing civil service reform by cleaning up the notorious New York Custom House, Tanner accepted an appointment as tax collector of Brooklyn. He held the job for eight years, serving under both Republican and Democratic mayors. By all accounts he was a great success. With "restless energy," he modernized the office's operations, reduced expenses, expanded services—he initiated a process by which taxpayers could pay their bills by mail—and increased collections by as much as 400 percent.[9]

In Gilded Age America, government jobs and politics were rarely separate, and Tanner's professional career was inextricably connected to his political career. He arrived at a time in the political history of Brooklyn when old-time politicians, led by the city's Democratic boss, Hugh McLaughlin, were just beginning to be challenged by Republican politicians in the state capital of Albany and by reformers in Brooklyn, led by Republicans like Mayor Seth Low. Nearly constant efforts to scrub clean the city's politics—by changing the city's charter, reducing the power of aldermen and increasing the power of the mayor; by consolidating the numerous city bureaus that controlled the jobs of hundreds, if not thousands, of political appointees; and by investigating charges of vote buying and other election-day corruption—roiled the city's politics in the 1870s and early 1880s. Most reforms failed, and Brooklyn politicians and city officials easily earned their reputations as perhaps the most corrupt civil servants in America, taking bribes, abusing their positions, committing fraud with builders and contractors, and, put simply, treating city business dealings as opportunities for enriching themselves. Despite Brooklyn's reputation as one of the worst-managed cities in the country in the 1870s, however, Tanner's standing as tax collector remained virtually pristine. His reputation was enhanced by stories like one published in a New York newspaper not long after he became collector, when a massive explosion in his department killed and injured several people. A woman carrying thirty-two dollars into the building had it all blown away; Tanner, who escaped injury, personally retrieved the cash and saved it until the woman recovered.[10]

Although Tanner's day job was with the city, he spent a great deal of his time practicing politics as a diehard Republican. Why Tanner chose the Republican Party is something of a mystery. He had grown up in a solidly Democratic county, had been mentored in the law by a Democrat, and his new home in Brooklyn had long been dominated by the party of Thomas Jefferson and Andrew Jackson. Perhaps he joined the party of Lincoln because he came of age politically—he became eligible to vote in 1866— just after the Republican Party had saved the Union. Perhaps as a young man he could somehow see beyond the tiny world of upstate New York to realize the potential benefits of the Republican commitment to encouraging business development through high tariffs and internal improvements. His innate sense of justice may have inspired him to adopt the party that had freed the slaves and offered them equal rights under the law. He may simply have seen the Republican Party as a safe haven for a double amputee who would have to rely on friends in high places to make a living. Tanner never indicated what had first attracted him to the Republicans, but it is safe to say that the party's dedication to preserving the Union and its later commitment to soldiers' issues earned his lifelong loyalty.

A recent history of Gilded Age politics argues that the issues over which Republicans and Democrats fought shifted from sectionalism and race in the 1860s and 1870s to almost solely economic matters by the 1890s. Yet, as one historian has suggested, "for both parties, the past played godfather to the present." The presence of hundreds of thousands of voters and officeholders who had worn the blue or the gray ensured that the war would never quite recede from politics until they died. Republicans would occasionally introduce civil rights bills, and the parties would from time to time clash over some issue related to Civil War remembrance (burying Confederates in national cemeteries or returning Confederate battle flags to southern states), and questions that had lent a sectional flavor to politics long before Fort Sumter—the tariff, to name just one—would continue to feature in the political debates of the age. Although Tanner would later become known as a "sound money" man—advocating the conservative gold standard over the more radical idea of loosening the nation's money supply by coining silver—he rarely talked about anything but respecting and supporting Union veterans. This single-minded political approach would qualify Tanner as a "single-issue" politician, to use a modern term, and certainly locates him within the overarching conservatism that came to represent most veterans' political ideas, which focused primarily on patriotism and sustaining the growing power of the United States. He may well have shared the wider views of his fellow Republicans, but his role in the party at the local, state, and national levels—to get out the "soldiers' vote" by publicizing the party's commitment to their needs—originated in the living memory around which he organized his life.[11]

And every vote counted. Although Republican presidents occupied the White House for all but eight years between 1869 and 1913, the parties often split Congress, with Democrats generally controlling the House and Republicans the Senate. Most states were solidly Republican (in the West and the Midwest, especially) or Democratic (this period saw the rise of the "solid South"), but a few "swing states" could make a difference in any given election. One was New York, which as Tanner's home state made his influence extremely valuable; another was Indiana, where a powerful voting bloc of Union veterans meant that Tanner would spend several weeks campaigning there during every election cycle. Although he never used the term himself, his campaigns were perfect examples of the Republicans' "Bloody Shirt" strategy, which emphasized the sacrifice of Union veterans in saving the Union from the Rebels—who, as they constantly argued, now controlled the resurgent Democratic Party. As a result, although Tanner himself would never hold elective office, his New York residence and influence with veterans—not to mention his dynamic personality and powerful rhetorical style—would make him a power in the Republican Party for decades.[12]

Tanner had gained local political prominence long before taking the tax collector's job. Brooklyn Republicans were organized into "ward clubs," and Tanner's political home was the Twenty-Second Ward. He appeared in newspaper accounts of various Republican meetings throughout the early 1870s, although reporters struggled to keep straight the details of his wounding and even his actual rank. When he addressed a meeting of the General Grant Club, he was described as having "had both his legs shot off at Fort Donnelson" in a quote that ended with the painful pun "but [he] has not lost his understanding, notwithstanding." A year later he had received a promotion to colonel, at least according to the *Brooklyn Eagle*, when he made a speech at a Twenty-Second Ward rally. By 1873 he was considered a "prominent Republican politician" and named to the nominating committee of the Twenty-Second Ward and for a time was a member of the general committee of the Kings County Republican Party. When he appeared at a party function to promote a candidate for local office, Tanner—this time called "Captain"—applauded the candidate as a man who had "risen from the ranks," and explained his own strong attraction to the party because it "look[ed] after poor men." He gave a "ringing speech" at a Republican rally in 1877, declaring that he "was glad . . . that the boys were marching, and that the political tramps of Brooklyn had got notice to march also." In 1879 he chaired the Kings County Republican convention and received credit for marshaling the "soldier vote" behind an underdog Republican candidate in Brooklyn.[13]

Despite his growing local fame, it was a little frustrating that no one could remember his actual rank in the army. Tanner commented on the confusion over twenty years later. "The newspapers and people got to referring to me as Major Tanner and Colonel Tanner, and I do not know but what I was sometimes called 'General Tanner.' No one seemed to know my military title." Since "[I] was pretty much around and to the front" in local affairs, "I must have some title, and Colonels and Majors were as thick as bees then. . . . About everybody in politics had a military title. I had mine. Several of them." He decided he needed to make a public announcement of his real rank, so as not to be "sailing under the false colors of so many titles," for, he explained, "Some day one of my political adversaries would in the heat of the campaign look up my record and discover that instead of a Major or a Colonel I was only a Corporal, and then where would I be?" Despite his wife's misgivings—she thought it would appear to be a publicity gimmick—he wrote a note to the *Brooklyn Eagle*, which informed readers that "corporal" was "not a 'nickname,' nor [was] it applied offensively. Mr. Tanner's rank in the army was that of 'Corporal.'" Tanner said, "From that time I became distinguished—at least, I was distinguished from everybody else—as 'Corporal' Tanner." Yet many of his friends continued to call him "Cap" rather than "Corporal."[14]

Tanner came into his own in local politics in 1873 when he exposed a plot by members of his own party to prevent the election of a Roman Catholic candidate for governor, the Democrat Francis Kernan—not because he was a Democrat, but because he was a Catholic. They also sought to purge Catholics from the Republican Party. The era's virulent anti-Catholicism often appeared in politics; less than twenty years earlier, the American, or "Know Nothing," Party had built an entire platform around anti-immigrant policies (focusing especially on Irish Catholics). In 1863, when thousands of New Yorkers rioted against the military draft, resulting in millions of dollars of damage and scores of deaths, most Republicans blamed immigrant Democrats, especially the Irish, who were depicted in political cartoons as more like drunken, violent apes than men. In fact, New Yorkers would not elect a Roman Catholic governor until Al Smith in 1918.

The bitter anti-Catholicism of the times made Tanner's challenge a bold move. Throughout 1873 New Yorkers and Brooklynites had waged a war of editorials and public meetings over the growing influence of Catholic parochial schools, efforts by local priests to eliminate the reading of the so-called Protestant Bible in public schools, and a campaign by Catholic schools to receive at least some public funding. The *New York Times* actually accused the Catholic clergy of trying to "overthrow" the public schools. Just two years later, the famous cartoonist Thomas Nast (known to modern Americans as the creator of the popular image of Santa Claus) would publish a cartoon in *Harper's Weekly* set on the shore of the "American River Ganges" (presumably New York's Hudson River), with a crumbling public school in the background. In the foreground stands a schoolteacher shielding his cowering pupils from an onslaught of crocodiles that, upon closer inspection, are actually Catholic cardinals whose miters become snarling, reptilian mouths filled with rows of sharp teeth.[15]

Tanner confronted the anti-Catholicism of Americans in general and of his own party in particular in a fiery speech at a Twenty-Second Ward Association meeting, perhaps at the old mansion on Fifth Avenue and Ninth Street that served as the association's headquarters. Declaring his support for the constitutional separation of church and state and freedom of religion, he exposed several instances of otherwise loyal Republicans and industrious workers being removed from office or prevented from taking office simply because they were Catholic. An employee at the Brooklyn Navy Yard and a clerk at the New York branch of the U.S. Pension Bureau lost their jobs, while a former soldier with an excellent military record and an up-and-coming Republican Party operative were rejected for a job in the police department and blackballed from becoming a delegate to the state convention, respectively, because of their faith. In the case of the man denied the appointment to the police department, Tanner claimed that members of a secret society had actually told him "frankly that they had nothing against" the man "morally, socially, or politically; but they believed he was Catholic, and they were bound that he should not have that position."[16]

Tanner's accusations sparked a heated exchange, but a somewhat watered-down version of his resolution condemning bigotry was eventually passed. The *Brooklyn Eagle* was still covering the story a month after Tanner's speech. It applauded Tanner for having "lifted the lid from a seething cauldron of prejudice and bigotry, around which ungenerous and narrow spirits danced in the seclusion of secrecy." It took Tanner, the "Republican, Protestant soldier" to "drag . . . it from its lair and hold it to the decay which the free air of heaven was certain to work on it." His speech exposing the secret society had been widely copied and helped lead to the removal of one of the plotters from a local office.[17]

Tanner's attack on religious prejudice seems to have stemmed from a sense of fairness more than an interest in religious ecumenicalism. His own religious convictions were somewhat uncertain. His occasional references to God and the afterlife were generically Protestant, and he rarely referred to actual participation in religious organizations, although the church publication *Zion's Herald* once claimed that he had been a member of Hanson

Place Methodist Episcopal Church in his own neighborhood throughout his time in Brooklyn. He would never again make a public comment on any issue related to religion—despite its continuing importance in the politics of his adopted city—which might suggest that the Corporal had hoped to improve his position in the party by challenging its leadership. If so, the ploy worked. During the controversy, the *Eagle* referred to Tanner's "sudden fame," and a few years later the *Eagle* called him the "local Hotspur of the Republican party." The nickname "Hotspur" was typically used to describe a rebel or a hothead, but the *Eagle* seemed to apply it as a compliment.[18]

Indeed, the incident seemed to endear Tanner to the Democratic-leaning but surprisingly open-minded *Brooklyn Eagle*. The *Eagle* covered Tanner's career closely, with rare nuance and an objectivity unusual for Gilded Age newspapers, which normally trumpeted with partisan vigor one party over the other. As the leading Democratic newspaper in Brooklyn, it had been critical of Lincoln and the Republicans who controlled the government during the Civil War. Yet its relative moderation ensured that it emerged from the war with a great deal of influence in the political, economic, and cultural life of Brooklyn. It was a leading booster of the city—the *Eagle* itself expanded its operations, its news coverage, and its profits as the city grew—and heavily promoted the Brooklyn Bridge project. During the 1870s and 1880s, the newspaper frequently clashed with "Boss" McLaughlin, which indicated the extent to which the *Eagle* could promote Democratic principles while maintaining a more or less independent editorial profile.[19]

That might explain the paper's ambiguous but generally positive relationship with Tanner, who was perhaps the most thoroughly Republican man in Brooklyn. Over the years the *Eagle* both criticized and lauded Tanner, providing perhaps the most complete analysis of his complex character. Early in his administration as tax collector, for instance, the *Eagle* included Tanner in its criticism of Republican politicians and officeholders in Brooklyn who opposed a bill before the state legislature that would have streamlined city government in ways that would encourage honesty and benefit taxpayers. At a time when virtually no job in a government agency—from collecting taxes to building roads to hauling garbage—remained above politics, the "Charter Amendment" would have consolidated several city departments, putting a number of employees and appointees out of work. One of the men who might have lost his job was Tanner, who had been in office less than a year. The *Eagle* went so far as to suggest that his appointment had come about because of illicit agreements or even bribes, although it stopped short of accusing Tanner of doing anything illegal. The *Eagle* predicted that he would probably be "turned out" of the tax collector's office after "the next turn of the political wheel ... before he [could] acquire any experience which [would] be of use to the city." Yet, four years later, at a time and in a place where political partisanship was a sport, a way of life, and the subject of constant speculation, the *Brooklyn Eagle* belied its Democratic tendencies to declare, after Tanner's appointment to a new term, that no one "had fault to find with the reappointment of Corporal Tanner as Tax Collector."[20]

As the leading newspaper in Brooklyn, the *Eagle* had more access to prominent politicians than most media outlets, and over the years it drew frank and apparently honest commentary from the colorful corporal. When Tanner ran for sheriff of Kings County in 1884, the *Eagle* published an "interview remarkable for its candor" with the tax collector, who had broken precedent by announcing his candidacy for the position long before the local nominating convention. Although unusual, the *Eagle* commented, "in view of the fact that most of the politicians are fond of working in the dark, he is rather to be commended for taking the people into his confidence." The paper grudgingly admired his honesty in admitting, "The office has money in it and ... what he wants is the money." The *Eagle* would always give Tanner a certain amount of leeway due to the "grievous injury" he had suffered "in defense of his country." Even though his physical condition encouraged sympathy from the public, and although Tanner was "strong with the members of the Republican organization," the *Eagle* doubted that a Republican could win a countywide election.[21]

Tanner would, in fact, lose that election, but the *Eagle*'s coverage of his career would continue even as he left Brooklyn for Washington, especially at times when it seemed necessary to puncture Tanner's ego or to defend him from unfair criticism. After he became commissioner of pensions, the *Eagle* posited, "Our gallant Brooklyn corporal, the irrepressible Tanner, continues to dwarf the administration by the increasing splendor and proportions of his personality." "As the iron moves with the magnet," it continued, "so is the country irresistibly attracted by the motions of Tanner. ... He never releases his countrymen from the spell that binds them." Although the *Eagle* seemed to find Tanner's ability to draw attention strangely attractive, it used sarcasm to burst Tanner's sense of self-importance. When he said that he was "too valuable a man" to spend time performing some mundane function, the *Eagle* responded, "And so say we all. There never was and never could be a more important man than our corporal." President Harrison's weak and rather generic administration had realized early on that "something was needed to hold it up. That something turns out to be Tanner. And, friends and countrymen, what an Atlas he is." Despite rather arch appraisals like these, Tanner granted the *Eagle* another interview three years later, after he had left the administration in disgrace. He talked about the Republicans' efforts to get him into the field to campaign for President Benjamin Harrison's reelection in 1892. The Corporal, by then a claims agent in Washington, all but flirted with the reporter, tilting comfortably back in his chair, smoking a cigar, "glanc[ing] complacently over a big roll of pension papers," and confirming that he had refused all invitations to speak because "business [was] too pressing." However, he had recently met with a number of Democrats who were also courting his influence with soldiers and would attend a soldiers' reunion in Indiana in a few days. Relishing his insider's knowledge of the campaign, he indicated that he would have "something interesting" to say about the state of affairs in that crucial swing state when he returned, and then cast doubts on Harrison's ability to carry New York. In fact, Grover Cleveland would eventually defeat the incumbent in the general election.[22]

The *Eagle*'s admiration, even affection, for the Corporal, mixed with its disapproval of most of his policies, gave the newspaper's coverage a distinctively sympathetic, knowing, and even humorous tone that Tanner probably appreciated. In 1895, when Tanner attacked the performance of the current pension commissioner, the *Eagle* found it "unfortunate . . . that he should periodically insist on instituting comparisons which in his case [were] doubly odious." Because of his good service in Brooklyn more than a decade earlier, "the *Eagle* [was] not inclined to be uncharitable enough to recall . . . his administration of the pension bureau. Suffice it to say" that his record "was not especially brilliant." Someone more sensitive "to his own defects" would not offer chances to reopen old wounds regarding his own career by highlighting the foibles of others. "But in Mr. Tanner's case," the newspaper asserted, "the excuse can at least be offered that he has long been a victim of too much mobility of mouth. We appreciate how hard it is for him to resist the temptation of saying something which will attract the public eye if not appeal to the public conscience, and making allowance for this weakness, it can in all truth be affirmed that the corporal is not beyond hope."[23]

The *Eagle* and almost everyone else in Brooklyn apparently loved Tanner's work as tax collector. He did well enough during his first four years to be reappointed by the reform-minded Republican mayor, Seth Low, in 1881. One historian—clearly no admirer—suggested sixty years later that Tanner's apparent honesty and competence derived more from the example set by the man who appointed him than from Tanner's natural abilities or character: "No better example of Seth Low's ability to make his appointees rise above themselves can be found than the case of James Tanner." Prior to his taking the job as collector of taxes for Brooklyn, Tanner had been a "time-serving Republican" and chairman of the Republican General Committee, whose primary purpose was to get loyal Republicans into good jobs. But inspired by Mayor Low, Tanner remained above scandal.[24]

Tanner deserved more credit than that; no one seriously challenged his personal honesty as collector. This certainly helped him rise through the ranks of the Republicans. By 1880, the *Brooklyn Eagle* declared, his prominence in the party was "undisputed," and he served as a delegate to that year's Republican National Convention in Chicago. He had also become influential in the state party. In an article published two decades later, the *Eagle* listed him as one of the longtime regulars at the so-called Amen Corner in the Fifth Avenue Hotel in Albany, where "lawyers and judges and United States Senators and Governors and ex-Governors and Congressmen and Cabinet members and ex-Cabinet members and newspaper men" chose candidates and plotted in the hotel bar or around a set of couches in an obscure hallway. "Corporal Tanner was in the inner circle for years," as were President Chester Arthur and U.S. Senator Roscoe Conkling.[25]

Despite this informal influence and his popularity as tax collector, Tanner retained an ambition for elective office. In 1871, only two years after his arrival in Brooklyn, he had run unsuccessfully for the state assembly from Kings County. He also lost the election for county register in 1876. However, while Democrats carried the presidential vote in Kings County that year by nineteen thousand, he had trailed by only two thousand votes, "a magnificent tribute to his popularity among all classes of his fellow-citizens."[26]

No doubt encouraged because he had run "ahead of the ticket"—he received more votes than the other losing Republicans—he ran for elective office one more time, mounting an 1884 campaign for sheriff against another veteran, James Farley, famous throughout the city as a fireman who, the *Brooklyn Eagle* declared, was "the hero of a hundred fires . . . and the brave rescuer of a score of perishing women and children." Tanner's name had been associated with the sheriff's office as early as 1878, when an unlikely rumor with uncertain origins surfaced that Tanner wanted to be sheriff so badly that he would desert the Republican Party if it refused to nominate him and run as a Democrat.[27]

Tanner based his campaign on his record as tax collector. A *Brooklyn Eagle* ad reminded voters of "his conspicuously good administration as Collector of Taxes," of "the simple truth . . . that Corporal Tanner has by his diligence and forethought saved his salary many times over to the city," and of his elimination of "the inconveniences which confronted those who had taxes to pay before his time." Otherwise, Tanner's operation was like any other big-city campaign in the Gilded Age, which relied heavily on door-to-door canvassing and a blizzard of campaign literature. Tanner claimed to have sent out one hundred thousand flyers to registered voters during the election for sheriff. In 1884 American voters did not cast their ballots in secret—the so-called Australian ballot, with uniform ballots provided by the government, would not be widely adopted in the United States until after this election. Instead, each party distributed "tickets" to likely voters, who used them to cast votes. Most years the Republican General Committee in Brooklyn had sent them through the mails, but in 1884 they had instead shipped them out to local supporters in the city's many wards, or voting districts; voters would not receive them until they arrived at the polls.[28]

An 1879 description of a typical Brooklyn campaign laid out the commitments of time and money required to run even for local office. Virtually no elected office, it declared, paid a salary "at all in proportion to the amount of money expended" on advertising, campaign events, and other expenses. Sometimes the amount spent was double or triple a year's salary, and the loser was often "hampered for a long time afterward, because of his fruitless expenditure." Because of recent reforms in maintaining the registry of eligible voters, it was less likely than in the past that candidates could actually buy votes, yet they and their party had to watch voting carefully to make sure only eligible voters cast ballots. The time between nominating conventions and elections had been reduced to three or four weeks, meaning that candidates had little time in which to hire men to go into the neighborhoods and print and distribute campaign literature. Campaign workers had to count and wrap ballots with rubber bands, bag them, carry them to various wards and districts, and get them into the hands of the voters. Other volunteers or employees distributed "pasters"—sheets with candidates' names and pictures—by posting them on buildings or handing them out to individuals. "Circulars" would list the candidates' policies and record and defend him against attacks by rivals.[29]

Newspapers commented on a candidate's every move. Early on the *Brooklyn Eagle* thought it curious that Tanner had joined a Methodist church near his home just six months before mounting his campaign for sheriff, implying that he had "found" religion as a way of winning more votes. He had also recently made derisive comments about the Democrats' standing with the Almighty, assuring his listeners that God was on the side of the Republicans. The *Eagle* thought such "flippant and irreverent" remarks were inappropriate for someone who had so recently joined a church, commenting, "The *Eagle* has always regarded Corporal Tanner as being a manly man and a genial and companionable fellow citizen. It will regret to see him join the hypocritical band" of stereotypical politicians. Early in the fall, the *Eagle* criticized Tanner for going to New Haven, Connecticut, to campaign on behalf of the Republican presidential candidate, James G. Blaine. Tanner had not only "outdid himself in blackguardism" with his over-the-top rhetoric about Democratic "criminality" and "indelicate" comments about Democratic nominee Grover Cleveland's alleged fathering of an illegitimate child as a bachelor in Buffalo, New York, but he had also violated Mayor Low's explicit instructions not to campaign during office hours.[30]

But, in truth, Tanner had always acted like a man campaigning for office. In an interview a few days before the election, he predicted that veterans would, of course, vote for him, as would a number of Democratic businessmen who appreciated the way he had run his department. "Besides," he added, "I know positively that there are many men who feel, perhaps unduly, grateful to me for little favors I have been able to do in the past, such as lecturing for almost every religious denomination in the city, for the Masonic Fraternity, St. Patrick's Alliance and the House of the Good Shepherd. This kind of work has never put a penny in my pocket." Indeed, his apparently steadfast commitment to administering the financial side of his job cleanly was part of his appeal. "As Tax Collector I have handled some forty millions of dollars of the people's money and not a penny has stuck; accounts have always been found correct and I am a mighty poor man to-day." Indeed, Tanner's incessant participation in veterans' causes and activities (described later in this chapter) could be seen as a part of his nearly perpetual campaigning; there were at least eight thousand veteran voters in Brooklyn at the time, and Tanner always seemed to be courting their approval.[31]

In a typical appearance less than two weeks before the election, Tanner touted his record as tax collector. But he began his speech with a fairly subtle reference to the "Bloody Shirt" by tapping his crutch against the leg of a table and saying, "I am not marching around as fast as I used to in the old days"—he paused here for a round of applause—"and I want here to deny the insinuation . . . that I lost my legs while running away from the enemy." Another round of applause indicated that the audience knew of a recent effort to cast doubts on Tanner's war record. "My face was to the front when I was struck," he continued, "and I was on the front line of battle. I believe we will be on the front line of battle on election day, and the other side will be our prisoners." After even more applause, he noted that the Democrats had nominated an old soldier for sheriff for the first time: "I accord my opponent his due when I say he was a good soldier and a brave fireman." But he simply was not up to the "complexities" of the office. He closed the speech with the kind of honesty for which he was known, bluntly admitting that he had been pursuing the sheriff's job for two years because "the office . . . [was] one of considerable emolument, and one term [was] sufficient to permit a man to retire to the bosom of his family with a competency sufficient to keep him comfortably after a hard fought struggle."[32]

Tanner was right. The position had little to do with law enforcement. Rather, a sheriff ensured that much of the mundane and not particularly pleasant work of the county was completed. He was responsible for executing and enforcing a number of civil processes, including evictions, administering foreclosure sales, and serving court papers, as well as managing the jail and several other administrative tasks. Until the 1890s, sheriffs in New York were paid out of the fees that they collected from citizens for performing these various duties, and those fees could lead to huge salaries: just two years after the 1884 election, the sheriff reported collections of well over forty-one thousand dollars for a single year![33]

Tanner badly wanted the job and hoped that his reputation would encourage fellow veterans to turn out on his behalf. A leading veterans' newspaper, the *National Tribune*, declared Tanner to be "one of the best of soldiers that the army had, one of the truest of comrades, and one of the most zealous of Grand Army men." His "unusual popularity" in a

Democratic-leaning county should help him overcome his party's minority status. "Without any legs at all," the *Tribune* predicted with a typical pun highlighting Tanner's disability, "he ought to easily outrun all competitors who have the advantages of two limbs." But it was not to be. In an election year when Grover Cleveland became the only Democrat and only non-Union veteran to win the presidency between 1868 and 1900, Tanner once again ran "ahead of the ticket"—but still lost.[34]

Tanner left the tax collector's office in 1885. He spent the next several years seeking ways to replace the income that had allowed his family to live in Brooklyn's best neighborhood. Despite the frequent references he and others made to his "poverty"—at about this time the *Eagle* reported that he was not a "man of means," which simply meant that he had no other source of revenue besides whatever he could earn (such as a family fortune or business investments)—he was not poor in any modern sense of the word. A year earlier a newspaper had reported that Tanner's "snug little position" earned him $15,000 per year. If true, that was the equivalent of an income of over $350,000 in 2010.[35]

But if he wanted to maintain that kind of income, he would have to look outside Brooklyn.

Veteranizing

Tanner was driven to make a name for himself and a good living for his family, but the central thread running throughout his public life was his association with veterans' causes. Like millions of their fellow Americans, Civil War veterans were organizers and joiners. Even before the war was over, officers especially and some common soldiers began forming associations. After 1865, the organizations multiplied rapidly, with veterans of specific armies—the Army of the Tennessee, the Army of the Cumberland, and the Army of the Ohio, for instance—and of specific units forming groups during the two or three years after Appomattox.

The largest and most important organization for Union veterans was the Grand Army of the Republic. Formed soon after the war, the GAR adopted a complicated, hierarchical membership structure that offended many common soldiers and caused the membership to stagnate at about thirty thousand during the 1870s. But a growing interest in the war and an expanded pension system for veterans disabled or injured during the war—which encouraged men to reconnect with former comrades whom they needed as witnesses for their pension applications—led to a rapid expansion in the 1880s to over four hundred thousand members.[36]

The GAR was organized into state "divisions" and local "posts," which were the building blocks of the organization. Groups of veterans would apply to the state organization for permission to form posts, which were assigned numbers based on the order of their founding, but also named after local soldiers, prominent officers, or even particularly patriotic or famous civilians. In Brooklyn, for instance, names of posts included prominent army and naval officers like Samuel F. DuPont, David Farragut, Jesse Reno, James B. McPherson, and Gouverneur K. Warren, as well as names of soldiers known only to the men in the post, such as Pvt. Stephen Thatford, Sgt. William Rankin, and Lt. Louis Hamilton. Veterans also honored the abolitionist and longtime minister at Brooklyn's Plymouth Church, Henry Ward Beecher, and the heroine of John Greenleaf Whittier's inspirational poem of Unionist resistance to Confederate aggression, Barbara Frietchie, by naming GAR posts after them. Tanner became a member of the GAR at least as early as his arrival in Brooklyn, when he joined Rankin Post 10, named after Sgt. William Rankin, of the Eighty-Fourth New York, who was killed at Spotsylvania.[37]

The GAR's official motto was "Fraternity, Charity, Loyalty," and every post devoted a great deal of energy and resources to raising money to help provide relief for members who had fallen on hard times. An 1884 pamphlet outlined some of the ways that the twenty-two posts of the Brooklyn GAR tried to help veterans. They had established a central committee working out of the city hall office, where they offered free aid for veterans applying for pensions; operated a "Bureau of Employment" that tried to connect veterans with jobs and lobbied local businesses and government officials to hire veterans; promoted the idea of "veteran preference," in which employers, "where the qualifications are equal, and the choice is to be made between a veteran of the war, and one who has not served," would hire the veteran; and provided funerals for destitute members. The Rankin Post's relief committee sponsored a fund-raiser in 1880 that featured singers, a violinist, an organist, a pianist, and an "elocutionist," who performed dramatic readings. This was the first of several concerts that the post would host on behalf of the relief fund, which was "exhausted, while the calls for relief [were] urgent and frequent." On another occasion, Tanner himself acted as auctioneer at a "pound party," where admission was a wrapped package weighing at least one pound. Bidders purchased them sight unseen; they were unwrapped to reveal items such as soda crackers, baby clothes, coffee, soap, cornmeal, chalk, kindling wood, and doughnuts.[38]

Posts held meetings every few weeks—sometimes as often as twice a month—while the state and national organizations held annual meetings called "encampments," which brought veterans together in quasi-military gatherings. GAR officers issued "orders" and assembled staffs to help administer the reunions, which included parades and formal reviews that occupied parts of each day, while the men slept in tent villages and ate simple army food like beans and hardtack crackers served on tin plates. Some featured "sham battles" similar to modern-day reenactments. National meetings could bring tens of thousands of veterans and double or triple that number of family members and other civilians. The favorite part of any veterans' encampment, large or small, was the "campfire," where veterans would gather around a real campfire or in a meeting hall to tell war stories, read patriotic poems, sing old army songs, and smoke old-fashioned, army-style clay pipes.[39]

The writer Sherwood Anderson's father had served in the Union army and enthusiastically took part in many local veterans' activities, which the younger Anderson called "veteranizing." There was a similar, if deeper, urgency to Tanner's participation in the GAR and other organizations. His short and inglorious military career, made notable only for the grievous wounds he suffered in a freak battlefield incident, seems to have made him want to create a shared past with other veterans whose service had been more memorable—men who had actually done something to save the Union besides getting their feet shot off. He may have been ashamed of the wretched performance in combat of the Eighty-Seventh, perhaps even of his mundane career as a soldier. His sudden departure from the army and unsatisfactory role in the North's victory seemed to leave a void that he filled by immersing himself in veterans' affairs and wrapping himself in the heroism and patriotism that came to be associated with virtually all old soldiers.[40]

Tanner would serve as commander and speak at several national encampments of the Union Veterans Legion, a much smaller organization limited to men who had served in the army for two years or had been wounded in action. But he poured most of his energy into the GAR, in which he would hold a number of offices at the local, state, and national levels. He won election as delegate to the state encampment in late 1875, sat on the national pension committee for many years, and was judge advocate general of the national GAR in 1892. Tanner would later join U. S. Grant Post 327 when it formed in 1883; he would apparently remain a member of this elite post even after he moved to Washington.[41]

The GAR helped extend the influence of the Civil War beyond Reconstruction and into the 1890s. Its members believed that one of their most important duties was to keep alive the memories of the men who had served in the Union army. Memorial Day—often called "Decoration Day"—had become a formal GAR and national holiday in 1868. It was the day when Union veterans would lead their families, friends, and neighbors in ceremonies recognizing the Yankees who had given their lives to save the Union. During Tanner's years in Brooklyn, Memorial Day was a major event. In 1882, for instance, 15,000 spectators gathered along the parade route to watch over 4,500 GAR members, along with a group of "cadets" (sons of veterans ranging in age from eight to sixteen), a battalion of U.S. Marines, and the Fourteenth Regiment of the New York National Guard parade through the city. At Greenwood Cemetery, Mayor Low delivered an address, a local minister gave a sermon, and veterans decorated the graves of dead comrades. Ceremonies were also held in other Brooklyn cemeteries, and most businesses were closed. Public buildings and private homes were decorated with flags, and the *New York Times* reported that "the day generally was observed as a holiday by people of all classes."[42]

The highlight of any Memorial Day was a somber and patriotic speech, usually delivered by a veteran or a prominent clergyman. Tanner would eventually speak at hundreds of veterans' functions, but his first recorded speech to a GAR gathering came in 1873, when he spoke at one of the most important commemorations in New York. The invitation to deliver the address certainly recognized the twenty-nine-year-old's rising prominence in veterans' circles (although the article announcing his speech called him "Captain," and the article reporting it a day later called him "Major"). The ceremony took place at Greenwood Cemetery in Brooklyn, where two hundred Union veterans were buried, at the grave of one of the first and youngest victims of the war, Clarence McKenzie, a drummer boy from Brooklyn who had died after being accidentally shot in camp during the first weeks of the war. Although he did not record his thoughts on the occasion, Tanner might have reflected on the fact that he had been only five years older than Clarence when he had gone off to war. Like Clarence, he had been one of the first volunteers from his hometown. And although he had survived, he, too, had sacrificed much for his country. Tanner probably delivered his speech as he stood next to the simple white marker at the boy's grave. Years later it would be replaced by a life-sized figure of a drummer boy modeled after young Clarence, and a Brooklyn GAR post would take McKenzie's name.[43]

Tanner's talk resembled thousands of other Memorial Day speeches delivered every year from 1865 through the early twentieth century, paying homage to the dead veterans, thanking God for the Union victory, refusing to cast blame. The tone was humble, patriotic, and forward looking. "In accord with one of the holiest sentiments of the human heart we gather here on this our memorial day, in this sacred enclosure to perform one of the most tender duties. . . . With bated breath and quickened pulses we stand here in the presence of sanctified death." Tanner emphasized the men rather than the cause: "Being dead they yet speak . . . to us . . . of a country's history illuminated and made dazzling by the recorded glories of their performances." He refused to mourn them but rather "rejoiced[d] that when the storm of civil war burst on the country men were found so noble as those whose deeds" were being commemorated. He also sought, as did many speakers on this somber day, to honor the Confederate dead, "not in memory of their cause, that [Union soldiers] loathed, fought and conquered, but because they were Americans and fought and died bravely."[44]

In this, his first known Memorial Day oration, Tanner set forth themes that he would stress throughout his career as a public speaker: the loyalty and sacrifice of the soldiers, the happy results of the conflict, the need for reconciliation between North and South, and admiration for the Grand Army, under whose auspices the dead were remembered. These appearances were less famous than Tanner's later speeches, but Memorial Day did bring out the best in Tanner's well-known ability to capture an audience. Three years later he was commander of the New York State GAR and his official Memorial Day message to members throughout the state reflected his often moving way with words: "In accordance with the established usage of our order," it began, "we go out to the graves of our dead comrades to present to them our votive offering of flowers, and to pay to their memories that mead of praise which the performance of noble deeds, gallantly accomplished, renders their just due."[45]

When his health permitted, Tanner almost always gave a speech somewhere on Memorial Day, although he made many other appearances at GAR events as he rose through the ranks of his beloved organization. In 1876, at the age of thirty-two, he won election as commander of the state organization. In a rare tribute to his popularity and effectiveness, he was reelected a year later. In a "history" of the U. S. Grant Post published in 1885, Tanner's two-page biography declared that he was "well-known to nearly every Grand Army veteran throughout the country" and asserted, "Probably no man connected with the Grand Army of the Republic has done more to advance its interests, or the interests of the homeless and disabled veterans, than Corporal Tanner."[46]

That reputation stemmed from his leadership in the campaign to build a state home for disabled soldiers. Small, volunteer-led efforts to care for sick and wounded soldiers had sprung up in a number of cities during the war, but the long-term problem of what to do with disabled soldiers was too big for purely local efforts, and in 1865 Congress had established the National Asylum for Disabled Volunteer Soldiers (later changed to National Home). The first four branches opened in Maine, Ohio, Wisconsin, and Virginia, with several more founded later in the century. By the 1870s and 1880s, the federal homes had earned reputations as large, impersonal institutions that provided inadequate care and isolated men from friends and loved ones. In response, the GAR began advocating the building of state homes for the use only of men living in those states. These homes tended to be smaller, homier institutions that often admitted wives and widows.[47]

In fact, New York built one of the first state-run homes for veterans. Inspired by his own injuries to take a leadership role, Tanner sought to help his fellow old soldiers who, "stung by the ingratitude of those in whose defense they had braved death and sacrificed their health, [had begun] to despair." He and many others cited the statistic that as many as six hundred New York veterans languished in poorhouses.[48]

The stage had been set more than a decade earlier, when the state legislature had passed a law establishing a soldiers' home but never built it. Veterans vainly continued to request funds over the next few years. In early 1875, the state GAR appointed a committee to begin a new campaign. Later that year, Tanner and several others composed an "address" that was formally presented at the state encampment the following summer. It complained about the legislature's lack of support for veterans, argued that this was a nonpartisan issue that all lawmakers should get behind, and, no doubt at the behest of Tanner, predicted that friends of old soldiers in Brooklyn would contribute ten thousand dollars toward the home. Energized by the statement, GAR members formed more committees; Tanner, by then state commander, became chairman of the location committee. By the summer of 1876, the legislature had passed the necessary legislation, and a number of New York cities had offered inducements and locations for the home. Eventually the GAR chose Bath, in far western New York near the Pennsylvania border.[49]

The New York GAR held its 1876 summer encampment in Yonkers, a short trip up the Hudson River from New York City. It celebrated the burgeoning campaign for a soldiers' home but also reflected the rather low-key ambience of reunions during this first phase of the GAR's history, which stood in stark contrast to the large, rowdy encampments held after the GAR's dramatic growth in the early 1880s. Commander Tanner remarked that the warm reception Yonkers had extended to the veterans reflected the support they had enjoyed from their home-front countrymen and women over a decade earlier while they fought to preserve the "Temple of Liberty." Here, he said, "We received a welcome showing that, though our swords may now be ploughshares and our spears pruning-hooks, you still preserve a grateful remembrance of the days when we stood in serried ranks at the front, sustained by your encouraging words and protected by your prayers." A band played "Marching through Georgia," a wartime commemoration of Gen. William T. Sherman's famous 1864 "March to the Sea" from Atlanta to Savannah; then the nonmembers in the audience were asked to leave, the band played two more songs, and the proceedings were "opened in due form." The official proceedings reveal just how tenuous the GAR's status was during these years before its 1880s revival. They also foreshadow many of the issues that would occupy the organization in general and Tanner in particular for the next twenty years. Fewer than ninety men were in attendance, and a roll call revealed that over half of the twenty-one past commanders and elected officers were absent and that only 41 of the state's 103 posts had sent delegates. Mundane administrative matters took up much of the business meeting. There was some trouble with posts submitting annual and quarterly reports on membership, dues, and expenses. For failing to pay dues, 3 posts needed to be "cut . . . off as dead wood," while another 3 voluntarily gave up their charters for the same reason. Yet another post was shut down because it had admitted persons ineligible for membership. "We cannot guard too closely," wrote the assistant adjutant general, "against the admission of improper persons to . . . our Order." Despite these problems, several formerly troubled posts had gained members and stability in the past year, and 7 new posts had been chartered, including one in Bath named after Gen. George A. Custer, the "boy general" of the Civil War who had been killed by Indians with many of his men on the Little Big Horn just a few weeks earlier. The adjutant's report applauded the "successful inauguration of the Soldiers' Home movement" and urged posts to ask each of their members to contribute a dollar toward the home fund.[50]

The second day of the meeting was given over to discussions of other procedural matters but also to issues related to the welfare of soldiers' orphans and veterans' graves. A sharp disagreement occurred over a motion to create a category of honorary members for nonveterans who had aided the war effort substantially. One "comrade" declared—to "vociferous" applause—that this would encourage poor posts to admit members with money but no military record and argued that there were plenty of veterans who had not yet joined. He argued, "The Comrades should go to work to get them in. After they are in it is time enough to talk about admitting those who helped us during the war." Another comrade suggested an amendment that would include sons of veterans. The final word on the subject came with an emotional speech by a veteran from far western New York, who argued that allowing anyone but a veteran into the GAR would lead to its politicization and undercut the mission of the organization as articulated by its motto. Evoking the sentiments of Henry V's famous "St. Crispin's Day" speech, in which—as told by Shakespeare—he called the ragged army of Englishmen facing the overwhelming French force at Agincourt, "We few, we happy few, we band of brothers," Comrade Baxter emotionally declared,

> The golden chain that fastens us together has three links—Fraternity, Charity and Loyalty. As we near the time when we must all pass away to the camp beyond, when we feel that the circle that draws us together is gradually growing smaller and drawing us nearer to each other, how much prouder and happier we will be to look around upon the gradually decreasing little band and acknowledge all as comrades and feeling prouder of our organization, because there are but few of us. And finally, when the last representative of this honored Order takes his farewell look at the old flag, and goes up to the battalions above, he will then join with all the old soldiers in an encampment that shall never end.[51]

A "thundering" voice vote of "no" defeated the resolution moments after Baxter sat down. Tanner broke the tension and drew a round of laughter when he deadpanned, "It is my opinion that" the resolution to expand membership criteria was "not carried."[52]

There was time for fun as well as for debate. The men bowled, went target shooting, and enjoyed several picnics hosted by local posts, lubricated by "that fluid which 'maketh the heart of man glad,' as Solomon said." At one of the picnics Tanner added to the sentimental ambience of the occasion by remarking, "Tender and tearful are our thoughts to-day," and introduced a representative of the GAR post in Bath, who officially confirmed that the home would be built in his city. Tanner declared, "I thank God from the bottom of my heart that the members of the Grand Army of the Republic are to be the means of providing such a place. Let us then determine, each and all, to do our best to make the Grand Army Soldiers' Home a success, and it will be a success." The closing banquet featured good food, martial music, patriotic poems, a humorous song about Jeff Davis, brief messages from President U. S. Grant and Gen. William T. Sherman, and a seemingly endless series of toasts to the president, to the state of New York, to the Army of the Potomac, to departed comrades, to the "Private Soldier; honest, brave and faithful," to "the ladies," and many others that kept the old soldiers drinking, laughing, and crying until after 2:00 a.m. Commander Tanner was "warmly applauded" when he rose to accept a toast in his honor. "I am prouder of the Grand Army of the Republic to-night, prouder this year, than ever before," he declared, "because this year it has been written in the calendar of fate that the disgrace which has so long sullied the fair fame of the Empire State is to be wiped out and in the Fall we are to rear a domicile known as the Soldiers' Home, where the men of New York who stood up for the Union can be gathered in."[53]

Funding the soldiers' home became Tanner's primary cause during the next two years. He traveled the state raising money and inspiring New Yorkers to petition the legislature on behalf of the "maimed defenders" of the Union. At a meeting held in mid-March 1877 and attended by scores of Brooklyn's political and cultural elite—including the poet William Cullen Bryant, future president (and Tanner's former boss at the custom house) Chester Arthur, and several former Union and current state militia generals—Tanner lamented the "disgrace" of the state's having ignored its most needy veterans for so long and gave an update on his and the GAR's fundraising. Buffalo, Utica, and Elmira had each pledged five thousand dollars and Albany ten thousand dollars. Tanner asked, "What would New York do?" A month later he exceeded his own prediction when he headlined an event at the Brooklyn Academy of Music that raised thirteen thousand dollars in pledges in a half hour.[54]

His efforts paid off. When the cornerstone for the first building was laid in June 1877, the state GAR, still led by Tanner, held its summer encampment in Bath in honor of the occasion. Residents and businessmen festooned their homes and offices with flags and banners. Tanner's speech to the assembled veterans applauded Bath's leadership in "perpetuat[ing] the memory of those who saved the State and Nation from destruction." After getting the audience to sing "Marching through Georgia," Tanner took a seat to receive their thanks. The next day, the formal laying of the cornerstone was held. Once again Tanner, joined by such notables as Henry Ward Beecher, spoke to a crowd of thousands. Tanner received the honor of laying the stone into place.[55]

The home opened a year and a half later with yet another grand ceremony attended by three thousand people. Tanner delivered the final address, which provided a brief history of the need for the home and the campaign to build it. Although the first residents numbered just over six dozen, eventually the home had beds for six hundred men. The *Brooklyn Eagle* acknowledged that no one had done more than Tanner on behalf of the home, which was one reason that he had "got into the good graces" of Brooklyn. "His maimed body [was] the best possible evidence of the part he played in the war," and his "course since the war [had] been one admirably calculated to make ashamed the political patriotism which sought to thrive upon coddled rancor after all strife between men had ceased." He had also "impressed himself upon the city as a gentleman not less liberal in mind than he [was] kindly of heart." Although a state investigation revealed harsh treatment and constant tension between residents and administrators—the conflict belied the descriptions of idyllic surroundings and patriotic generosity that dominated the media—Tanner's role in the creation of the home would be a lasting legacy.[56]

In addition to leading the effort to care for sick and disabled veterans, during his time in Brooklyn Tanner became one of the more prominent advocates among veterans for the principle of "reconciliation," a cause he would promote throughout his GAR career. Many historians have explored reconciliation's long and complicated history. The best-known interpretation is that of David Blight, who argues that the declining tension between North and South depended on the former accepting the latter's attitudes about race. Slavery had ended, of course, and southerners adapted quickly to the new economic realities of hiring rather than owning their workers. But despite laws and constitutional amendments establishing legal equality for African Americans, in the 1870s and 1880s those legal guarantees began a steep decline that by 1900 would lead to strict racial segregation and the disfranchisement of southern blacks. In effect, a substantial majority of northerners decided that national unity was more important than racial justice. Old soldiers played an important role in this process. As the men who had actually risked their lives and often sacrificed their health for their countries, by the 1880s they had taken the lead in pushing political and moral issues to the background and highlighting the courage, hardships, and nobility shared by soldiers on both sides. It came to matter less *what* the men had fought for than that they had fought for *something*, and that in doing so they had demonstrated the character and patriotism that distinguished the American "race." GAR and Confederate veterans' organizations—the largest, the United Confederate Veterans (UCV), was formed in 1889—began holding joint reunions, and the intricacies of strategy and tactics and the pathetic and humorous experiences of common soldiers seized the public's imagination, driving the original issues that had led to the war out of sight.[57]

Although Caroline E. Janney has recently warned that reconciliation was never as complete or as uncomplicated as Blight and others have argued, Tanner, who rarely mentioned slavery or emancipation in particular or race in general, was one of the minority (according to Janney) who committed himself fully to reconciliation. In doing so, Tanner identified himself with a very specific collective experience that may have eased whatever discomfort he perhaps felt about his own short and fairly undistinguished service. It was a way to capture a piece of the glory he had missed, to make his sacrifice seem more purposeful rather than simply accidental. In the warm embrace of the GAR, the boy who probably never fired his gun in anger became the man who with hundreds of thousands of others had saved the Union. Tanner earned far more recognition as a veteran than as a soldier, and he enhanced that reputation by leading the charge for reconciliation.[58]

The Corporal took every opportunity to demonstrate and encourage friendly relations between the sections. As commander of the New York and, later, national GAR, Tanner ordered the graves of dead Confederates, many of whom had died and were buried at northern prison camps, to be decorated on Memorial Day. He came around to the idea of returning captured Confederate battle flags to southern states, which symbolized the reunification of the sections. "Unitedly we march along the highway of nations," he said, "rose bushes blossoming over and around, and the birds nesting in the mouths of the cannon that once roared defiance and death at each other, the world applauding, our conscience approving." At an appearance in Dallas in 1906, he recalled his first visit to Texas sixteen years earlier, when he was welcomed to Galveston by a line of veterans in blue and a line of veterans in gray. "I have long ago found," he said, "that the men who fought each other have learned that the men who can place life on the altar of conviction on principle are worth forgiving when the fight is over and of loving when the country is together again."[59]

Tanner's advocacy of reconciliation led to an unlikely friendship with Sumner A. Cunningham, the former Rebel and founding editor of the *Confederate Veteran*, the most influential publication for former Confederates. Cunningham was, as contemporaries and historians have termed it, an "unreconstructed Rebel," aggressively defending the Confederate cause and promoting the interests of Confederate veterans. His magazine reached tens of thousands of subscribers and was the official publication of the UCV, the southern equivalent of the GAR. Cunningham rarely expressed approval of northern politicians or veterans, but he developed a soft spot for Tanner, beginning in 1895 when Tanner wrote a thoughtful letter to the *Veteran* about recent criticisms by GAR posts of the erection of monuments to Confederates. "Nothing you or I can say or do," he told Cunningham, "will change the opinions of mankind in respect to these matters." Tanner admitted that, as a northerner and a Union veteran, "I look at [the issue] and say to myself, Why are these men thus honored?" However, "calm reason arises and says, these men represented a tremendous unanimity of sentiment in their section, and they died for that sentiment. And all my life, without regard to what quarter of earth, or to what people it applied, I have felt and maintained that those who do not remember and honor their dead, especially if they died fighting for them, should be regarded only with contempt." This classic statement of a veterans' preference to ignore political differences and emphasize shared sacrifices and commitments—even to opposite political credos—thawed Cunningham's normally icy reaction to northerners and to the "namby pamby sentiment for conglomerate mixture of the 'blue and gray,'" as he once wrote.[60]

A little over a year later Tanner made a historic appearance at the 1896 reunion of the UCV. Years before he had led a fund-raising effort among Union veterans to help build a home for destitute Confederate veterans in Richmond, which eventually opened in 1885 as the R. E. Lee Camp Soldiers' Home. His address was "the leading sensation of the Reunion." The UCV commander, John B. Gordon, introduced the Corporal, reminding the audience of his efforts on behalf of Confederate veterans. "Cheers followed cheers, and from ten thousand tongues exclamations came, and, by ten thousand hands handkerchiefs, fans and hats were waved." Tanner made the customary reference on occasions such as this to old times, when it was likely that some of the men before him had been shooting at him on some distant battlefield. He also argued that the men who had fought each other at Malvern Hill or Gettysburg had more in common with one another than with the unworthy men of the North and the South who had found reasons to remain at home rather than serve their country or region. He acknowledged that political opinions were largely a matter of nurture and geography; had he grown up in the South, he was certain that he would have worn the gray rather than the blue. Tanner told the story of his fund-raising on behalf of the Confederate soldiers' home, mentioned with approval the erection of the monument in Chicago to the Confederate prisoners who had died at Camp Douglas, and accepted applause and laughter when he complimented the women in attendance by admitting, "If you had not had the ladies with you as they were, we would have licked you eighteen months sooner than we did." After a digression into vague pieces of advice to the younger people in the audience, Tanner returned to his theme of reconciliation, calling both Lee and Grant worthy examples of their sections and of their country. His stirring finish combined the spiritual and the political, the past and the future: "I believe we have met here today ... in the spirit of fraternity and fraternal love in the fullest sense, absolutely without regard to sectional lines. As I step from this platform my soul is filled with this one thought, that if it be granted in the immortal regions of beatific peace that spirit eye can gaze upon material scenes and forms, I am confident that Grant and Lee, Sherman and Johnson"— all dead generals, two from each side—"and their colleagues gone before, are looking upon us today and thanking God that this spirit exists at this time."[61]

An Alabama newspaper headlined its story about the encampment with "Corporal Tanner Caught the Vets" and called him "the Figure of the Day." A correspondent to the *Confederate Veteran* overheard one old Confederate say, "Comrades, I want to tell you that since I heard Tanner I'm a changed man. I'm shot in the heart. I've shouted myself hoarse for him, and hereafter I shall hurrah for Tanner!"[62]

Tanner's reputation as an advocate of sectional reconciliation continued into the twentieth century. His impromptu remarks at the 1912 ceremony marking the laying of the cornerstone of the Confederate monument in

Arlington National Cemetery recalled earlier celebrations of reconciliation. He summarized his feelings about the monument—which was controversial among some northern veterans—with the statement, "Wherever on this broad earth there exist a people who will encourage their manhood of any and all ages to go out and battle for a cause and then will permit those who gave their lives in sacrifice to that cause to lie in unmarked sepulchers and the memory of them to die out, they are a people regarding whom I have no power of expression with which to convey to you the measure of scorn and contempt I feel therefore."[63]

His comment at a Memorial Day celebration in Chicago—that he raised his hat every time he passed the monument to the Confederate soldiers who had died there, "not to the Lost Cause, but to the brave men who died in its defense"—inspired a poem called "Corporal Tanner," which went, in part

> Voice of a patriot-prophet, dreaming
> Of a Union born of love
> With the starry Standard streaming
> All the States above . . .
>
> To salute the nation's banner,
> Streaming in the light of May,
> And to gallant Corporal Tanner,
> Lift our hats today.[64]

Tanner even appeared in the minutes of the 1914 convention of the United Daughters of the Confederacy (UDC)—perhaps the leading advocate of recognizing and even romanticizing the contributions of Confederate soldiers and the legitimacy of the "lost cause"—when a speaker contrasted the "diatribe" of a recent GAR commander against the UDC to Tanner's comments to the UDC at its Washington convention two years earlier, when he had said, "I honor the sentiment which prompts you to cherish your flag. It is akin to that which prompts the mother to go to the bottom drawer of the bureau, take out the little dead baby's shoes, kiss them and weep over them." He finished the thought with a smile and a remark he used on other occasions: "I buried my legs in the Shenandoah Valley and I buried my animosity at Appomattox."[65]

But Tanner could not reconcile himself to all elements of the Confederate past. For instance, long after the war he retained a hatred of Jefferson

Davis, the Confederate president. "I would not march in the funeral procession of Jefferson Davis," he announced when Davis died late in 1889, although "[I] would uncover my head at the grave of Stonewall Jackson, who commanded the forces whose guns knocked my legs off." But even his disdain for the Confederate president could not eclipse his conciliatory ideals. "I certainly have no quarrel with the people who honored Mr. Davis and mourn his departure."[66]

Another trace of long-lasting bitterness surfaced when Tanner attacked the idea promoted by Georgia's UDC of erecting a monument to Capt. Henry Wirz, the commandant of the infamous prison camp at Andersonville and the only former Confederate to be executed for wartime actions. Tanner began by saying, "When the accursed soul of Captain Wirz floated into the corridors of hell, the devil recognized that his only possible competitor was there." At the GAR National Encampment in 1906, Tanner took the floor to criticize the women's groups that supported the monument. Although he did not want to "get into a warfare with women," he asserted, "It is time to speak out man-fashion in a dignified way, and let the country know that the Grand Army of the Republic makes its dignified protest against the exaltation of the man who sent to horrible death so many of our comrades and who caused such inexpressible anguish in the hearts of the people of the North." Tanner's remarks shocked southerners. Remarked one Confederate veteran, "We cannot understand how Corporal Tanner expects us old fellows in Gray to love and hobnob with him when he attacks our women in this way."[67]

The controversy soon subsided, and most southerners seemed to go along with the sentiments expressed by John B. Gordon, the hard-fighting Confederate general, U.S. senator and governor of Georgia, and commander of the UCV from its formation in 1890 to his death in 1904, who in his reminiscences recalled his first meeting with Tanner, on a train heading to Richmond. When Gordon "jocularly" asked him if he feared going into former Confederate territory without a guard, Tanner replied, "I left both my legs buried in Virginia soil, and I think a man ought to be allowed peaceably to visit his own graveyard." They immediately became friends, and as he came to know Tanner better over the next few years, Tanner's demeanor, public comments, and efforts on behalf of building a home for Confederate veterans in Richmond led Gordon to admire the "exuberance of his spirits, the cordiality of his greeting, and the catholicity of his sentiments."[68]

A Favorite on the Stump

With a young family accustomed to a fairly affluent lifestyle, Tanner had to scramble to find ways of making a living after he left the tax collector's office. Around the time of his departure from the office, he and his family journeyed west. In addition to giving speeches to GAR posts, he visited his good friend and fellow veteran celebrity John "Captain Jack" Crawford at his New Mexico ranch. Tanner eventually invested in horse ranches and mines with the Crawford family, but any profits he earned from those ventures would come later.[69]

Ever the entrepreneur, Tanner apparently became a bookseller. He never spoke of it, but from time to time a newspaper would hint that he had gone into this potentially lucrative line of work. The *Brooklyn Eagle* mentioned Tanner's "book business" in 1887 and also reported a legal wrangle between Tanner and one of his customers. A few years later, the *Eagle* reported that Tanner had "peddled the 'Life of Grant' for a living" in the late 1880s.[70]

It is likely that Tanner sold books by subscription. Under this system, publishers contracted with an author to write a big book, often filled with illustrations, on popular subjects—war histories and biographies of generals and presidents were quite common during the Gilded Age—and then sent agents into the field to line up subscribers. Only after salesmen reached a critical mass of orders would the books actually be printed. It seems that a number of former soldiers engaged in this work after the war, especially men too disabled for factory or farm work. Soldiers' newspapers frequently advertised for agents to sell war-related memorabilia, books, and magazines. *Eighteen Months a Prisoner under the Rebel Flag*, an ad in the *American Tribune* promised, "sells at sight. . . . Never fails." The Iowa-based *Grand Army Advocate* assured "OLD SOLDIERS" who "Wish[ed] Profitable Employment" that *Iowa in War Times* was "the best book to sell in Iowa." Focusing on recruiting agents and increasing sales through GAR posts, the ad reported that one old soldier made forty dollars during his first two days on the job. "Hustlers" could make thousands of dollars as agents for the "Humorous, Pathetic, Fascinating" and profusely illustrated *Corporal "Si Klegg" and His Pard*; the publisher promised "big money for G. A. R. men and agents in general."[71]

The *Eagle*'s reference to Tanner selling a book on Ulysses S. Grant suggests that Tanner may have been an agent for either *The Life of Ulysses S. Grant* or *The Life of Ulysses S. Grant, Ex-President of the United States and*

General of the United States Army, Comprising His Early Training, Military Career, Presidential Administrations, Travels round the World, Sufferings and Death (both published in 1885). Joel Tyler Headley, a former minister and popular writer of biographies and histories sold by subscription, authored both. Tanner would have shown prospective customers a sample that included a few representative pages or perhaps two or three full chapters, a few illustrations, and testimonials from prominent individuals and authors. Buyers reserved a copy of the book by making a small down payment. Thousands of book agents went into the business, especially in rural areas and small towns where there were no bookstores. Publishers produced guides to selling books for ambitious agents, and although few people actually made a career of it, some managed to do quite well.[72]

Tanner could probably count on his many personal contacts and his gift of gab to do fairly well as a book agent, but there is simply no way of knowing how much money he made. But he also developed another line of work during this time as a public lecturer. Beginning in the 1880s and through the first decade or two of the twentieth century, Tanner gave lectures and speeches throughout New York and eventually the United States. Many of the speeches were political, from which he may have derived at least a little income.

His fame as a speaker and status as one of the most popular Republicans in the state attracted the attention of the national party, who put him on the "stump" in many elections. One admirer wrote that "his ability as an orator, his intense, infectious earnestness and loyalty to the principles of the Republican party, made his services eagerly sought for in every political campaign during that stirring period." He made a famous trip to California in 1886—where he gave twenty-seven speeches in a single month, mainly to GAR posts. He drew "the largest audience . . . ever assembled" in the San Francisco Opera House, with men and women alike crowding into the back and the aisles to listen to his 110-minute speech. Two years later he "went through Oregon like a cyclone" and spent several weeks in California and in Indiana on behalf of the Republican candidate for president, Benjamin Harrison. A local paper called him "the man that everybody wants to hear."[73]

When he went back on the campaign trail in 1896 for William McKinley, who would become the last president to have served in the Civil War, a Democratic paper in Ohio made the dubious claim that Tanner earned nine hundred dollars a day for his work. Whether or not he was paid, he certainly kept a hectic schedule: in the third week of September he appeared in Chicago and in five different Kansas towns over the course of five days. By early October he and the other main speakers of the campaign, Generals Sickles, Howard, Alger, and Stewart, had brought their "Republican Patriotic Battalion" to Illinois, where in one town two thousand people had to be turned away from the overcrowded opera house.[74]

One writer reported, apparently without irony, that Tanner was "a favorite on the stump." But the Corporal was more than a political speaker. He had gained a reputation as a logical and witty public lecturer. Tanner spoke often and on almost any topic. He once addressed a temperance meeting, declaring that although he was not going to make a traditional temperance speech, he "was glad to join with all good people in resisting the most terrible evil in the world, the evil of rum, and especially to resist it when it [put] itself against law and order and public decency and decorum." He appeared at a rally in support of newspaper dealers during their disagreement with publishers, arguing that "the laborer is worthy of his hire" and assuring the former, "We want no cheap newspapers at your cost." He also presented a five-piece, engraved tea set to Ada Anderson, the famous "pedestrienne," after she ended a monthlong walking demonstration at Mozart Hall; handed out marksmanship awards to a local National Guard unit; toasted former congressman and *Brooklyn Eagle* editor Thomas Kinsella at a reception upon his return from a trip to Ireland; introduced the famous revivalist the Reverend Sam Jones; and participated in various Civil War monument dedications.[75]

According to an announcement of an address by the well-known "Corporal Tanner," he was "about the best drawing card lyceum managers and Grand Army posts throughout the country could offer." The vast network of railroads built during the Gilded Age made it possible for even the smallest towns in the most remote places to enjoy nationally known entertainers and lecturers hired and managed by professional agents. Tanner signed on for the 1887–88 season (and for at least several other seasons) with the Star Lyceum Bureau, which had offices in the Tribune Building in lower Manhattan and was managed by Alonzo Foster, who claimed in an ad that he offered "Star Lecturers, Readers, Concert Companies, and other First-Class Entertainments."[76]

Foster no doubt enlisted Tanner to enhance his offerings of speakers on the Civil War, who were always popular on the lyceum and GAR circuits. Foster already represented Judge John L. Wheeler, who had traveled the country for several years giving a series of lectures about the campaigns and battles of the Civil War, illustrated with hundreds of slides—both sketches and photographs from a vast collection maintained by the federal government. "They are not alone of interest to the Veteran Soldier," declared the twenty-page pamphlet promoting Wheeler's lectures, "but are of equal interest to those who were not at the front, and to the generation which has grown up since the close of hostilities."[77]

Foster's flyer about Tanner offered potential audiences three different lectures: "Soldier Life—Grave and Gay," "Standards and Standard Bearers," and "A Glance at Mormonism." (Although there is no record of his giving a lecture on Mormonism, he did make typically negative comments about the Mormon Church's tolerance of men marrying multiple wives and other aspects of the church in the 1880s, declaring at the Denver GAR encampment, "We live in the hope of . . . wiping out . . . the great curse of polygamy.") The flyer also included testimonials from newspaper reports of a previous lecture. One promised that if he should ever return to Lawrence, Massachusetts, he would have to lecture in the "open air," because no building could hold the throngs of people clamoring to hear him. "To say that [Tanner's] lecture was interesting," said another, "would convey but a faint idea of the manner in which the speaker entertained his listeners. His descriptive powers are excellent, his choice of language faultless, his relation of comical army incidents laughable in the extreme, and his more serious recitals are given with a pathos that brings tears to the eyes."[78]

Of course, without recordings of Tanner's lectures, and without objective descriptions of his performances—most accounts were designed to attract paying customers or make political points—it is hard to know exactly what drew individuals and crowds to him. His well-known perseverance certainly helped. A number of public men had one empty sleeve or one artificial leg, but virtually none had two. The fact that he had gained fame as "Corporal Tanner"—not "General," "Colonel," or "Major"—must have helped attract American audiences delighted to see a common man succeed in their vaunted democracy. He seemed to exude a combination of confidence and humility, extraordinary patriotism, just the right amount of piety, and a knack for turning phrases that, while they may seem overwrought to modern *readers*, no doubt moved contemporary *listeners*. It helped that he was truly funny. Most accounts of his political speeches and lyceum lectures remarked on his ability to get a laugh.

Although one listener declared, "It is impossible to give an abstract that would do justice to the wit and eloquence of Corporal Tanner," observers kept trying. Most accounts echoed the following description of his effects on the audience, published about the time he signed on with the Star Lyceum Bureau: "One minute his audience would be roaring with laughter and as suddenly they would be moved to tears as he related some touching incident in his career." Another reported that his words had veterans at one reunion "shouting themselves hoarse, throwing hats in the air, pounding the tables at some eloquent and patriotic utterance." Yet "strong-hearted men" also "[wept] in his presence who [had] not shed tears before for years." In his heyday he was compared to Robert Ingersoll, who made a living giving three-hour lectures on subjects ranging from Shakespeare to women's rights to religion (he was a famous agnostic). "Next to Bob Ingersoll," claimed a New Mexico paper when reporting an upcoming lecture by Tanner, "the corporal is classed as the greatest orator in America, and many hold that his natural eloquence even surpasses that of the gifted unbeliever." Perhaps the most meaningful description of his popularity as a speaker was the simplest: "It is enough beforehand to know that Corporal Tanner is to speak. Afterward it is a matter of sighing and wishing it would occur again."[79]

By August 1887, just before the lecture season started, the *National Tribune* reported that Tanner's "dates [were] rapidly being booked," explaining, "There is no man in the whole country that old soldiers would rather listen to than the brilliant orator who left his legs on a Virginia battlefield." By early 1888, the Star Lyceum was running a regular ad in the *National Tribune* warning potential audiences that Tanner had only a few dates still available. Tanner started the most intense portion of his lecture tour during a mid-February snowstorm in Pittsburgh, where despite the weather 1,300 "hearers . . . gave every evidence of interest and approval." Tanner would deliver a dozen more lectures before March 20 in towns stretching from northern Illinois and Wisconsin through Michigan, Ohio, and Pennsylvania and into upstate New York.[80]

Tanner was part of the Gilded Age phenomenon of superstar speakers crisscrossing the country for fairly high fees. But thousands of other famous and near-famous orators, performers, magicians, and others joined in. In many towns and small cities, local lyceums, Young Men's Christian Association chapters, GAR posts, theaters, and other entities sponsored "seasons" that offered residents a great deal of variety. For instance, one of Tanner's first stops was in Brattleboro, Vermont, where he was featured in a series of programs held between late fall and spring along with a humorist, an elocutionist, a male quartet, a violinist, a "whistling soloist," and Albion

Tourgée, the former soldier, Reconstruction politician, writer, and lawyer (he would later serve as counsel for the plaintiff in the famous *Plessy v. Ferguson* case that would lead to the legalization of racial discrimination by the Supreme Court).[81]

Tanner appeared with over six hundred men and women in *Werner's Directory of Elocutionists, Readers, Lecturers and Other Public Instructors and Entertainers*. Another one thousand "elocutionists and readers"—people who would present poetry and prose in staged readings, complete with ethnic dialects and other dramatic flourishes—were also listed. Among the speakers included in the directory were Anna Dickinson, the abolitionist who had become famous as a teenaged lecturer in the early 1860s; Edward Everett Hale, the writer, Unitarian minister, and reformer who had written the universally known *The Man without a Country* a few years before; Mary Livermore, who had gained fame working on behalf of soldiers and the U.S. Sanitary Commission during the war; Blanche Bruce, who had been one of the first two black U.S. senators during Reconstruction; and Lew Wallace, the former Union general, governor of New Mexico, and author of the blockbuster novel *Ben Hur: A Tale of the Christ*. Most of the reputations of the others have been lost in time. They were professors and ministers, writers and poets, journalists and reformers. They spoke on literally thousands of different topics, although history, religion, and the natural world were particularly popular. The brief titles make it impossible to capture the precise topics, but some of the lectures seem a little odd to modern tastes. A sampling of the possibilities presented by other lecturers on the same page on which Tanner appears includes "Three Lectures on Horace," "Turns on Life's Highway," "From the Useful to the Beautiful," "Bright Side of Things," "Is the World Better or Worse?" "Croaking and Crowing," "Beauty," "Cranes, Their Construction and Uses," and "The Woes of Wooing." A few lecturers addressed hot topics of the day, such as "The Absurdities of Evolution," labor strife and "The History of Communism," prohibition ("Rum's Ruin and the Remedy"), and "The Use of Electricity in the Arts."[82]

This wildly varied community of speakers and entertainers helped to create what one historian has called a "public culture" in the days before television, movies, and radio. Beginning in the 1820s and extending until well into the twentieth century, the "American Lecture-System," as one writer called it, brought to the entire continent "the measured footstep of advancing civilization." Although its origins were in local organizations in which men and older boys gave lectures or participated in formal debates, the system grew to include educational and religious gatherings called "Chautauquas," named after the lake in New York State where they began, which featured mixes of entertainment, serious speeches, and even slide shows. But whatever their content, all these presentations and performances were intended to elevate the character and values of Americans of all classes, creeds, and backgrounds. As such, they became a classic part of the entrepreneurial and self-improvement-minded Gilded Age that Tanner proudly represented.[83]

An 1889 article on the lyceum system shows why Tanner—always looking for ways to earn money—would have been interested. Speakers made between $50 and $250 per appearance, plus expenses, with an average of $75. In the 1870s top earners could make as much as $30,000 to $40,000 per year. They would have to deliver scores, even hundreds of lectures to earn that kind of money. Tanner spent at least one season working at nearly that pace; he reported to a friend that the bureau had lined up at least seventy appearances in the fall and winter of 1890–91 and hoped to schedule an even hundred! Tanner would be paid $100 per speech, plus expenses. The bureaus contracted with theaters or groups, made travel arrangements, and provided posters and other advertising. Agencies compiled catalogs of lecturers and their topics and distributed them to a wide variety of organizations, from fraternal groups and the GAR to YMCAs and teacher institutes. The performers most in demand in 1889 included the "king of the stereopticon" (an early version of a slide show), a "hunchback" who specialized in mimicry, a few ministers and readers, and a handful of others. First on one list, however, was "Corporal Tanner of Brooklyn, who [stood] gracefully on artificial legs." The description stated, "He is a good story-teller, and has graphic power, while his valiant career as a corporal never fails to inspire interest. His most popular lecture is 'Soldier-life—Grave and Gay.'"[84]

In fact, the Corporal had been entertaining audiences with yarns of soldiers' lives for years before he hit the lyceum circuit. Perhaps the earliest reference to it appeared in 1879, when he spoke to the St. Patrick's Alliance of America, an Irish American fraternal association. A published account of an appearance before a group of young Baptists a few years later suggests a few of the lecture's themes. Reconciliation, not surprisingly, was a major emphasis. "No man who speaks of the war truly represents the feelings of the veterans who served in it if he speaks anything in bitterness," Tanner told his audience. He argued that if "the settlement of all questions" related to the war "had been left to the front line of each army at Appomattox, they would have been settled lastingly [and] amicably" and would have put the "politicians ... out of business during the reconstruction period." Although that statement conveniently ignored his own position as a politician throughout most of the Gilded Age, the next one reflected his own personal response to the plight into which the war had cast him: "My blood boiled when I read printed assertions that when the boys came back they would be utterly demoralized by their experiences" and "exemplify, not the survival of the fittest, but the survival of the worst." Fortunately, that was not the case; Tanner asserted, "Proud as I am of the way they bore themselves on the field of battle," "[I am] equally proud of the way in which they have borne themselves since."[85]

Tanner's audiences were no doubt unaware of the unimpressive record of the Eighty-Seventh New York, and Tanner certainly never betrayed that fact in public. "Soldier Life," in its various manifestations, became Tanner's very public way of expanding on his own rather generic war experiences. Like his enthusiastic embrace of the GAR and the Union Veteran Legion, Tanner's dramatic, patriotic, and entertaining accounts of the Union soldier were a way for him to make a deeper connection with his comrades and rewrite his own past. Although he seems never to have lied about his service, he incorporated a broad range of hardships, battles, and incidents into his lectures that were not his own. While he did not claim otherwise, audiences probably came away with a very different sense of Tanner's war record than the facts support.

For instance, Tanner described the origins of the well-known hymn "Hold the Fort," based on Gen. William T. Sherman's famous message to a hard-pressed garrison: "Hold the fort, for I am coming." He also told one of the most-repeated stories from the war as though he alone had thought of it: "In the heaviest of the fight" at Malvern Hill, "a rabbit was scared from our lines and ran directly into the ranks of a North Carolina battalion. The colonel in command saluted the trembling little animal and shouted, 'Go it, Molly Cottontail. If it were not for reputation's sake I'd be after you mighty quick!'" He regaled the audience with tales of foraging for food in southern smokehouses and farms, of army mules' habit of braying all night, of a drunken chaplain who gave all military preachers a bad name, of the creative swearing of a legendary New Hampshire regiment, and of the tragic death of a drummer boy who, against orders, insisted on joining the fight when the shooting started. It is safe to say that Tanner did not witness all these events, but he seamlessly integrated them into his own experiences.

Tanner spent perhaps a third of the lecture telling the story of his own wounding and survival and finished with a humorous version of his encounter with the well-meaning but clueless lady with the antidancing brochure. Finally, he suggested that the four hundred thousand men who died for the Union were not the "chief martyrs" of the war; those were the untold hundreds of thousands of widows and orphans they left behind.

An account of the same lecture delivered in Lowell, Massachusetts, five years later suggested that he had expanded on a number of themes, although the core stories of chaplains, mules, and his own experiences in the hospital remained. He seems to have paid more attention to the religious aspects of soldiers' lives, about which there was "much . . . to commend. There were grand Christian lives lived and grand Christian deaths died on the field and in the hospital. Character in its purest and noblest aspect was displayed on every side." The most ordinary men became heroes; "the battle ground and the thick of a contest is most astonishing ventilation of human traits," he maintained. He also urged the present generation to understand "the tremendous sacrifices made when the rebellion lived" and asked them to ensure that the "unprecedented spectacle of American patriotism and valor . . . never die out of . . . American recollection."[86]

An 1886 invitation to a lecture in Sacramento, California, promised, "Those who desire to spend this evening with pleasure and profit cannot do better than . . . the lecture by Corporal Tanner." Just a few years after he entered the lyceum business, a newspaper advertising his lecture at the Saint Paul Lyceum called Tanner "one of the best-known men in the United States to-day." But his renown was not based solely on his reputation as a lecturer or a Brooklyn politician. By 1890 Tanner had moved to Washington, risen to fame as head of one of the government's largest agencies, and then lost it all.[87]

Eyes on Washington

A year before his ill-fated run for the sheriff's office, Tanner gave the *Brooklyn Eagle* a confident interview in which he predicted great things for the Republican Party locally as well as nationally. His personal pick for the 1884 Republican nomination for president was Benjamin Harrison, a former Union general—he had commanded a brigade during the Atlanta

Campaign—and currently a U.S. senator from Indiana. Tanner had campaigned for Harrison during the latter's unsuccessful run for governor in 1876. "He is a man of fine character and attainments," Tanner declared, "a man of poise, who in a remarkable degree combines the requisites of a good candidate." Harrison was popular in and outside Ohio, a state the Republicans had to win, and he had "made a good record" during his two years in the Senate. Tanner believed that the Ohioan would be the best candidate in 1884. He was off by four years—Harrison would not be the Republican nominee until 1888. But when Harrison did win the nomination and the presidency, he appointed Tanner, one of his biggest supporters and hardest campaigners, to be commissioner of pensions, responsible for managing the hundreds of clerks who administered the hundreds of thousands of pensions and pension claims of Civil War veterans.[88]

The Tanners moved to Washington and would never live again in Brooklyn. Yet he remained very much a Brooklyn man. Nearly forty years after his departure, the *Brooklyn Eagle* reported on an appearance he made at the GAR national encampment in Boston. "Old Brooklynites get a thrill when they read that Corporal James Tanner . . . was carried up to the pulpit of the Old South Church and delivered an address as full of fire as any speech of his younger days." The *Eagle* recalled the old days, when Tanner could "bring cheers from any Brooklyn crowd by exclaiming, 'I'm a Republican from the hair of my head as far down as I go,'" and called him "Kings County's stump speaker par excellence" during a time when there were many "crowd-pleasing orators." Tanner's days in Brooklyn had been a time "when Brooklyn was an independent city and her sense of civic virtue kept things stirring. He is not forgotten here," the *Eagle* assured readers. "It is pleasant to think of him as very much alive."[89]

Tanner would, indeed, live for many years after leaving the city in which he had won his first taste of fame. But there were no doubt times in the troubled years that followed when he wondered if the move had been worth it.

CHAPTER FOUR

God Help the Surplus

Corporal Tanner and Civil War Pensions

Tanner rode the wave of the pension issue all the way to Washington, where he became President Benjamin Harrison's highest-profile political appointment. As always, Tanner had played a crucial role in the campaign, and the soldier vote contributed significantly to the Republican victory. Many observers saw his appointment as a reward for both Tanner and his comrades in the GAR. Not surprisingly, the Corporal relished his place in the spotlight. But his ill-fated stint as commissioner, and his subsequent career as a claims agent, ensured that he would be a lightning rod for both the pension issue and the role of veterans in politics.

To Care for Him Who Have Borne the Battle

During his Brooklyn days, Tanner had promoted soldiers' homes and sectional reconciliation, both of which were generally popular with veterans and civilians alike. But a third issue came to dominate veteran politics during the Gilded Age: pensions for men who had served in the Union army. The fights over pensions—their size, their scope, their meaning in American culture—became the greatest source of conflict between the American public and hundreds of thousands of Union veterans.

Few people denied the justice of pensions for soldiers who were unable to support themselves due to permanent injury or illnesses, or to the widows, children, and other family members dependent on soldiers who had died in the line of duty. The martyred President Lincoln had applied a dramatic rhetorical flourish to this idea in the famous concluding paragraph of his second inaugural address, which begins, "With malice toward none, with charity for all." He went on to urge the nation "to care for him who shall have borne the battle and for his widow and his orphan." Veterans heard that phrase as a solemn promise; it appeared on the masthead of the GAR's official organ, the *National Tribune*.

Tanner, at about the time he was commissioner of pensions. Thomas and Samuel White, *Ancestral Chronological Record of the William White Family, from 1607–8 to 1895* (Concord: Republican Press Association, 1895).

Complications arose, however, when veterans, largely abetted by the Republican Party, demanded larger pensions that covered even those conditions incurred after a veteran left the military. When the GAR and other veterans' groups—who counted perhaps half of all living veterans as members—pushed for a so-called service pension for every honorably discharged veteran regardless of his health or need, many Americans, particularly Democrats, began to resist. They worried that unworthy men might end up with pensions. And they worried that the spirit of volunteerism and patriotism that had animated the Union cause had been replaced by a more sinister, mercenary approach.

Those concerns would have been unfathomable during the early days of the Civil War, when Congress approved the first of three major laws shaping the pension system for Union volunteers. The General Law, passed in 1861 and amended several times, established pensions for widows and orphans of soldiers and for soldiers disabled as a direct result of military service. The law set a precise table of payments based on specific disabilities, military rank, and the extent to which the injuries prevented men from performing manual labor (even if they had not worked as manual laborers prior to becoming disabled). Privates received $8 a month if they were rated as totally disabled, while an officer could receive as much as $30. Over the years rates were changed, specific conditions were added, and examining physicians were given the authority to rate disabilities at nearly twenty different levels or "percentages" of disability. By 1888, there were over 120 different amounts paid out to veterans, ranging from $1 to $100 a month (only two pensioners received that much; the most common amounts were $4 and $8). Congress passed the first major revision of the system in 1879, when the Arrears Act left the basic structure in place but set the date for the beginning of pension payments at the time of discharge or death (in the case of widows' pensions) rather than at the time an application was approved. This had huge ramifications for the federal budget. For instance, if a man could prove in May 1880 that the pain in his elbow could actually be traced back to an accident he had suffered in the army, he would be awarded the monthly pension of $8 for "anchylosis"—an abnormally stiff joint—and have it backdated to his muster-out date in May 1865. That would mean a lump-sum payment of $1,440, plus almost $100 a year for the rest of his life. The Arrears Act benefited not only new pensioners but also men already receiving a pension, who could receive a lump sum for the years between their discharge and the date they had started receiving a pension under the old law. The second—and last—major systemic revision of the General Law came with the Disability Pension Act of 1890, which extended pensions to any disabled man who had received an honorable discharge after serving at least ninety days. His disability need not have been incurred during his military service, but it could not be caused by his own "vicious habits."[1]

The arrears payment and annual pension for this hypothetical veteran would have made a huge difference in his life. Although income estimates are difficult to nail down, one commonly cited study based on U.S. Census returns suggests that the average annual wage for a factory worker in 1880 was just under $350. Farmers would have reported much lower incomes, although most would have been relatively self-supporting in terms of growing their own food. A different study investigating average incomes by state shows an extraordinary range, from less than $100 to over $600; the

The Pension Building, now the National Building Museum. Prints and
Photographs Division, Library of Congress.

lowest incomes were found in the South and border states, while the highest incomes were earned in the far western states. Incomes in the industrial northeast hovered near just over $300 per year. No wonder veterans
sought to protect and increase access to pensions that could mean the difference between comfort and poverty.[2]

The various laws governing pensions led to a rapid expansion of the Pension Bureau, which employed many hundreds of clerks and administrators.
This growth was part of a general expansion of government after the Civil
War. Although the federal government was much smaller than it would
become in the twentieth century, the Gilded Age saw the gradual growth
in its size. Led by the massive Interior Department, which contained, in
addition to the Pension Bureau, the Departments of Education, Indian
Affairs, and Labor, by the late 1880s, about 136,000 people worked for the
government, with just under 21,000 in Washington. (Federal employment
accounted for just over 0.2 percent of the total number of employed Americans in 1890. There are now roughly 2.8 million federal employees, about
2 percent of the American workforce.) Only the Post Office Department
and the Treasury Department employed more people than the Pension
Bureau.[3]

Symbolizing its importance to the government, the Pension Bureau had
moved into one of the grandest buildings in Washington just two years

A section of the bas relief sculpture portraying marching Union soldiers that extends around the Pension Building's exterior. Prints and Photographs Division, Library of Congress.

before Tanner became commissioner. The sprawling department had been scattered over several locations for the decade and a half following the war, but in 1881 Congress ordered Montgomery Meigs, quartermaster general of the army—near whom James Tanner claimed to have stood during President Lincoln's final moments—to design a new building. His masterpiece went up over the next several years on F Street between Fourth and Fifth Streets NW, and when completed in 1887 the $900-million building was the largest brick structure in the world. Marking the line between the first and the second floors on the building's exterior was a sculpture inspired by the famous frieze on the Greek Parthenon, which shows a procession of mortals, gods, and other Greek archetypes. For the Pension Building, artist Caspar Buberl carved a repeating loop of Civil War soldiers and sailors, cavalrymen and artillerymen, drummer boys and sutlers, some fiercely determined, others weary and wounded, and still others anxious and fearful, marching on to the next battle. They represented the men whom the building had been built to serve. That commitment to veterans was also

The Pension Building's grand hall. Prints and Photographs Division,
Library of Congress.

reflected in the low, wide stairs and two elevators Meigs designed for the old, crippled men who would be using the building (although the actual elevators would not be installed for several years). The Great Hall occupied the 316-feet-by-116-feet first floor—about the size of a modern football field. Several white columns stretched upward for over 150 feet; they would later be painted in a faux marble design. The central area was open on all four floors; well-lit office suites lined the mezzanines, and the open doors, windows, and ventilation systems were designed to provide a kind of natural air conditioning. Although the Great Hall was meant to be a work of art more than a working space—it included a decorative fountain— almost immediately the always-expanding bureau began to set up desks and file cabinets on the clay-tiled floor.[4]

The fireproof building more fully met the requirements of the bureau and was a spectacular monument to veterans, but the builders were not quite done when it opened for business. Even a few years after the bureau moved in, the ceiling was still unfinished, and pieces of tile regularly fell off, endangering the clerks working in the large open space below. The building had major entrances on all four sides, but Meigs's ventilation scheme mandated only one door per entrance, as opposed to the two or three doors separated by foyers that prevent drafts in modern office buildings. As a result, although the building may have remained relatively cool in the summer, in winter the coming and going of applicants and workers caused drafts to whip through the building, resulting in colds and rheumatism among the poor clerks freezing at their desks. Because there was no freight elevator, literally tons of records had to be moved by hand from the fourth-floor storage areas—where sweating workers toiled under the lead roof during steamy Washington summers—to offices scattered around the building. Finally, the building lacked a coal vault in the boiler room, which resulted in coal having to be hauled to the fire room from a makeshift storage area one hundred yards away.[5]

Of course, the pension system was also unfinished—at least according to the men who had fought for the Union—and with Tanner in the vanguard, the pension issue became one of the most important in American politics.

We Will Stand Up as High as God Built Us

The debate over what would become the 1890 law—should the drastically expanded pensions be based on disability, need, service, or some combination of all three?—played a major role in the presidential election of

1888, which pitted the incumbent, the Democrat Grover Cleveland, against Benjamin Harrison. Cleveland was the only Democratic president between 1868 and 1901 and the only president during that time not to have served in the Union army (Republicans made much of the fact that he had hired a substitute to take his place, which was perfectly legal for men drafted into both the Union and the Confederate armies). Worse, he was seen by many veterans, particularly members of the GAR, as an enemy to pensions in particular and veterans in general. The fact that a third of all congressmen in the 1880s from northern and border states had served in the Union army guaranteed that the Republicans would hammer away at Cleveland's stance on the pension.[6]

Just before the start of the campaign, Congress debated various versions of a greatly expanded pension bill. Early in 1887, Cleveland had vetoed a GAR-supported bill providing twelve dollars a month to every disabled veteran unable to support himself through daily labor. Although it contained a hint of charity—veterans would have to prove their inability to support themselves—the disability did not have to be the result of military service and required only ninety days of active duty. It was close to the "service" pension that many veterans wanted. The following months saw Congress, the GAR, and the president bicker about whether pensions should be based on poverty (the so-called pauper pension), on disability, or simply on service. The GAR backed the latter, Congress tended to prefer the first, and the president refused to consider either option. The failure to pass any pension bill gave veterans their main issue during the campaign.[7]

Adding to the partisan bickering was the conflict over continuing wartime taxes and tariffs—raised by the Republican-controlled Congress to pay for the war but extended after 1865 to promote their economic policies—and the growing surplus in the federal budget. In the 1880s, the annual surplus hovered around $100 million and came chiefly from high tariffs on imports, which Republicans believed protected American manufacturers and their employees from foreign competition. Democrats opposed high taxes and tariffs out of principle and believed that the excess revenue should be eliminated by lowering both. One obvious way of spending down the surplus and justifying the high tariffs was to reward Union veterans with generous pensions. Not coincidentally, that policy would win support for the Republicans among old soldiers.

Republicans also focused on the alleged indifference toward old soldiers—or at least poor management—by Democratic appointees in the Pension Bureau and elsewhere. Veterans had long complained of the months or even years that it sometimes took to review and approve pension claims and about the puzzling ambiguities in the application process. The bureau gave examining surgeons no specific instructions or definitions for disability; the term "total disability" as applied to the ability of a man to perform "any" manual labor also turned out to be much more subjective than intended. Disabilities caused by illness were difficult to demonstrate and could be the result of a combination of military and civilian experiences. Men rated as less than "totally" disabled had to be examined every two years and risked having their pension payments reduced if their health improved. Finally, the requirement that a veteran submit two affidavits from commanding officers, regimental surgeons, or comrades who had witnessed the applicant's wounding or sickness put a heavy burden on old soldiers that only worsened as men moved around the country and memories dimmed with age.[8]

As in modern political campaigns, it was easier to explain complicated issues with heart-tugging stories of individuals victimized by the system than with dry statistics. Several poems offered stories of pathetic veterans unable to get pensions because of unfair decisions or byzantine paperwork, anguished descriptions of destitute families, and demands that the patriotic contributions of the old soldiers be recognized. One went,

> There is many a brave heart,
> Dying of misery untold,
> While only across the country,
> Are many that roll in gold.

"Yes, I am Bob Ridley, who once wore the blue," began another poem published in a soldiers' home newspaper,

> Or what there is left of the comrade you knew;
> I've lost my discharge, and can't tell where;
> Just look in the record and see if it's there.

The poet went on to describe how Bob's hard service had left him unwounded but without "the old vigor." Because his disability was only a vague inability to keep up with more-energetic men, he was unable to get a pension.

> Somehow I'm a failure and scarcely know why,
> Doomed to live when it's harder to live than to die.

Another offered the point of view of the son of a veteran who had been wounded four times, including a head wound that had left him mentally disabled. Although he had applied for a pension, it had never come through. Gazing at the old musket that his father had carried through the war, the son bitterly thought,

> I guess they thought he would soon die,
> Then they could save arrears;
> Four wounds has been his pension,
> For these twenty-seven years.[9]

Countless articles appeared in soldiers' newspapers telling tales of wronged veterans and widows. A long piece in the *Ohio Soldier* during the last weeks of the campaign told of Mary Woodworth, whose husband, Ebenezer, a private in a Michigan cavalry regiment, had disappeared from his tent in 1862. He had been wrongly accused of desertion by an officer who owed him money when, in fact, numerous witnesses reported not only the hard feelings between the private and his captain (other officers described the latter as brutal and "licentious") but also the impossibility that he could have safely deserted considering the regiment's proximity to the Rebels. His body was never found, but all the witnesses believed he had been killed by Confederates. The Pension Bureau had denied Mrs. Woodworth's application, and when Congress had passed a private pension bill on her behalf, it was vetoed by the president. The *American Tribune* told of the widow of a pensioned soldier wounded in the back by a shell at Murfreesboro in 1862. When her husband finally died in 1882, the president had vetoed her widow's pension because she could not prove that her husband's death was "entirely attributable to military service." The woman had lost two sons to the war, while another son had lost an eye and a fourth had lost an arm in the war. Now the seventy-year-old woman, "helpless as an infant, without means of support or friends able to assist her," had seen her last-ditch effort to get a pension via a private bill fall to a presidential veto. In his message, Cleveland claimed that the widow had not actually claimed that her husband's death was due his wound; rather, she had emphasized her poverty and the faithful service of her husband and sons. He vetoed the bill because he thought it inappropriate to provide charity out of a fund intended for military pensions.[10]

Like the subjects of these poems and stories, many soldiers and survivors of deceased soldiers failed to receive relief from the Pension Bureau because of incomplete evidence or other problems. But even when their applications were rejected, they could petition Congress to pass a "private" pension bill written just for them. In fact, sparsely attended Friday-night sessions of the House and the Senate passed thousands of such bills—and President Cleveland vetoed hundreds of them. His legalistic approach to pensions and the sometimes sarcastic rhetorical flourishes he applied to his veto messages outraged soldiers and Republicans. For instance, when the president vetoed a group of pension bills during the summer of 1888, he wrote, "[Too often] medical theories are set at naught, and the most startling relation claimed between alleged incidents of military service and disability or death. Fatal apoplexy is admitted as the result of insignificant wounds; heart disease is attributed to chronic diarrhea; consumption, hernia and suicide is traced to army service." The *Ohio Soldier* called Cleveland's message "bitterly sarcastic," and accused him of trying "to show the nation how little congress"—at the time Republicans controlled the Senate, Democrats the House—"knows about medical pathology, and to hold it up to contempt for its ignorance and its careless improvidence in granting pensions for diseases that it is manifest could not have come from army service." Yet, veterans suggested, it was the president who failed to grasp the complexities of modern medical science. Each of the conditions he dismissed in vetoing these particular pensions could easily be traced to military service and the hardships it inevitably imposed on soldiers. The *American Tribune* roared that the president had "assailed men—whose only faults were their loyal service to the Government and present needs—with foul epithets and charges."[11]

Soldiers' newspapers hammered away at pension issues throughout the campaign. From the *Ohio Soldier* came the argument that extending pensions to an ever-increasing number of soldiers would take the money out of the U.S. Treasury, where it was doing no good, and put it in the hands of Americans who would actually support American businesses by spending it. "The money paid to the veterans would not be hoarded" as it now was, in effect, "nor would it be spent in foreign lands. Every dollar would find its way into general circulation." Later in the year, the same paper published a letter that accused the "soldier-hating press" of claiming that the "government [was] breeding a set of paupers and beggars by giving pensions to those who saved it." The reverse was actually true, argued the author. "Abundant evidence can be collected to prove that by taking a poor crippled or diseased soldier out of the slough of despond, giving him a lift out of his low spirits, making him think he is somebody, that there is a chance for him yet." From Kansas the *Soldiers Tribune* contrasted the money spent on pensions to government spending on useless and wasteful construction ventures that today would be called "pork barrel" projects: "When a crippled, maimed and broken down soldier asks his government to fulfill its promise ... the whole pack of yelping jackals join the chorus: oh! you will impoverish the tax payers.... They are willing that twenty-millions should be wasted in deepening frog ponds, and other millions worse than wasted in building government buildings at every country road village, but not a dollar more for pensions." Another article painted a grim picture of the "ragged beggar, homeless, houseless, and weary of life. The door is shut in his face with the remark that 'Those who won't work must starve.' Work! with what! Arms that are sinewless, legs that are marrowless, hands that are nerveless, a form that distributed the splendid vitality over the broad domain of Dixie, twenty-five years ago. Can't work! The last bright ray of life is gone, his services are forgotten, he went his way to the poor-house and a pauper's grave."[12]

Tanner had overcome his disability—with the substantial help of a pension—but nevertheless helped lead the veterans' campaign on pensions. Since the early 1880s, he had been a member of the national GAR pension committee, which was the organization's most important committee. Many members had been or would be national commanders, and their reports were eagerly anticipated at national encampments. Throughout the 1880s, they more or less successfully pressed Congress to allow the Pension Bureau to increase the number of clerks in the Washington office and the number of medical examiners around the country (as well as the fees they earned), to give the commissioner of pensions more latitude, and to raise pensions for specific conditions. Along with George E. Lemon, who ran perhaps the biggest pension-claim agency in the country and also edited the *National Tribune*, Tanner was one of the most outspoken advocates for pensions. He had testified before congressional committees and often presented the national organization's case for larger pensions to the press. Late in 1887, in the aftermath of Cleveland's veto of the pension bill, Tanner gave a pep talk to the GAR about its chances in the coming year. "Now, having the ammunition in our hands to go before congress, let us do it; do not dampen the powder; keep our cartridges in good condition.... We are the representatives of 375,000 men, and with an election pending next year both parties won't slap us in the face."[13]

During a contentious appearance before the Democrat-controlled House Committee on Invalid Pensions just a few days before Memorial

Day in 1888, Tanner had argued with committee members about the nature of the bill they were considering. Tanner generally supported a "service" pension, but he declared that the bill currently under consideration was an unsatisfactory hybrid of a "disability" and a "pauper's" bill. When the chairman of the committee, Courtland C. Matson of Indiana, declared that many veterans did not need a service pension, Tanner retorted, "Yes, a good many of them [have] gone to their graves." That confrontational attitude infused Tanner's many speeches throughout the long campaign. According to the *Grand Army Advocate*, the Corporal declared in virtually every speech he made "that if he had the power," no old soldier or sailor or widow would ever have to "accept public or private charity. He would make them all independent out of the public treasury."[14]

Both parties published long campaign guides that provided talking points for candidates and their supporters and detailed examples of the execrable policies of their opponents, complete with quotes from speeches and excerpts from newspapers. The *Campaign Text Book of the Democratic Party* promised to "enforce frugality in public expense and abolish unnecessary taxation." The Democrats would lower the tariff and help the working man, taking steps to ensure that the government would not benefit only a few Americans. The party attacked the Republicans' support of "vast tax-consuming, non-producing standing armies"—Democratic code for Union veterans collecting pensions. Nevertheless, the textbook devoted nearly forty of its six hundred pages to "Democracy and the Soldier," arguing that the Democratic approach to pensions ensured their fairness. The Democratic side of Cleveland's famous vetoes took up fifteen pages. Some failed applicants had been deserters, others had submitted inaccurate paperwork, and yet others had suffered from conditions that predated their military service or could not be proven to be related to the army. Sometimes they were applying for duplicate pensions; sometimes their disabilities had been caused by alcoholism; some had committed suicide. The message, of course, was that Cleveland and his party had only been watching out for Americans' pocketbooks, discouraging fraud and honoring only those veterans who deserved to be honored.[15]

The Republican campaign spent only seven pages on veterans' issues, but the party forcefully made its point by naming that section of the book "Dem[ocratic] Hatred of Union Soldiers" and with none-too-subtle hints that the Democrats actually favored *Confederate* over Union soldiers. It listed the various Republican-sponsored laws that had expanded pensions and eliminated obstacles for deserving Union soldiers and assured voters that the overwhelming majority of veterans deserved their pensions. And, as in the days before the Civil War, the Republicans accused the Democratic Party of taking its marching orders from former Confederates, who insisted on dismissing Yankees from federal jobs and installing former Rebels in their places.[16]

The passions aroused by the campaign could inspire extraordinary anti-soldier rhetoric, as in the following *Chicago Tribune* editorial after Cleveland's veto of the 1888 pension bill: "Thank God! The claim-agents, the demagogues, the dead-beats and . . . deserters and coffee-coolers and bounty-jumpers, composing our great standing army of volunteer me[n] dicants have been defeated." The *Tribune* refuted the claim that the veterans had "saved" the country: "No country, no nation, political constitution, system, or establishment, has ever been saved by . . . citizens that are not in the habit of depending on themselves." Indeed, the "army of pension-beggars" were "more dangerous enemies of the nation than undisguised rebels." Former Rebels, deprived of the opportunity of living off government pensions, had become thrifty, hard-working, independent men. The majority of Union veterans, on the other hand, encouraged by Republican Party demagogues, had been "indoctrinated . . . with the pestilent notion that it is becoming to a savior of his country to fulfill the character of a dependent upon its bounty . . . of a pauper without character or self-respect." The article ended with an astonishing attack on veterans: "It will be a happy day for the republic when the last beggar of the Grand Army humbug is securely planted."[17]

Although most Americans did not share the antisoldier views of the archly Democratic *Tribune*, the fact that anyone could actually suggest that everyone would be better off if veterans would only die played a huge role in uniting old soldiers behind the Republican Party and their beloved Corporal Tanner. It was widely believed that Tanner's influence helped swing the soldiers' vote in Indiana and other midwestern and western states in Benjamin Harrison's narrow victory over the incumbent Grover Cleveland. Although Cleveland won a small plurality of the popular vote, Harrison's victories in several key states ensured a comfortable majority in the Electoral College.

Taking Hold of a Mighty Machine

Tanner eagerly sought the job of commissioner of pensions, which, given the size of the country's pension commitment and of the bureau itself, was one of the most important positions in the federal government. In January 1889 he went to Washington to campaign for the office personally. The *Brooklyn Eagle* followed the progress of Brooklyn's sometimes-favorite son in an article cleverly headlined "Tanners Both," in which the special correspondent compared Tanner's efforts to win a "big office" in Washington to the well-known actress Cora Tanner's parallel efforts to attract "big audiences" in the city's theaters. "Corporal Tanner and Cora Tanner reached the National Capital simultaneously," began the article, "each on a mission of fascination bent." The "stellar luminaries . . . will attract considerably more or less attention during the entire current week." Cora had the advantage; her advance agent had, of course, been in the city, renting the National Theater for the actress's performance in the popular play *Fascination*, putting up posters, and buying ads in local newspapers. "Washingtonians are going to pay big prices to see her," predicted the *Eagle*, "but with the Corporal matters are different. Nobody is going to pay a cent to look at him, although it ought to be worth twice that amount." He had no advance agent, could not rent a hall, had no glowing reviews to support his claim. Yet, despite these disadvantages, "the masculine Tanner [was] expected 'to get there,' as they say in the Senate." Tanner was "fond of convincing himself that he carried all the States west of the Missouri for Harrison" and assumed that was worth "substantial remembrance." His mission in the capital was to "stir up Republican statesmen . . . to incandescent temperature in favor of his candidacy for the Commissionership of Pensions." He needed a few more endorsements to "complete the almost unanimous approval he [had] from all the remaining parts of the country in which the insidious influences of the G.A.R. are at work."[18]

The *New York Evening Telegram* reported that Tanner had hinted that if he was not made pension commissioner, the soldiers, whose votes had helped win the election for Harrison, would retaliate. Whether or not the president succumbed to such blatant use of political leverage, propelled by that strong support from the GAR and by the work of the New York and Oregon delegations to Congress, the president did, indeed, appoint Tanner to the commissionership.[19]

Tanner was no doubt the only commissioner of pensions to have a poem dedicated to him upon taking office. "To Corp'l Tanner," which appeared in the *National Tribune*, was a manly Valentine: "We like the manner, the feeling you express," it began. "It is teeming full of meaning to your comrades in distress." Believing soldiers had a "friend in you," the poet showed both an appreciation for Tanner's work thus far and a hope that he would continue:

> Since your induction your construction seems to be without a flaw,
> In your ruling without fooling of complicated pension law.
> Without assuming or presuming we are watching every hour
> All the pledges and alleges *our* party now in power.

The second verse continued the theme of expectations for the Republicans and for Tanner:

> To keep moving it's behooving that the pledges you have taken
> Be a token bravely spoken, shall never be forsaken.
> Keep revealing kindred feeling, for you've felt the shock of war....
> Do your duty without booty, and we'll bless you, one and all.[20]

A more complicated image of the new commissioner appeared in a parody of a recent parade held in New York to commemorate the centennial of the U.S. Constitution. It offered snide comments on various politicians and celebrities—including the Corporal. President Harrison leads off, followed by cabinet secretaries, "carrying their Portfolios and Bloody Axes" (bloodied by the merciless firing of Democratic appointees); the Irish alderman "Wearing Shamrocks and Shillelahs and waving Green Flags"; "Baby McKee," the president's newborn grandson, and Baby McKee's bottle; and "The Grand Army of the Republic and The Sons of Veterans Acting as a body guard to Corporal Tanner and carrying a banner with the inscription Down with the Surplus."[21]

Tanner came into office with a seven-thousand-dollar salary, a great deal of confidence, and, he believed, a mandate from his fellow veterans and his president, who, Tanner never tired of saying, had told him to be "liberal" with the old soldiers. He moved his family to a house in a tony Georgetown neighborhood at a rent of a thousand dollars a year and began making statements such as "I am going to take hold of this mighty machine." When asked what policy he would follow, he quoted one of General Harrison's favorite lines from the campaign: "It is no time to use the apothecary scales when you come to weigh the services of the men who saved the nation." On another occasion he said, "If I were asked to define my ideas on this pension question in a sentence, I should reply: 'A pension for every surviving soldier who needs one, and no soldier's widow, father or mother should be in want.'"[22]

God Help the Surplus

Tanner had taken on one of the biggest jobs in the federal government. In the grand if not quite finished Pension Building, Tanner supervised more than 1,500 clerks, agents, and secretaries (several thousand medical examiners, agents, and clerks in the eighteen field offices around the country also worked under him) and was responsible for a payroll of more than $2 million and an operating budget of just over $400,000. During the fiscal year in which Tanner served as head of the bureau, the government distributed $88,275,113.28 in pensions to 489,725 veterans (including a few thousand veterans of the War of 1812 and the war with Mexico), widows, children, and "dependent relatives" (meaning, for instance, destitute parents of deceased veterans). This outlay comprised 34 percent of the entire federal budget.[23]

Obviously, business was booming for the Pension Bureau. Every day he went to work, Tanner passed through the Great Hall, where veterans, attorneys, and employees bustled to and fro. Above him baskets clacked and whirred along metal tracks attached by ornate wall brackets to the undersides of all three balconies. Each basket could hold up to 125 pounds of documents (a typical pension file might include scores if not hundreds of separate forms, letters, and other documents), and each track might transport a ton of paper a day. Tanner would also have heard the scraping and slamming of file drawers, the murmurs of scores of separate conversations, perhaps the clicking of canes and the creaking of artificial legs.

On his own creaky legs, Tanner would have slowly ascended the low stairs built for men just like him—the elevators still had not been installed—on his way to an impressive suite of offices in one corner of the building. He would pass through a reception area with a vaulted ceiling, trimmed with ornamental plaster work on the way to his personal office, which included a gaslight chandelier, wall-to-wall carpeting, a private bathroom, and a fake fireplace with a mantle decorated with a cast of the Parthenon frieze (the inspiration for the sculpture that marched around the Pension Building a story or so below his office window). Behind a giant bookcase was a vault that often contained tens of thousands of dollars.

Tanner's only annual report, submitted just a few weeks before he would leave office, offers even more evidence of the magnitude of the job he had taken. Statistical tables and explanations dominated the fifty-page document, which quantified the activities of the various departments, including the number of pensions applied for, granted, and denied; examinations made by doctors; pension claims dating back to 1861; pension certificates issued and pieces of mail processed by the bureau; queries handled and information provided to applicants, agents, and others; residences of pensioners, listed county by county and state by state; and, interestingly, a list of the names and addresses of the twenty-seven widows and two children of Revolutionary War veterans still receiving pensions.

Tanner's report also featured recommendations indicating that, in addition to being an advocate for generous pension policies in general, he was also a bit of a policy "wonk," to use a modern term. For instance, he laid out the case for increasing the number of regional pension agents—some of whom were required to sign personally as many as 250,000 checks per year—and for instituting a system to ensure that pension work would go on even if an agent was ill or unable to perform his duties. He also asked that three hundred additional clerks be hired in the main office in Washington. Many other recommendations would tweak policies that accidentally discriminated against widows or featured provisions that failed to accommodate the particular circumstances of some deserving veterans, established inconsistent rates of payments, unfairly penalized dependent children whose mothers had lost their widows' pensions "on account of [their] immorality" (widows who were proven to be living with another man outside marriage forfeited their pensions, as did women who remarried), and failed to deal appropriately with accrued pensions in cases when pensioners died while the government still owed them money. He was particularly interested in expanding the rating system so that the disabilities of certain catastrophic amputations—of shoulder and hip joints, in particular—be recognized for the disabilities they incurred. Finally, and he was, of course, particularly interested in this, he urged Congress to recognize the seemingly obvious fact that losing both feet was a worse disability than losing just one foot (as Congress had recently recognized to be the case with hands). Tanner also presented the GAR version of the service pension bill that would grant a pension "to every honorably discharged soldier and sailor who [was] now or who [might] hereafter become disabled, and without regard to whether such disability [was] chargeable to the service of the United States or [had] been contracted since discharge therefrom."[24]

Despite the acclaim and high expectations that accompanied him to office, virtually everything Tanner did sparked criticism. Although the story eventually took on the status of an "urban legend," Tanner supposedly attended a banquet early in his tenure as commissioner and "in a burst of enthusiasm" declared to the assembled GAR members, "Boys, I am with you. My legs are shaky, but if my good right arm"—the one he used to sign pension certificates—holds up, "God help the surplus!"[25]

In addition to reducing delays, Tanner undertook a major "re-rating" of existing pensions—effectively redefining and nearly always raising the extent of disability of thousands of pensioners—and urging others to submit applications for increased pensions. This excessive and expensive re-rating process outraged budget-minded critics, who worried not only about the cost but also about the claimants' worthiness. A telling, if unique, example of the extremes to which the bureau went to expand the system appeared in a book published just after Tanner left office. It told the story of Henry O. Wills, a Methodist evangelist who referred to himself on the title page of his autobiography as "a sneak-thief, a convict, a soldier, a bounty-jumper, a fakir, a fire-man, a ward-heeler, and a plug-ugly" who was eventually converted to Christianity. Well into the book, as Wills told of his reformation and cheerfully detailed all his previous sins against God and crimes against humanity, he wrote a brief aside to the effect that, "shortly after the appointment of Corporal Tanner as pension commissioner," he had received a card asking for information about his military record, which would help begin the process of his applying for a pension. He returned the card with a summary of that undistinguished record, which included enlisting for the bounty offered by state and local government and deserting—*three times*! Although he might have been "a bad soldier in time of peril, now [he was] a soldier of the cross, and enlisted for the war." He pasted stickers bearing Bible verses all over the card, and although he denied wanting or deserving a pension, he closed with "God bless Corporal Tanner for his love of the soldier!" The rather lackadaisical approach to pension applicants described by Wills was one of the reasons Tanner almost immediately became a target of Democrats and pension opponents.[26]

They had already been angered when Tanner opened his commissionership by dismissing many Democratic employees in an open and enthusiastic embrace of the so-called spoils system. Although the Civil Service Commission had been established in 1883, most appointments to the 130,000-plus federal positions were still made on the basis of political loyalty rather than merit. Both parties needed the system to fund campaigns and partisan newspapers; most appointees gave "voluntary" contributions to the party before receiving an appointment. Tanner acted no differently—although perhaps somewhat more enthusiastically—than any other member of the new government and argued that he was merely replacing "incompetent and inefficient Democrats" with "competent Republicans." He implied that many of the men he fired were actually former Confederate soldiers. Yet critics, including the *Brooklyn Eagle*, accused Tanner of "making a clean sweep" in the Pension Bureau. "The regular guillotine" used by his predecessor was "too slow" for the Corporal, who had "invented a machine similar to the ticket choppers on the elevated railroads." As the *Eagle* described it, an assistant "pumps the handle as the corporal shoves in the clerks" to be discarded as so many used ticket stubs. When Tanner's boss, Secretary of the Interior John Noble, discovered that Tanner had fired 130 men in his first three days, he told him to slow down. It was the first of a number of confrontations between the secretary and the commissioner. The second controversy of Tanner's short administration occurred when a sex scandal forced Tanner's personal secretary—a crony from Brooklyn days—to take a different job, and a third occurred when Tanner replaced him with twenty-two-year-old Ada Tanner, who had just graduated from Packer Collegiate Institute, a college prep school for elite Brooklyn girls. Her $1,800 salary seemed a little high, at least to Democratic observers, some of whom pointed out that Tanner's second daughter, Antoinette, also made $700 a year working in the regional pension office in New York. Tanner also appointed his friend Jack Crawford's daughter Eva to a Pension Bureau job.[27]

Tanner's appointment policy and apparent nepotism sparked a few sharp but brief barbs. One paper dismissed Ada as "a young and pretty feminine sphinx" whose main job was to "soothe the . . . outraged feelings" of "her erratic, irascible and much-troubled father." A *New York Sun* article reported sarcastically, "[Tanner is] doing all he can now to relieve the country of the reproach that it is not doing enough for the Corporal Tanner family," while another Democratic paper referred to the Corporal as "a very prudent man" who is simply "mak[ing] hay while the sun shines, for he knows there are breakers and storms ahead."[28]

Cracks about making hay aside, Ada became a minor celebrity in her own right. The *Philadelphia Times* reported on Tanner's busy work schedule (he kept "open house" at the Pension Bureau and often worked into the evenings and until midnight on Saturdays) and published a poetic tribute to veterans by Mrs. Tanner, but under the headline "The Tanners, Especially Pretty Miss Ada." A pencil sketch of Ada appeared halfway down the column (no pictures of her parents were offered), along with a condescending paragraph indicating that, although she was partly responsible for keeping out the many people clamoring to see the commissioner, because she was "amiable and pretty and just from school" she would probably "not be an impenetrable breakwater" against the wave of visitors.[29]

More-serious charges indicated that Tanner provided streamlined access to the bureau for favored agents, particularly George Lemon and Col. W. W. Dudley, the former commissioner of pensions who had made a fortune as a private pension agent. One Democratic newspaper assured readers that Tanner owed his appointment to a "local ring of pension agents" who had "devoted a fortune to dethroning Cleveland." With thousands of clients and revenue from the *National Tribune*, Lemon was said to be worth a million dollars by the early 1890s. As though to highlight his close relationship with the new commissioner, three weeks after Tanner took office, Lemon's newspaper published a two-column advertisement for his agency with the headline "One Hundred Million Dollars—Money Lost by Delay—Important Information for Soldiers." Packed with information and statistics, the ad projected great confidence that times had changed and that the new administration would make soldiers' needs a higher priority. The *Brooklyn Eagle* reported that on days when Tanner was absent, Dudley had the run of the office, ordering around secretaries and using bureau stationery. "There appears to be a convenient working arrangement whereby Corporal Tanner signs papers, makes speeches, and accepts abuse," while Dudley "runs the business." Indeed, in an *Eagle* report of an interview with the two "professional soldiers," Dudley kept interrupting or correcting Tanner on matters related to bureau policies.[30]

Critics also alleged that Tanner misidentified hundreds of "special cases"—applications were supposed to be considered in the order of their receipt, except in rare "special cases" such as the imminent death of an applicant or some other emergency—including nearly one hundred cases handled by Lemon. Others charged that employees of the bureau were busily re-rating their own pensions or those of their friends.

Tanner apparently did not break any laws, although he did rather carelessly ease the amount of evidence required for original or re-rated pensions. "His contemplation of the overflowing coffers of the Treasury and his feeling that he was appointed to office as the 'soldier's friend,' to scatter with a free hand the bounty," suggested one observer, "tempted him to overlook the arbitrary restrictions by which generous souls in official station are handicapped." Employees revealed that a culture had quickly developed under Tanner in which employees were encouraged to approve pensions despite unconfirmed or even questionable medical evidence. And he never wavered in believing he was right. "The corporal is a thorough going smasher," declared one critic. "There are no halfway processes in his method of doing things. All he appears to see is what he wants and then he goes to work and clears the way for its attainment."[31]

Although not illegal, Tanner's actions violated the secretary of the interior's explicit policies regarding re-ratings, medical evidence, the use of "special cases," and other procedural matters. Tanner resisted, and Secretary Noble enlisted the Justice Department and the president himself to support his stances. Along the way, he removed several of Tanner's appointees.[32]

The tensions caused by these very public disagreements deepened because of Tanner's increasingly careless rhetoric. He kept repeating the outdated notion that ten thousand veterans were still living in almshouses (it may never have been true) and, contrary to the official Republican Party line, cheerfully admitted that the liberalization of the Pension Bureau was at least partly the result of campaign promises. In a speech in Omaha midway through his administration, he compared himself to an "alchemist, for [he had] been turning gold from the old channels and distributing it among the worthy and need[y]."[33]

He seemed to relish his high profile in the administration and told everyone who would listen that he had the confidence of the president. "I tell you frankly," he said in a speech in Chicago in July 1889, "that I am for the old flag and an appropriation for every old comrade who needs it. I don't claim that I represent the views of the administration, but I do know that I have the support of the President and Cabinet on this line—a pension for every old soldier who needs one." The *Eagle* suggested that Tanner believed himself to be part of a "partnership of glory" with the president and the rest of the administration. Prior to becoming commissioner, "he went about the land casting pearls of speech," but then he would at least occasionally pause "to get a breath." Now, however, he never stopped; "his lungs [were] always inflated to vocal pitch."[34]

The *New York Times* actually reported in midsummer that there was talk of Tanner being nominated for president in 1892. Veterans in Kansas and other western states had proposed the idea during the recent campaign, and enough old soldiers were talking about it "with so much apparent earnestness that Tanner [had] at last got a very vigorous and growing 'bee in his bonnet.'" Rumors suggested that Tanner had even spoken of the possibility to his friends. Toward the end of the summer, the *Times* floated the idea that the president's rising dissatisfaction with Tanner was due to the latter's growing popularity, which could pose a threat to the former's renomination in 1892.[35]

Nothing reflected the *Brooklyn Eagle*'s love-hate relationship with one of the city's favorite adopted sons more than a typically perceptive and ambiguous article that appeared in August 1889, when Tanner was mired in controversy over his administration of the Pension Bureau and Secretary Noble had appointed a three-person committee to investigate him and the bureau. Democratic concern that investigators would cover up what they believed to be Tanner's misconduct inspired the article, titled "The 'White-washing' of Tanner." "The *Eagle* takes a deep interest in the subject," the piece indicated, "because the little corporal is a peculiar product of the Brooklyn school of Republican statesmanship, and the tendrils of local pride cling lovingly around him." He had been a lightning rod ever since he rose to prominence in the 1870s. "The passions which he evokes and the suspicions he arouses conspire to make him the target of a large number of archers whose quivers are always full and whose arrows are always barbed and sometimes poisoned." Most politicians were corrupt, to a greater or lesser extent, but that was not why the Corporal attracted so much criticism. "The fact is that he talks himself into all sorts of queer situations," the *Eagle* asserted, and "his failure to observe the rules of strategy in the multiplex movements of his mouth" only exacerbated the political dilemmas in which he found himself from time to time. After agreeing earlier in the summer to quiet his aggressive rhetoric about pensions and other matters, Tanner waited only a few hours before he was "gabbling away again." Inevitably, "the 'clack, clack, clack' of the lively little corporal's tongue kept up" until he said something that detractors could manipulate into an admittance of misuse of his position. Somewhat surprisingly, the *Eagle* defended its longtime "frenemy," to use a modern term: "Of course there is nothing in them which can possibly disturb the foundations of Tanner's reputation for moral rectitude.... Our corporal may be a sad babbler, but he is not a rascal.... He does not need to be whitewashed, and, therefore, there is no sense in the cry that the committee intends to whitewash him." Nothing came of the investigation, which intensified Democratic anger.[36]

Despite support from hundreds of thousands of veterans—an "old soldiers" meeting in Garden City, Kansas, telegrammed Tanner with a line from his popular lecture: "Hold the fort for we are coming"—certain elements of the Republican establishment, and even the *Brooklyn Eagle*, Tanner's days at the Pension Bureau were numbered. Although former GAR commander George Morrill explicitly requested that he not attend the national encampment in Milwaukee in August, the Corporal went anyway. Outrage over criticism of Tanner dominated two whole sessions at the encampment, as veterans took turns defending Tanner, attacking his critics, and composing a resolution to the president praising the commissioner's integrity and calling for an investigation that could clear his name. (In fact, Tanner had to talk them out of passing a much stronger resolution that condemned "in unmeasured terms the wicked and malignant criticism of [their] distinguished comrade.")[37]

Things came to a head when Tanner submitted a draft of his first and only annual report to Secretary Noble just before leaving for Milwaukee. When he returned, the secretary had apparently returned it, covered with blue marks and stern suggestions to roll back the "radical recommendations." It is unclear which passages concerned the secretary—the published report differed little from those that came before or after him—but one reporter suggested that his recommendations for major expansions of the staff and of pensions convinced Harrison that "Tanner was totally unfit to hold a position of responsibility under an Administration where discretion was valuable, where a small majority in Congress would be fatally embarrassed by such liberal recommendations." In other words, Tanner had gotten himself too far out in front of the rest of his party and had to go.[38]

The actual resignation took some doing. The *New York Times* reported that Tanner worked through three drafts before settling on language that preserved his dignity without admitting any actual wrongdoing. One report suggested that Mrs. Tanner had urged him to stick it out, saying that "if her husband resigned his office she would choose to take in washing rather than that he should accept" another job in the administration. Eventually, on September 12, he submitted a letter that attributed his departure to ongoing disagreements with Secretary Noble that threatened to "embarrass" the president. Harrison's formal acceptance of the resignation carefully referred to vague "causes which [had] led to the present attitude of affairs" about which Tanner had already been "kindly and fully advised" in person by the president, who did add, "Your honesty has not at any time been called in question."[39]

Not surprisingly, members of the GAR were outraged and flooded Washington with protests. Eventually Green Raum, another respected veteran and GAR man, was given the post and served the rest of Harrison's term. Tanner had to settle for having a post office named after him in a small town in Indiana.[40]

A Martyr to the Republican Party

It was clear to some contemporaries and now obvious with more than a century of perspective to see that Tanner was being used by both parties. Tanner's disgrace was simply part of the Democratic "scheme to charge the Republican administration with extravagance." To another newspaper, he was a "martyr" to the Republican Party and a scapegoat willingly sacrificed by the administration. Still others suggested that he had been removed because he had overshadowed a weak president, whom one historian has called "a forgettable Indiana senator elected after a forgettable soldier's career," whose role as grandson of William Henry Harrison (who served only a few weeks before dying in office) was more important than his own four years in office![41]

There had certainly been plausible reasons to appoint Tanner commissioner: he was well known in the GAR and the party, he had been a successful and honest agency head in one of the country's largest cities, and he was knowledgeable about pension affairs after his years of service on the GAR pension committee. The fact that he was wildly popular with the party's single largest voting bloc made his appointment an obvious choice for the president.

The *Brooklyn Eagle* saw it differently. Tanner's steadfast loyalty to the party and to the old soldiers had actually played into the hands of the Democratic Party. "General Harrison is a weak man of whom it would be foolish to take much account," said the *Eagle*, and Tanner easily overshadowed him. Opponents realized that "the way to tumble this Administration in the dust [was] to unhorse Tanner." In fact, Tanner had known what was going on. He told the paper, without the "slightest sign of fear or quivering," that he understood that the Democrats had targeted pensions and the pension commissioner. As he talked, according to the *Eagle*, "his courage increases, his eyes sparkle, his nostrils distend, and anticipating the spectacle of the advancing enemy he exclaims, 'Let them come on. There will be music by a full band.'"[42]

Yet his defiance failed to hold off the critics, and the *St. Paul Globe* assured readers that Tanner's dismissal was "a terrible warning to all who attempt to be honest in politics." No one had suggested that he was personally dishonest. Rather, "his offense was simply and solely in attempting to carry out the . . . election promises of his party." Another paper declared that "President Harrison thought that it would be a good political move to supersede a wounded Democratic general"—Tanner's much-maligned predecessor, John Black—"in the Pension Bureau with a wounded corporal, and so Tanner was lifted to dizzy height." No one was surprised when he failed; "his inexperience and unfitness were so marked that he seem[ed] to have been the victim of designing politicians rather than his own folly."[43]

Inevitably, Tanner became the butt of numerous stories and cartoons in the popular press. As commissioner, he had already been featured in a number of jokes, especially in *Puck* magazine. A *Puck* cartoon had depicted a sinister-looking Tanner, draped in a toga, standing before the U.S. Treasury building holding a horn of plenty whose long tail, labeled "Pension Bureau," reached all the way back to the Treasury. As Tanner grinned devilishly, coins, paper currency, and bags of money spilled from the horn into the grasping hands of greedy pensioners. Tanner wrote a wry letter, published in the magazine three weeks later, that complained not about the cartoon's critique of the pension system but about the caricature of him, which, he said, resembled "Jack the Ripper"—the "Whitechapel Murders" perpetrated by the mysterious villain had taken place late in 1888—more than it did him. He teased that "any intelligent jury" would find in his favor if he sued for libel, and with irony that the editors at *Puck* had to appreciate, he enclosed a photograph so that, he explained, "the enormity of your offence may seize upon your soul." He finished with the biblical injunction: "Puck, go; and sin no more." Above the letter, photograph, and detail from the original cartoon, the editors of *Puck* "hasten[ed] to ease the gallant Corporal's mind by showing the public just how much injustice [they] did to his manly beauty." And they assured the Corporal, "If he runs his office on business principles and disburses the public money with strict justice and honesty, his face will shine with the light of conscious rectitude, and Puck will portray him in all his pulchritudiness [*sic*] glory."[44]

Nevertheless, *Puck* continued to make Tanner the symbol of a failed and expensive pension system. In a clever reference to a current health fad, it

THE HORN OF PLENTY.

This *Puck* cover shows a rather sinister-looking, toga-clad Tanner carelessly tossing money to greedy pensioners from a bottomless "Horn of Plenty" that snakes back to the U.S. Treasury. Tanner complained that the picture made him look like "Jack the Ripper." *Puck*, May 29, 1889, author's collection.

Puck compares Tanner's generosity with pensions to a popular "elixir of youth."
Puck, August 28, 1889, personal collection of Bert Hansen, New York City.

compared the "elixir of life," a cure for male impotence that featured injections of "testicular extracts" from animals, to the widespread belief among pension conspiracy enthusiasts that many applicants faked their disabilities. *Puck* showed Tanner injecting gold coins into the pockets of decrepit veterans who dance away afterward, visibly younger and throwing away their canes and crutches. And just after Tanner left office, *Puck* joked about a butcher telling a customer that he has had to kill a dog because it kept running off with the best cuts of meat and leaving them on neighbors' doorsteps. The customer remarks, "Queer dog, that! What did you call him?" "Corporal Tanner," replies the butcher.[45]

Tanner also appeared several times in the humor and news magazine *Life*. Just two weeks before his resignation, *Life* suggested that Tanner was "to be adopted bodily as one of the planks of the next Republican platform, in lieu of any device for the reduction of the surplus." Three weeks later, after Tanner had been forced out, the magazine reported that "one of Corporal Tanner's subordinates decided for his superior's guidance that a dishonorable discharge was no bar to a pension. President Harrison thereupon decided that Corporal Tanner's pension should be no bar to his dishonorable discharge." An elaborate cartoon on current events and popular culture in early October portrayed the bearded president, crowded with his cabinet into a tiny boat named "Administration," tossing Tanner into the stormy sea, as did the terrified crew in the biblical story who feared that God's wrath against a passenger, Jonah, would sink their little boat. The text that followed showed a "genial oyster" saying to Tanner, "If you and I had only known how to keep our mouths shut we wouldn't have been in this fix." *Life* also included the Corporal on a list that matched political celebrities with song titles representing their misfortunes during the past year; Tanner's was "Out in the Cold World."[46]

A humorous letter from "Bill Snort"—the pen name of popular late-century humorist Alexander Sweet, whose satiric pieces appeared in newspapers throughout the country—reported from Washington on the "sensation" of Tanner's downfall. Snort defined what it meant to be "resigned" from an office: "'Resigned' is the sugar coated substitute for 'bounced.' To 'bounce' an official is to kick him out and pound him with the hard end of a broom as he goes, but to 'resign' him is to express bogus regret that he prefers to go, while you are shoving him out with the soft end of the broom."[47]

The piece ended with a flinty encounter between Tanner and Harrison in the White House, during which Tanner bitterly compares himself to yet another biblical character, Joseph, whose jealous brothers had sold him to Egyptian slave traders, and accuses the president of seeking a more pliant, less dedicated, old-fashioned "ward" politician. The scene begins with Tanner's entrance.

> "Comrade Harrison," he said, in a very sarcastic tone, "I came to say farewell as you seem to take more interest in my farewell than you do in my welfare."
>
> "I'm sorry, Jim, that you look at it that way," whined the President.
>
> "Don't call me Jim. Call me Joe. My name ain't Joe, but it ought to be, for, like Joseph, I have been sold out by my brethren."
>
> "It's no pleasure to me to see you go out," said Harrison.
>
> "Well, for whose pleasure is it then, that I am bounced. I'll be d——d if it's for mine. The truth is, Mr. President, you don't want a man with a war record. You prefer a man with a ward record."

The conversation ends with Harrison weeping and Tanner leaving "haughtily."[48]

Even Ambrose Bierce, the wounded veteran, writer of short stories, and creator of the hypercynical *Devil's Dictionary*, included Tanner in a list of mordant and entirely unsympathetic epitaphs of prominent politicians and orators of the age:

Of Corporal Tanner the head and the trunk,
Are here in the unconsecrated ground duly sunk,
But stranger you needn't be blubbering here.[49]

Tannerism

Tanner's dismissal was simply a part of the larger debate over pensions that continued to rage after he left the bureau. The *New York Times*, long an enemy of the ever-expanding pension system, was unsatisfied with the removal of Tanner. "It is not Tanner, simply," it declared, "but Tannerism, that ought to go." The *Times* defined the term as the "vicious . . . theory" that "whatever surplus exists in the Treasury belongs to the war veterans as a right, and that the people of this country have been niggardly in their treatment of Union soldiers."[50]

Ironically, less than a year after Tanner was forced to resign as commissioner, the now Republican-controlled House and the Senate passed a bill, signed by President Harrison, that provided a twelve-dollar pension for every honorably discharged veteran unable to support himself by manual labor. The disability did not have to be related to military service, and financial need did not have to be proved. It was the closest thing to a service pension that veterans would ever achieve, but it hardly ended the fight over pensions.[51]

The *New York Times* launched its harshest attacks on the pension system as well as on veterans and the GAR during the weeks just before and after the bill became law. The Dependent Pension Bill, rather than "saving the veterans from the humiliation of [actual] pauperism," would "offer a large premium for professed pauperism, and the number of the unworthy who [would] receive its benefits [would] be so large that they [would] throw discredit upon" even those who deserved government aid. Indeed, as soon as the bill went into effect, reported the *Times*, the "grand army of pension hunters" had besieged the pension system with thousands of new applications. "When the war ended, these men had enlarged views, [and] good health," but "as time passed an avaricious enthusiasm . . . caused them to elbow back to the rear the sick and infirm, the disabled, and the widow and the orphan." These were the "pension sharks" clamoring for government handouts. By the end of the summer, the *Times* could make the inspirational wartime song "We Are Coming, Father Abraham, Three Hundred Thousand More," into an anthem promoting expanded pensions. It even complained that the 1890 census of Union veterans currently under way, which would include the names and addresses of every living veteran and his physical condition, was simply "a means to help the grasping pension agents" find new clients. Other critics called the pension system a "Raid Upon the Treasury," one rather shrill observer compared pensions to gambling, another called it "An Indignity to Our Citizen Soldiers" that "cheapens the sentiment of patriotism," while yet another compared it to socialism and accused it of failing to distinguish between soldiers "who serve for gain whether as wages, booty, or political advancement, and those who serve for honor and patriotism."[52]

By the early 1890s, critics had decided that any man or GAR post that did not stand up to fraud or even admit that pensions were a drain on the Treasury and a blight on the Union was no better than a man who actually defrauded the government. "It is hard to realize how the Grand Army of the Republic could have been placed in its present shameless attitude," *Puck* declared in 1893. "Is it any wonder that the people should doubt the patriotism of men who seek to join it? Can not the rank and file of the G. A. R. be brought to see that the element which controls it is gradually placing the Order on a par with the women who sell their bodies?"[53]

Old soldiers fought back. An 1885 article in a soldier's newspaper summarized their most basic response. "As time passes we grow more impatient with the grudging objections which many are so ready to make whenever some material benefit is bestowed on an ex-soldier," complained the *Milwaukee Sunday Telegraph*. All soldiers carried some physical "memory" of the war, whether a chronic disease, a scar from a wound, or a searing recollection of horror. But an equally long-lasting effect of the war was the devastation it had wrought on men's economic prospects. Few soldiers could save money while in the army, which "consumed . . . four years of [their] business life." Yet, back home, their "friends . . . had had great business opportunities; fortune had knelt at their feet." But when a veteran limped home, he "found the choice places occupied; the strategic points strongly entrenched; he could not well ask any one to step down and out that he might step up and in." Of course, many soldiers succeeded in building good lives for themselves, but some ended up "losing their grip in the weary campaigning and falling down and down, even to the depths of tramphood." Although much had been done for the soldier, the newspaper acknowledged, "the debt has not been so fully paid that we can hear the sharp and thoughtless criticism often made when some ex-soldier had received a pension from the government . . . without being angered by its free and ready injustice."[54]

The report of the commissioner of pensions for the fiscal year ending on June 30, 1892, argued forcefully for the new law. Submitted by Tanner's successor, Green B. Raum, the report showed that during the twenty-eight months since the new law was passed, 920,367 claims had been filed, and 403,859 pensions had been approved. The law, wrote Raum, "has brought relief to a host of needy and deserving persons—many of whom were living upon charity, and thousands of others who were upon the verge of that condition." It had relieved those who could not produce solid evidence that "disabilities were of service origin" and proved that the "old laws were not broad and liberal enough" to meet the needs of the men who had saved the Union. Despite the "great deal of unfavorable comment" about the pension system that had followed its passage, the law was neither a plot to raid the Treasury nor an example of undeserved charity. Rather, it was a demonstration of the nation's patriotism and gratitude to men who had never recovered from the rigors of service. "A great many of the men who carried the muskets have been unable to keep up with their neighbors who remained at home, in the great struggle of life," the report declared, "and the claims of these persons for assistance from the Government rest upon the broadest foundation of justice."[55]

The pension bill was a bonanza for the claims agents who helped veterans assemble the necessary evidence and complete the complicated forms. Based on the figures presented in Raum's report, at ten dollars per successful claim, during the first two years after the law went into effect, claims agents had collected over four million dollars in fees.[56]

With the opportunities presented by the bill, it comes as no surprise that, between July 1, 1891, and June 30, 1892, nearly 1,100 new attorneys were authorized by the bureau to prosecute claims. The race to cash in by these hundreds of opportunists opened the profession to attacks from pension opponents, at least partly because of their aggressive and rather modern marketing campaigns. This had been going on for some time. In the late 1870s, according to the commissioner of pensions, "the country was flooded with addresses, circulars, and other printed matter, addressed to pension claimants and soldiers in general," along with personal letters and other correspondence. And the avalanche of letters and flyers—exactly like the "junk mail" from advertisers, charitable organizations, and political groups that crowd twenty-first-century mailboxes and email inboxes—continued to stream out of agents' offices.[57]

Philander H. Fitzgerald, who for decades ran one of the country's largest pension agencies in Indianapolis, made his expansive interpretation of the 1890 pension law part of the sales pitch. "Every Soldier Disabled while in line or discharge of duty, and who is now laboring under disability, either by accident or otherwise, is entitled to a pension," declared a huge ad in the *American Tribune*. "The loss of a finger gives a pension. The loss of a toe gives a pension. Rupture, though but slight, gives a pension. Inguinal hernia or varicocele gives a pension. Varicose veins of legs will give a pension. Deafness a pension. A gunshot wound entitles to a pension. Where piles or hemorrhoids were contracted while in service of the United States a pension is granted if the disability still exists." Even before the law was passed, Fitzgerald published a long questionnaire that soldiers could complete and send to Indianapolis, where agents would calculate the appropriate pension rate and fill out an application. When the bill finally made it through Congress, he promised, the forms would immediately be sent to every old soldier for a signature and then be submitted to Washington, beating the rush of new applications and avoiding long delays.[58]

Hundreds of men and a few women worked as pension agents, including local lawyers, retired Union generals, and even residents of soldiers' homes. But a few giant agencies—including those established by Fitzgerald, Lemon, and Dudley—controlled perhaps half of all pending claims. They trumpeted the fact that the only law they practiced revolved around pensions. Fitzgerald declared in an ad, "It costs no more to get a competent attorney ... who devotes his entire time to the [pension] business, than to take up the average 'Cross-Road Jack' lawyer"—apparently meaning a small-time lawyer engaged in a general practice—"who is only in your way."[59]

The hard-sell techniques inspired critics to blame claims agents for the fraud that almost everyone believed polluted the pension system and Americans' attitudes toward it. Contemporary estimates of the extent of fraudulent claims—by nonveterans who forged or purchased discharge papers, by veterans who lied about the source of their injuries, by supposed widows who had never been married to dead soldiers or had married again since the war—ranged from 5 to 33 percent. In 1889, Gen. H. V. Boynton, a veteran who worked as a reporter in Washington, blamed the counterfeit claims on the pension agents, "who, with their advertising dodges and their circulars, [had] kept the veteran element in constant ferment on the subject of pensions." The agents, he argued, "have held out false expectations, and led thousands upon thousands to apply for pensions who, except for these confidence men, would never have entertained the idea." Among the epithets applied to Lemon and his colleagues were "parasites," "pension sharks," and "the Grand Army of Pension Attorneys."[60]

Less unsavory, perhaps—at least less dishonest—was the fact that claims agents themselves admitted that they lobbied hard for changes in pension laws that would expand their potential client base by changing rules and allow them to submit applications for existing clients when rates were raised or new disabilities added. It was a well-known fact that men like Lemon and Dudley constantly pushed Congress to tweak the system, and Lemon once admitted that he had paid lobbyists to promote his schemes in Congress.[61]

Incensed by such unabashed lobbying and the huge profits it earned for a few agents, *Puck* expanded its criticism of Tanner to include most other claims agents. In 1882 it published a fictional monologue by one of the members of this devious club. "I am a pension agent . . . and I am proud of it," declared the fictional entrepreneur.

A disreputable business? What! To succor the distressed, to get justice for the faithful servants of the government—that a disreputable business? But I'm not obtaining justice for the faithful servants of the government, I'm getting fat pensions for people who never earned them? Well, now, don't you judge my business too lightly. When you take into consideration the trouble of mind, the wear and tear of intellect that is required to run up cases of neglected vets and impoverished widows—when you consider the labor I have in teaching them what to say—why then you'll admit that I'm earning my money.[62]

The same issue featured a rather grotesque cartoon with the caption "The Insatiable Glutton," which depicted a many-armed man wearing a Civil War–era forage cap labeled "U.S. Pensioner," crouching on the floor, scooping coins out of an overflowing bowl engraved with the words "U.S. Treasury." The sleeves on the two dozen or so arms are stitched with "Fraudulent Attorney," "Bogus Widow," "Bogus Grandpa," "Bogus Grandma," "Bogus Orphan," and "Agent." A few years later, a *Puck* editorial argued that most "deserving veterans . . . got their pensions long ago." Desperate to keep the flow of money coming, "the pension agents had to make business. They made it by seducing old soldiers; by persuading them to swear that their present weaknesses and ailments were the result of injuries incurred during the war. These agents have got their commissions, and have tarnished the honor of thousands of men who were brave and honest before they were tempted beyond their strength."[63]

Where He Belongs

Perhaps inevitably, Tanner stayed in the pension business as a private entrepreneur rather than a public servant. He had few other choices. In an article published the day after his resignation, the *Brooklyn Eagle* dismissed any rumors that he might return to Brooklyn to relaunch his political career. Too many bridges had been burned, and after all, he had never won an election in New York. He had also become too single-minded, "marred" by "that habit of partisan abusiveness" that he had displayed "since he became a figure in national politics." The *Eagle*, which had always had a soft spot for Tanner, predicted that although the rancor of his political utterances might diminish, he nevertheless should leave politics. Working for a few years in business would "place him in [a] much better situation than any in which politics [had] put or left him—and . . . he would not need to care a rap who was President, or even who was Commissioner of Pensions."[64]

The *Eagle* was right. A few months later, Tanner agreed to be interviewed by the *Pittsburgh Dispatch*. He refused to discuss his "difficulty" at the Pension Bureau but admitted that being commissioner had been "six months in purgatory." Moreover, in a phrase recalling his honestly stated reasons for running for sheriff in Brooklyn back in 1884, he had "discovered that he [could] make more money in Washington out of office than he could while in office." Tanner expounded on his good fortune in an interview with the *Brooklyn Eagle* later in the spring. The day he resigned the commissionership, he said, "was the darkest day [he] ever saw." He claimed to have left office poorer than when he entered it; even worse, everyone knew about his embarrassing dismissal, since the news had been telegraphed "far and near." He had few options for making a living, so, taking the advice of a friend, he had "flung out [his] shingle as a pension agent." His fame assured that his decision to go into business "was also telegraphed all over the country," and within forty-eight hours over two hundred clients had signed up. "Since then the business has increased at an enormous rate and I have all I can possibly attend to," he stated. As it turned out, "it was a blessing for me when I resigned my position as Commissioner of Pensions."[65]

He certainly worked hard enough. Tanner pursued new business as avidly as any agent. He ran ads in newspapers all over the country, opened a New York office, and in the summer of 1890, according to the *New York Times*, "flooded" the city with "circulars, blank applications, and letters 'inviting' his comrades to file their applications with him, because with the valuable experience gained in the Pension Bureau he [would] be able to push their claims with great facility." The *Times* published the text from one of the flyers, which offered to send clients "prepared application[s]" under the terms of the law just passed by Congress. Apparently clerks would have found in public sources and filled in most of the personal information about a potential client's military service; the veteran simply needed to check it for accuracy, make sure the list of "the name and nature of all the disabilities" from which he suffered was complete, and take it to the regional pension office, where he would swear to the application's accuracy and submit it.[66]

As it was for most of the major Washington agents, the amount of money made by Tanner was a frequent topic of conversation in Washington. In a short article headlined "Where He Belongs," a Missouri newspaper remarked that Tanner had "found his proper level as a pension claims agent in Washington" and quoted the Corporal as saying that he had received 3,444 claims applications when Congress passed the 1890 law. If all were successful, he made $34,444. Two years later, another report quoted unnamed sources asserting that the Corporal was "coining money" as an agent, having "netted" $200,000 in his first three years in the business. Yet another report claimed that Tanner had said he had earned $100,000 in his first year and hoped to increase that to an annual take of $400,000. Whatever the actual amount of his annual income, he was apparently "rolling in wealth," as one article declared, just a few years after his ignominious departure from the bureau. Less than a year after dusting off his law certificate and hanging out his shingle as a pension agent, one report suggested that he made $40,000 or even $50,000 per year. The article quoted Tanner as saying that he wished he had abandoned politics and gone into the pension business sooner, for, as Tanner claimed, "If I had done so, I would now be a millionaire."[67]

He was not quite so sanguine in letters written to his old friend Jack Crawford during his first year or two in the business. He frequently bragged about the number of clients he had acquired and the speed at which he had gotten them—a few months after starting his business he had filed 2,177 applications and had lined up over 2,000 more; by mid-1890 he claimed to have processed 8,000 claims. But in addition to providing periodic updates on the "big lot of business" he was doing, he also complained about how expensive it was to set up a business. He had hired twenty-two employees in just a few months; by May 1891 he had twenty-five clerks. In addition to payroll, he had to pay for advertising and the hundreds of thousands of forms and flyers he had sent out; at one point he noted spending $12,000 on advertising alone. Things were going very well, he once wrote, stating, "If it had not been so very expensive to build up [the business] I would be in clover." He hoped eventually to earn $250,000, but he also had to acknowledge that the claims processing at the Pension Bureau took many months, and he would not be paid until the claims were approved. He was still owed $167,000 in fees nine months after starting the business. "I am weary waiting for the proceeds," he admitted.[68]

In a letter to Crawford's son Harry, who apparently managed his father's business affairs in New Mexico, Tanner predicted that by the end of 1891 he would be able to invest twenty-five thousand dollars in the mines and horse ranches that the two old soldiers dreamed would make them rich. He would first have to pay off his debts and establish financial security for his family. It is likely that Tanner probably invested in western ranching interests, at least, although it is impossible to tell how much he actually put in or took out.[69]

Your Humble Servant

Tanner never became a millionaire, but his material well-being no doubt served as balm to his bruised ego and ruined political aspirations. A few weeks after Tanner's departure from the Pension Bureau, one of his greatest supporters—and another veteran proud of his lowly rank, Pvt. James Dalzell, a lawyer, writer, and Ohio legislator—published a searing letter in the *New York Herald* defending his friend Tanner, castigating the weak-kneed Republicans who had forced him out, and predicting dire consequences among soldier-voters. "If Tanner had been found guilty of drunkenness, stealing, or other crime the soldiers would be satisfied," stormed Dalzell. But "if his crime is that he is not an aristocrat with a pedigree, a martinet with a title, or a millionaire with a million, a million men who wore like him the private's blouse will condemn and avenge his decapitation."

The outrage was so great that Dalzell suggested that soldiers might raise a quarter of a million dollars as a fund to support Tanner in his retirement. "In his degradation they see their own. In his fall they see theirs. They see all privates are despised and scorned and ostracized." Indeed, Dalzell claimed that he had never seen the soldiers so angry since the assassination of the beloved President Lincoln, "for their best friend [had] been stabbed to death in the house of his friends." Tanner may have been careless in his choice of words from time to time, but "he left two more legs on the field than any man did who forced his decapitation."[70]

Tanner's bruised ego did lead to at least a little political resentment. He relished the fact that at the 1890 national encampment of the GAR, the old soldiers refused to offer the customary applause whenever President Harrison's name was mentioned. And when Democrats did well in the off-year elections in 1890, he bet a friend "dollars to donuts that if [he] had been in the Pension Office [the Republicans] would have come out flying in Indiana at least."[71]

The Republicans' downfall was completed when the Democrat Grover Cleveland did, indeed, defeat Harrison in 1892. But after a mild flirtation with the Democratic Party, which vainly hoped to turn Tanner against his former colleagues, he returned full force to the Republican cause in 1896. Weirdly, following the decisive victory of William McKinley—for whom Tanner campaigned hard with other prominent Republican veterans—one observer confidently predicted that he would be appointed commissioner of pensions![72]

That was about as likely as his being elected mayor of Brooklyn. By the mid-1890s Tanner was happily engaged in making money hand over fist. He was in his early fifties, and one newspaper reported that he was still a "well built man, with a large, heavy head and thick, gray hair" who got "around very well for a man who walk[ed] on two wooden legs." He remained in Washington with Mero, Ada, and Antoinette and continued to deliver lectures for pay and for politics. Yet for the rest of his life he would be closely identified with the pension issue. Of course, he himself received one of the highest pensions available. By 1890, according to his pension records, he received seventy-two dollars a month. That paled in comparison to the money he allegedly made as an agent, but it provided peace of mind and a sense of his country's gratitude for his sacrifice.[73]

Thirty-six years earlier, just a few months after turning twenty, Tanner had written a straightforward letter to the commissioner of pensions, Joseph H. Barrett, asking for clarification of a recent change in the law raising the amount of the pension for someone who had lost two limbs to twenty-five dollars. "I have had the misfortune," he wrote, "to loose [*sic*] both of my legs," and inquired if the pension would be dated from his date of discharge or the date of the passage of the act setting the new rate. "If you will also inform me, or cause me to be informed of what measures I must take to get the increased pension you will greatly oblige me," he continued. "An early answer will be very agreeable." He signed it, as men typically did in such formal situations, "Your Hum[ble] Serv[an]t, James Tanner, West Richmondville, Schoharie Co., N.Y."[74]

Tanner probably did not remember writing such a letter—although perhaps he did. Much had happened since this first brief but confident foray into soldiers' pensions, an issue that would dominate a substantial portion of his life. Yet the thirty-plus years that followed his calamitous stint as a high-ranking federal official would provide many opportunities for him to bask in the recognition and approval of his fellow veterans and, indeed, of almost all Americans.

CHAPTER FIVE

The Most Celebrated GAR Man in the World

Legacies

James Tanner lived for another thirty-eight years after he left the Pension Bureau. He flourished as a claims agent, maintained his influence in the Republican Party, and continued to be a popular lecturer and campaigner. He would win the office he had truly wanted—commander in chief of the national GAR—and remain a beloved figure among old soldiers. In 1904, the *Niagara Falls Gazette* called Tanner "the most celebrated G. A. R. man in the world." Yet he would never entirely live down his few months as commissioner of pensions.[1]

Not Altogether Forgotten

In popular culture, political discourse, and even history textbooks, Tanner became synonymous with bad government, the misplaced sense of entitlement among veterans, and the Gilded Age culture of greed. As his dismissal became more and more inevitable in the late summer of 1889, one critic wrote, "Corporal Tanner is doubtless glad that there are so many fools and rascals in this country that no one man can hold public attention very long at a time." Yet the Republican Party should know that "Tanner is not altogether forgotten," as it might well find out in upcoming elections, when voters would reveal their disapproval with the Corporal's "efforts to turn the treasury surplus over to the Grand Army of the Republic."[2]

For years Tanner appeared in large and small publications as an archetype of government excess. A Church of Christ publication compared shirking church members to soldiers who had shirked their duty during the war yet after the war managed to collect pensions when "Corporal Tanner got into the pension business." A dozen years after he left the commissionership, the Democratic newspaper in Akron, Ohio, compared the city's crumbling finances and overspending politicians to "Corporal Tanner's noted interjection about 'God help the surplus.'" A rather alarmist 1910 article out of South Carolina traced the government corruption that the author feared might destroy the state back to the days when the GAR "fell largely into the hands of pension promoters—Corporal Tanner . . . at their head." A series of articles published later in the year by the muckraking magazine the *World's Work* described the evolution of the pension system and offered numerous anecdotes about fraud and unnecessary pensions. It, too, accused Tanner of "hand[ing] over" the bureau "to the attorneys in the Grand Army." Referring to him as though he was a long-dead figure from the past, the article described Tanner as "a warm-hearted, uneducated Irishman, intensely loyal to his old comrades. Public duty as an official meant nothing to him. His personal honesty has never been impeached, but his idea of Government was that it existed to pay pensions to anybody who claimed ever to have worn a blue suit." In addition to the more famous quote about the Almighty helping the surplus, the article added Tanner's quip that he would "drive a six-mule team through the Treasury." More than twenty years after Tanner's stint in government, advocates of lower tariffs (high tariffs had helped pay for pensions) blamed the "clear incentive to extravagance" in spending tariff revenues on "such an insane cry as that of Corporal Tanner."[3]

As time went on—no doubt partly because Civil War veterans were dying off and fewer Americans had any sort of personal connection to the conflict or to anyone who had fought in it—Tanner became less a person in his own right and more a sample of bad government, the spoils system, or Benjamin Harrison's poor judgment. He made cameo appearances in a history text published in 1915 and in a political science text published in 1919, as an example of one of the ways that Harrison paid "party debts" to old soldiers. Testimony about the condition of state institutions for the mentally disabled in 1916 suggested that "the institutions of Illinois were model institutions until Corporal Tanner came in and played ball with them"—perhaps an obscure reference to Tanner's commitment to veterans' preference in government employment. A 1922 history of the *New York Evening Post* by Allan Nevins, who would become one of the best-known historians of the twentieth century, offered the typical line about "God help the surplus" but added information—taken from the *Post*'s files—that amounted to libel (the old soldier was still alive and well in Washington): Tanner "had lost his leg from a stray shot while, a straggler from his regiment, he was lying under an apple tree reading in what he thought a safe place." That flippancy was also reflected in a column titled "Easy Come, Easy Go" about the loose-spending ways of the government published in the same year. It claimed that "the whole country was amused and had a hearty laugh when [Tanner] announced his policy: 'God help the surplus!' Them was the halcyon days!" A 1924 *New York Times* article compared a spendthrift congressman to the Corporal: "He flings himself" upon the surplus "with the glee of Corporal Tanner, crying: 'God help the surplus.'" Three years later an attack on fiscally careless city officials was headlined "Heaven Help the Deficit."[4]

The litany continued long after his death. A 1933 textbook reported that Tanner had "shoveled out money as fast as he could, but red tape got in his way and his gallant efforts to cut it brought him into conflict" with the president. A book about how to plan for returning veterans of the Second World War called Tanner "a professional veteran"—decidedly not a good thing—while a monograph on interest-group politics from the 1950s called the GAR and Tanner the "forerunner of the modern mass-based politicized interest groups" devoted to the idea that "having saved the country," they wanted to be rewarded and "were taught how to get some of it" by the Corporal.[5]

Tanner may not have paid much attention to the legends that grew around the facts of his pension advocacy. But it would have been hard to ignore the contempt—not to mention the writer's fuzzy grasp of the facts—that oozed from the pages of the *Houston Post* in 1899: "Corporal Tanner, who can boast the proud distinction of being the greatest living curse to his country . . . has made more capital out of a game leg than any man on the planet. Whether he broke it in battle with the rebs or in deadly conflict with old John Barleycorn will perhaps never be known; but certain it is that he has made that old game leg trot so as to put money in his purse as well as in the purse of every other deadbeat of his acquaintance."[6]

A certain amount of infamy came with the criticism, and Tanner found himself—in print, at least—in rather odd company. A brief piece in a Montana newspaper—likely published in many other papers—enigmatically declared, "It's a hot race between Prince Russell and Dis De Bar, [and] George Francis Train, Corporal Tanner, Senator Blair, and the rest of the big field are hopelessly behind." Many, if not all, of those names mean nothing to modern Americans, but in 1891 they belonged to people who, for one reason or another, had been in the news for unsavory or fraudulent behavior, for embarrassing failures, or for seeking publicity for its own sake. The competition was apparently for the number of headlines in which they appeared. "Prince Russell" was Russell B. Harrison, the president's son, who was involved in controversial investment schemes in Montana and elsewhere; Henry W. Blair was a senator from New Hampshire who not only failed to be renominated but was rejected by the Chinese government as minister to the emperor because of his callous comments about the Chinese; Ann O'Della Dis De Bar was a swindler and fake spiritualist; and Train was an eccentric businessmen and adventurer who in 1890 circled the world in sixty-seven days.[7]

A fictional GAR post also took Tanner's name in a satire published in the *Pocket Magazine* in 1896. Filled with virtually every negative stereotype of "professional veterans," the plot offered grasping pensioners, veterans whose service was far from notable, GAR members who bragged about their dubious claims of heroism at reunion campfires, fake veterans begging on the streets, ambitious "coffee-coolers" running for office on the basis of exaggerated or nonexistent war records, and a fish-out-of-water tale of country rubes being duped by big-city sharps when the men finally got their longed-for trip to the national GAR encampment.[8]

But Tanner also enjoyed a more positive fame to go with his infamy. He had become colleagues and friends with a wide variety of famous men, ranging from war heroes and presidents to powerful businessmen and writers. When his name appeared on newspaper lists of notable attendees at public functions, the "Corporal" stood out among the "generals," "mayors," "judges," "senators," and others. One of his closest friends was the well-known western scout and author Capt. Jack Crawford, who as a very young soldier was also severely wounded during the Civil War. He went on to become the chief of Indian scouts in the U.S. Army, to be featured in dime-novel-style stories about the West, and to publish many poems, stories, and tales based on his adventures. Indeed, the most extensive biography of Tanner appeared in an odd volume with the history of a Union artillery unit and an account of the "poet scout" Crawford's escapades in the Black Hills of Dakota Territory. Tanner presided at a benefit appearance by Crawford in New York in 1886 and provided one of the promotional blurbs for Crawford's most recent book, along with Generals John B. Gordon, Winfield Hancock, and Lew Wallace (who would later write the best-selling *Ben Hur*), as well as U. S. Grant's son Fred. In the same year that Tanner was forced out of the Pension Bureau, Crawford dedicated the poem "The Veteran and His Grandson" to Tanner.[9]

At the other end of the spectrum of fame, although he was probably unaware of the honor (he would certainly have seen the humor), in the late 1880s at least four farmers in Ohio and Missouri named prize livestock "Corporal Tanner" (for the record, they were a bull and three hogs). A slightly more dignified honor came from far southwestern Nebraska, where in May 1889—about the time Tanner visited Nebraska as commissioner of pensions—Union veterans in the tiny town of Curtis named their new GAR post after the Corporal. The post was never very large; although it reached its peak membership just two years later, it survived until the 1920s.[10]

Even as he became a kind of legend, Tanner continued to manage a successful claims office. In the 1899 Washington city directory, he was listed as a "lawyer and claim agent," with offices at the Washington Loan and Trust Building on the corner of F and Ninth Streets, about four blocks from the Pension Bureau. He still testified from time to time before the House Committee on Invalid Pensions and never hesitated to criticize publicly the work of his successors as pension commissioner.[11]

The Chief Star of the Party

Despite press speculation that he would actually campaign for Democrats following his ouster from the commissioner's job, Tanner never wavered in his loyalty to the Republican Party, and he enjoyed circulating in the inner circle of Republican politics. Just two years after he was fired as commissioner, an amusing *Brooklyn Eagle* article portrayed him smoking cigars and hobnobbing with other former Brooklynites at the bar in Washington's Willard Hotel "almost any night." He took a leading role in the 1896 campaign that pitted William McKinley against William Jennings Bryan. McKinley was just a year older than Tanner and, like him, had entered the Union army as a private, eventually rising to the rank of major. Although the soldiers' vote remained important to the Republicans, the 1896 campaign revolved around economic issues: the tariff (as a congressman from Ohio, McKinley had authored the very high and very controversial 1890 "McKinley tariff") and whether the United States should abandon its traditional gold standard (as the People's Party, or Populists, advocated). The Ohioan favored "sound" money—gold—and other pro-business policies.[12]

Tanner played a major role in the campaign that would make McKinley the last Civil War soldier to serve as president. The Republican National Committee organized a speakers bureau with hundreds of paid and volunteer speakers flooding the country, in towns large and small, to pound the sound money and high tariff policies into the minds of voters. Tanner was, according to one account, the "chief star of the party" and the main attraction of the so-called Generals' Train. In addition to Tanner, the group included former Generals Daniel Sickles (who had lost a leg at Gettysburg), O. O. Howard (who had lost an arm at Fair Oaks), Franz Sigel, and Russell Alger, although a couple of other, less well-known generals also appeared from time to time. Alger, who had just finished a term as governor of Michigan, was a lumber magnate who loaned his private railroad car to the campaign. The special train carrying the old soldiers through Kansas, Nebraska, Iowa, Wisconsin, and other parts of the Mississippi Valley and Midwest in September and October included a platform car with a cannon that would be fired as the train entered a town to attract crowds. The five old soldiers spoke either directly from a platform on the train or in a local auditorium.[13]

The men traveled in two private cars named "Elmwood" and "Michigan" and ate meals prepared by Alger's private chef. Despite the luxury of their conveyance, as older men, most with disabilities or indifferent health, they were sacrificing a great deal, at least according to one admiring newspaper article. The author maintained that, rather than being a "junketing trip of a lot of major generals" or "a few old veterans sent out . . . to work the professional old soldier racket," as some Democrats had suggested, these men were campaigning out of "love of country." Yet despite their seriousness of purpose, they also had a good time. They rarely talked about the war, but they did enjoy "cracking jokes at each other's expense."[14]

The "Goldbug Generals," as some labeled the group in reference to their "sound money" policies, spoke to crowds large and small. A late-September stop in Council Bluffs, Iowa, drew an estimated ten thousand people, including thousands of school children, to the makeshift stage erected in front of a downtown hotel. They had been met at the train station by a thousand old soldiers, militiamen, high school cadets, and a marching band and paraded to their appearance. An unfriendly newspaper described Tanner's brief remarks at a whistle-stop in Sutton, Nebraska, where a GAR reunion was taking place, as "one of his characteristic extreme and unfair talks." He ended with a straw poll of men who favored McKinley and "an honest dollar" or men who preferred Bryan, "a 53-cent dollar and 47 cents worth of wind," to vote by raising their hands. The former indicated support for the hard-money gold standard, the latter indicated support for the idea—popular among many farmers in the 1890s—of coining silver as well as gold, which would loosen up the economy and cause a certain amount of inflation. Surprised when a number of men raised their hands and apparently shouted, "You bet we'll vote for Bryan," as the train pulled out, Tanner "halloed back: 'We have such people in New York, but they are in the lunatic asylum.'"[15]

Toward the end of the campaign, the Union Veterans' Patriotic League hosted a massive rally at Carnegie Hall in New York that featured on the platform thirty-four generals, four colonels, "and Corporal Tanner." The top brass and the Corporal helped McKinley edge Bryan with 51 percent of the vote. He would be reelected in 1900, when Tanner once again was called upon "to rally the veterans throughout the West." He also campaigned on behalf of Theodore Roosevelt in 1904.[16]

But political campaigns could not pay the bills. As the claims business finally plateaued and then declined, Tanner sought other positions. The *New York Times* declared rather snidely, "Mr. Tanner's friends have long felt that it was time he had a job." One of those friends, Jacob Riis, the well-known journalist, pioneering photographer, and reformer—his most famous book was the 1890 expose of conditions in New York's immigrant neighborhoods, *How the Other Half Lives*—stepped in. Riis and Tanner had apparently been friends since the 1880s. In the concluding chapter of his 1922 memoir, Riis thanked a number of reformers, politicians, and notables, ranging from Jane Addams to the king of Denmark (his native country) to the Corporal. He recalled attending church with the "infallible James Tanner, called Corporal by the world, Jim by us," and Mero Tanner's friendship with Riis's wife, especially when the latter "was homesick in a strange land." He also alluded to an inside joke: "I would be willing to let the rest" of a certain story "go if you will promise to forget about that bottle of champagne. It was your doings anyhow, you know." Riis encouraged another friend, President Theodore Roosevelt, to appoint Tanner register of wills for the District of Columbia, and he held the job for more than twenty years, also serving Presidents Wilson, Harding, and Coolidge.[17]

A brief controversy erupted over the appointment, as critics accused Tanner of being incompetent and, inexplicably, as having "first come to public notice by joining in the Federal retreat from Bull Run," which wrongly implied that Tanner had been present at the Union army's ignominious defeat at the *First* Battle of Bull Run. But it blew over, and Tanner held the position for over two decades. As register of wills, he acted as clerk to the probate court in the District of Columbia, supervising the mountains of paperwork associated with the filing of wills, the disposition of estates after the deaths of people without wills, the appointment of executors for estates, the process of managing the cases of orphans who inherited property, and all matters related to divorce proceedings. Although it was hardly as large a job as the commissioner of pensions, it required a fair amount of organization and paid him four thousand dollars a year. As an admiring newspaper declared a year after he took the job, "The amount of hard work done by that 'totally disabled' veteran, Corporal Tanner, is an object lesson for younger men with a full complement of legs and arms."[18]

Our Country Will Not Fail

Because he continued to be relevant to national politics, because he lived in the center of political journalism in the United States, and because he made good copy, reporters often sought Tanner's opinions, especially on military issues. He reveled in the growing influence of the United States, as American economic power exploded and U.S. foreign policy sought markets and influence around the world, especially in Latin America and the Caribbean.

Like a number of famous veterans, he linked the country's surging power and growing prestige in the world to the Union victory in 1865. In this way also, Tanner's Civil War continued to extend its influence for decades after it ended. The Corporal applauded American efforts to force Spain to give up its colony in Cuba and presided at a mass meeting in the fall of 1895 in support of the Cuban rebels against Spain. In a subsequent talk to a veterans group in New York, Tanner somehow connected his usual speech about Civil War soldiers' experiences to the need to support the Cubans. Much of the gathering enthusiasm for intervention on the island perched less than a hundred miles from the tip of Florida was encouraged by American newspapers' often sensationalized coverage of the mistreatment of Cuban civilians by the Spanish, and in 1897 Tanner spoke at a reception for a Cuban girl who had escaped from a Spanish prison in Cuba.[19]

Spain eventually gave in to most of the United States' demands, but the momentum to intervene—exacerbated by the sinking in Havana Harbor of the USS *Maine* by, it was believed at the time, Spanish agents—led to a declaration of war in April 1898. Tanner seemed to be both thrilled and alarmed by the turn of events. His son Earl raced to join the army, which lent Tanner's Memorial Day speech in Rochester a few weeks after war was declared a poignant tone when he compared the patriotism of his generation with the patriotism of his son's generation and acknowledged that the latter might have to make similar sacrifices to the former. Yet the "country [would] not fail to answer to the call of distress by whomever made."

He reflected on Earl's going off to war: "There is a sob in my heart but I can keep it down when I think that he is marching in step to the same grand music, in defense of the same flag his father went down under thirty-six years ago." He mentioned many of the examples of fear and bravery that appeared in his usual speech about the soldier's life, but this time the old stories had regained an immediacy that may have faded over the two decades he had told them. The possibility that twenty-two-year-old Earl might also fall in defense of the flag forced the fifty-year-old father to pause and wipe away tears from time to time.[20]

The three-month war ended in complete victory for the United States and semi-independence for Cuba (which would remain under American influence for decades). But at the same time that Americans had prepared to invade Cuba in spring 1898, a naval force had steamed from Hong Kong to Manila Harbor and defeated the Spanish squadron stationed in that faraway colony. Eventually American forces would occupy the colonial capital. The peace treaty with Spain that ended the Spanish-American War also gave the United States control of Puerto Rico, Guam, and the Philippines. Although the Filipino rebels who had been fighting Spanish rule at first welcomed the Americans, when it became clear that they would not achieve independence after the Spanish departure, they revolted against the American occupation. The resulting three-year conflict caused tens of thousands of civilian casualties, and American commanders instituted concentration camps for civilians and committed numerous atrocities against guerilla fighters and civilians alike. Gen. Jacob Smith ordered all Filipino boys over the age of ten to be killed in the area under his command.

Many Americans opposed not only the brutal tactics but also the policy of occupying the Philippines as a colony. But not Tanner. Perhaps because by then Earl was leading men into combat against the Filipino guerillas, Tanner never wavered in his support for the American soldiers and even defended the atrocities they committed. On the policy of killing ten-year-olds, he declared in a 1902 speech, "Out there in the Philippines boys of ten years are oftentimes more dangerous than grown men. I say, 'Clean them.' The thing to do with them is to make them respect our glorious flag." One newspaper claimed that Tanner was the only person of any prominence to express support for Smith's appalling order.[21]

The Filipino war would wind down in a few years, and Tanner's rash statements were quickly forgotten. But the superpatriotism that his imperialistic, even racist comments reflected would emerge again when the Great War broke out more than a decade later.

Everybody Loves Jim Tanner

Tanner had set his sights on becoming commander in chief of the GAR long before he was elected. From the 1880s onward, the GAR rumor mill about who would serve the next one-year term often included Tanner. Nominations were made by state delegations to the annual encampments; balloting would go on until a candidate had won a majority of the votes. As a result, much of the politicking took place even before encampments started.

Tanner had been formally nominated in 1886 but attracted few votes in the election. Three years later he made a brief and unsuccessful run for the job—even as he was being ousted from the commissionership.[22]

His time finally came in 1905. When Tanner's easy win over three other candidates was announced to the assembled veterans, "the convention went wild," according to one observer. "The old veterans leaped from their seats, shouting and cheering and throwing their hats in the air." One of his defeated opponents took the podium and asked that Tanner's election be made unanimous, which inspired another demonstration. Tanner was escorted to the stage by the other three candidates, but before they got there, "the delegates made a rush for Tanner and, lifting him into the air, carried him bodily to the rostrum," where he accepted their cheers for several minutes.[23]

One wag commented that he had made "an excellent race" for the office "for one who lost both legs at Bull Run," while another made a slightly veiled reference to his failed commissionership by writing, "His newest title will never stick like the old one." Yet the results of the balloting reflected true enthusiasm, and at least two songs honored his election. "To Commander-in-Chief Tanner" was sung to the tune of the popular 1905 song "Everybody Works but Father" (which would become part of the comedian Groucho Marx's vaudeville act):

Everybody loves Jim Tanner
They praise him night and day.
Fighting for our banner
He fell in the bloody fray.
Up and down the country
His voice for freedom rang.
Everybody loves Jim Tanner
In our old gang.

Tanner's official portrait as national commander in chief of the GAR. *Roll of the 40th National Encampment of the Grand Army of the Republic* (Philadelphia: Town Printing, 1906).

The other was sung to the tune of the Stephen Foster song "Oh! Susannah":

> We're glad to see our chieftain here
> You bet your bottom dollar.
> So let her go for all you're worth
> Just whoop her up and holler.
> Oh, Jim Tanner!
> Hope you'll never die.
> But if you do
> You'll surely have
> A mansion in the sky.

Inevitably, as soon as the "poet scout" Jack Crawford heard the news, he sent Tanner a new poem that began:

> Let me be the first to write and say
> How gratified I am today
> That you are Chief, and ain[']t it good
> To know that love and gratitude
> Are yours in overflowing measure.[24]

Most of the commander's time was spent traveling the country, visiting GAR posts, and making speeches. But two issues came up while he was commander that demanded his attention as the national representative of Union veterans. When the federal government attempted to close the "canteens" that sold low-alcohol beer to residents of the National Home for Disabled Volunteer Soldiers (NHDVS), Tanner joined most administrators of the homes and veterans' organizations to oppose the policy. Tanner's own drinking habits seem to have varied over the decades, but he believed that depriving the old men of this one small pleasure was small minded and would lead, in fact, to their getting much stronger and cheaply made alcohol illegally. "The time is coming," he claimed (wrongly, it turned out), "when men of honest convictions in Congress will not listen to the impracticable ideas of persons holding to certain dogmas and will listen to the reason of experienced men. The old soldier is not an imbecile. He does not need to be handled like a baby." Despite his efforts, Congress banned the selling of beer at the NHDVS in 1906.[25]

The other issue stemmed from a congressional bill reducing the pay of veterans working for the federal government when they reached the age of sixty-five. Tanner made headlines around the country in a much-published letter to the chairman of the House Committee on Appropriations that deployed the kind of rhetoric that had been used to argue for pensions and job preference for decades. "There is a dead line," he wrote, invoking the infamous line established in Civil War prison camps that meant certain death if a prisoner stepped too close, "in legislation respecting the saviours of the nation as perfectly marked as at Andersonville." Changing the rules would cross that line, and he warned that "this unjust, cruel, monstrous law" would unleash a political firestorm against the party that passed it. The flurry of attention passed, and the veterans' wages were not lowered.[26]

The climax of his year as commander in chief came at the August 1906 national encampment, held that year in Minneapolis. His lengthy annual report, at least part of which he read to the encampment toward the end of the ceremonies, reported on membership issues, the deaths of notable comrades, a plan to honor Civil War nurses and to lobby Congress for pensions for nurses, comments on Memorial Day (posts had increasingly begun decorating graves and performing the more somber activities of the day on the Sunday preceding Memorial Day, which had become "a mere holiday for games and amusements" in many places), the GAR's efforts to educate youth and to promote the new "Flag Day" holiday, campaigning to get men to remove their hats during the playing of the "Star-Spangled Banner," various anecdotes about sectional reconciliation, a testy update on pension issues, and a series of thank-yous to various staff members and other comrades.[27]

Earlier in the encampment, he had stood for hours on the reviewing stand as state veterans' organizations, militia units, and various notables and celebrities passed in his honor. The *Minneapolis Journal* emphasized the age and weariness of many of the veterans—they had finally aged into being actual "old soldiers," although they had been calling themselves that since the war had ended—but Tanner must have loved the attention. His daughters and son Earl, by then a lieutenant in the regular army, were with him on the reviewing stand, as were his good friends Capt. Jack Crawford and Clara Barton, the founder of the Red Cross. But Tanner's thoughts that day were no doubt more on the one person who was not there than on the many thousands who were.[28]

My Individual World Lay in a Wreck and Ruin

Tanner always gave his wife credit for having rescued him from the despair and hopelessness that struck during the two or three years after the loss of his feet, and he would call her the "controlling factor of [his] life" in his short autobiography. Mero never matched her husband's public acclaim, but she spent more time in public than most wives of successful men. She appeared in an 1887 article titled "Tales of the Gentle Sex," which, tinged with the male condescension typical for the period, hailed women's intelligence and "superiority" to men. The article described a random group of women who seemed to have made significant contributions to their husbands' careers. Its point seemed to be that, since women could not demonstrate their intelligence and skills in public life on their own terms, they could inspire their husbands to greatness. Like the wives of several other nationally known politicians—including Secretary of the Navy William Whitney, Senator John A. Logan, and President Grover Cleveland—Mero had seen the potential in her husband and provided the support he needed to push ahead. "Corporal Tanner is quite well known," said the article, "but very few of the thousands who have heard him know of the patient devotion of the wife who showed him how to secure success as an orator and also as a politician."[29]

Mero had weighed in on political matters from time to time—Tanner once told the story of their discussion of how he should respond to the frequent misreporting of his army rank early in his career—but like many middle-class women of the time with talent and a sense of duty, she worked mainly behind the scenes. She was a published poet, and in one of her pieces articulated a prosoldier attitude about government jobs; the poem, titled "Heroic Service, or Civil Service," asked, "Shall Faithful Soldiers or Delving Book Worms Be Promoted?"[30]

But she did not merely follow her husband's lead in public affairs. One of her pet projects was the Brooklyn Nursery and Infant Hospital, established in the 1870s to care for the infants of parents who could not support them. At various times she served as a manager (one of a group of women who made decisions about admissions and other day-to-day matters), as a member of the executive board, and as a volunteer at fairs and other fundraisers. In 1883, she persuaded the Corporal to give a lecture on its behalf. On that occasion Tanner made a joke told by countless spouses over the centuries: "I did not intend to be here," he began. "I said I would not be here this morning, but my wife said I would. She generally wins in matters of this kind, and so I am here." He went on to give a jovial but heartfelt lecture that included a few war stories, a few political remarks, and a general description of the institution's functions. He closed by saying, "I have always been with the infants. I have several of them at home, and

Mero Tanner around the time of her death in 1906. *Roll of the 40th National Encampment of the Grand Army of the Republic* (Philadelphia: Town Printing, 1906).

I say God bless them and the ladies who care for them." He would later accept a position on the nursery's advisory board.[31]

Mero took a public role, too, publishing articles in support of the nursery in a local publication called the *Echo* and in 1886 giving several public lectures to raise money. Two years later she opened a fund-raiser with an impassioned plea for support for this institution, which, in less than twenty years, had grown from its origins as "a cupola, piazza and a mortgage" to its current "dignified proportions." She also scolded her fellow Brooklynites: "In this city of 700,000 population, with its millions of dollars ... that are thrown away and wasted, Brooklyn has not an institution, save the poorhouse, where a poor mother, unable to properly care for her sick baby, can take it. This may be an appalling fact to you, but it is, nevertheless, a fact."[32]

Mero later became heavily involved in the Red Cross, particularly during the Spanish-American War, when she met with Clara Barton, the founder of the organization, and several other women in Washington and became a member of the organization's executive committee. Later she took charge of the campaign to gather food and other supplies for forty thousand recruits flooding into the understaffed training camps suddenly springing up around the country.[33]

But Mero was more than a typical Gilded Age do-gooder. Her poetry addressed a wide variety of subjects. She called her lecture on behalf of the Brooklyn Nursery the "Product of an Auction Room" and in it imagined a machine that could crank out poetry on demand. Of course, the poems were her own and reflected her particular interests, ranging from religion and women's rights to veterans' issues and art. Her sense of humor and understanding of the tawdry side of politics—this was, after all, 1886, just two years after her husband's bitter defeat in the sheriff's election—offer at least a hint of the ways in which she and the Corporal seem to have been well matched. She joked that people in the audience could leave at any time, but only if they paid another thirty-five cents. She also compared her poetry machine to "a political machine. You put the material in the public hopper and let the boss work the crank and out pops a mayor, an alderman, a justice, or a ward supervisor, just as the man at the crank desires."[34]

Mero spoke on other occasions, too, most notably in spring 1889, just after Tanner became commissioner. He had been hired through his speaker's bureau to lecture to a GAR post in Vermont but fell ill. The bureau suggested Mrs. Tanner as a replacement, and she basically gave the standard soldier's life talk, "telling ... how her husband was wounded, of his sufferings then, and his cheerfulness and perseverance and indomitable will." She delivered "a charming talk." Although the stories were familiar, "Mrs. T. [had] a way of her own which [was] very pleasing." Indeed, one of the veterans in the audience commented, "I have often wondered at Tanner's eloquence, but now I understand it all."[35]

Women's rights also found their way into her writing. At least two of the poems she read on multiple occasions dealt with the issue. The text of "Jones's View"—which she read to the District Women's Suffrage Association in Washington—has not survived, but "Justice" took the form of a humorous dialogue between an old married couple about women's rights. Although Tanner's position in politics did not require him to have an opinion on women's suffrage, he did on occasion weigh in on the increasingly controversial issue. Perhaps it is not surprising, as both of his daughters remained single and worked in various government offices throughout their adult lives, that their father seems to have adopted a pro-woman attitude. In fact, he saw himself as something of a pioneer in women's rights. He had hired the first woman to work in Brooklyn government while he was tax collector, and more than twenty years before the Nineteenth Amendment gave the vote to women, he declared to a convention of the Women's Relief Corps—an auxiliary to the GAR—"his belief that women [would] do everything toward the elevation of the ballot and bring it from the neighborhood of the saloon to that of schools and churches." In a 1904 speech to a GAR meeting, Tanner denied "that God made woman subservient to man. He made man and saw that He could do better, and then he made woman." A few years later, Tanner spoke at a rally protesting police actions that violently disrupted a women's suffrage parade. In an interview a few weeks after the incident, he claimed to have realized the injustice of women being refused the vote when he was only twelve years old. Throughout his long life, he said, he had observed "that as a whole the influence of women over public and private affairs of the nation and men [had] been proven incontrovertibly to be beneficial," and he hoped that they would soon be given the right to vote and, in that way, "be made a mighty force in behalf of public and private morality, and, therefore, beneficial to the nation today, more so in all the years to come."[36]

Clearly, at least as far as the limited sources can tell us, James and Mero Tanner were partners in thought and deed. That partnership continued after he became commander in chief, when they set out for a triumphal national tour on behalf of the GAR. The Corporal and "Mrs. Corporal" were feted by dozens of posts, as he basked in the affection of his comrades and in the knowledge that he, as much as anyone, had brought the organization to its current prominence.

The trip took a tragic turn in late June when the Tanners took a drive near Helena, Montana. They had been welcomed to the state capital by the governor's wife and a vast crowd of GAR men; the day after their arrival, they were treated to a long tour of the city, a nearby fort, and other local sites. Tanner may have been a reluctant participant in the sightseeing trip. Newspaper accounts would later mention Tanner's longtime disdain for automobiles. Toward the end of his short reminiscences, he waxed eloquent about the beauty of winters in upstate New York, especially when a new snowfall provided breathtaking views of the countryside that could be appreciated only from a horse-drawn sleigh. "How can the lumbering, odorous, gassy machine"—the automobile—"compare with the trim cutter, the spirited horse encircled by resonant bells, and with the chosen one, snuggling, ensconced by your side." He apparently believed he was a jinx when it came to riding in cars, claiming once, "I have seldom ridden in an automobile when accident did not happen." He reportedly wagered a box of cigars just before Mero and he departed on the fateful trip that his "hoodoo" regarding cars would cause something bad to happen and, indeed, it did; one of the cars in the expedition broke an axle while touring the Capitol grounds. The passengers shifted places, and the tour continued. But a little while later, when the driver tried to pass two horse-drawn wagons, the car spun out of control and overturned. At first Tanner thought Mero was unhurt; she asked immediately, "Are you hurt, Jim?" and there were no visible signs of injury. Yet she soon fainted and never regained consciousness. The Corporal bitterly blamed the chauffeur, who had apparently ignored his pleas to slow down—he was "young, reckless, surcharged with his own importance [and] a disposition to rush"—and the coroner's jury would rule that the accident was caused by bad roads and the driver's carelessness.[37]

A funeral was held in Helena, and Mero was buried a few days later in Arlington National Cemetery, which had been the final resting place for veterans of the Civil War since the 1860s. Several officers of the Legion of Loyal Women and the Ladies' Auxiliary of the Union Veteran Legion attended. Among the floral tributes was a handsome wreath from President and Mrs. Theodore Roosevelt, who had facilitated Mero's burial in Arlington (wives who preceded their husbands in death were not normally allowed to be interred there). Tributes and condolences came from across the country. The *Confederate Veteran* expressed its sympathies and said that "for more than a quarter of a century Mrs. Tanner had been well known and esteemed in the South through her cordial cooperation in her husband's patriotic and progressive movements for the restoration of fraternal sentiment between the sections."[38]

Tanner appeared at the national encampment of the GAR in Minneapolis just a few weeks after Mero's death. After finishing his annual report, he paid tribute to his wife of nearly forty years. Because of his disabilities, he said, it was "absolutely necessary that [he] should have some arm in touch, [so his] wife had . . . accompanied [him] on all [his] journeyings." He continued:

> You know what occurred. We toured the city and its vicinity in most congenial company. A bright sky overhead, magnificent scenery greeting the eye at every point, accompanied by her who forty years before had joined her life to mine, and who in all those forty years had been such a guide and counselor as few men have been blessed with, she, in the calm serenity of the Indian summer of her life, radiant in health and spirits every bit as fair to my old eyes in her crown of whitened hair, as she had looked on our wedding morn in her raven tresses—what wonder the world looked fair and radiant to me one instant! Then the fatal crash—as out of the sky, leaped the Angel of Death, and in a few moments I realized that my individual world lay in a wreck and ruin, not equalled by that which crushed me at Bull Run. It was a great soul that passed to God that afternoon. True to her own heroic self, mortally wounded though she was, the first thought in her heart, the first cry from her lips was not of herself, but found expression in the words: "Are you hurt?"
>
> God was merciful in the end, and without so very much physical pain her soul was released. Then there came to me a knowledge impossible for one to obtain under less agonizing circumstances of the full measure of comradeship. God grant that none of you may ever come to the realization of it except from speculative imagination! No lips were ever molded capable of expressing the debt of obligation I feel toward the great and sympathetic hearts that gathered around me in those awful hours when the world seemed rocking under me. For the countless kindnesses which to some degree brightened the gloom of the journey of that terrible home coming, my pulsing heart is unable to throb a sufficiency of thanks. Many of you, my comrades, have trod the "wine press of sorrow" and realize the crushing effect of such a blow.

But I rally to the thought that if the lips now silent forever could speak once more they would voice to me the injunction not to wrap myself in a mantle of fruitless sorrow, but rather to spend myself in even more strenuous efforts in the future for the helping of our needy comrades than it has been my privilege to indulge in the past. To that I pledge myself.

An organ softly played "Nearer, My God, to Thee"—the hymn sung at her funeral in Montana—and the GAR chaplain ended the session with a prayer.[39]

Paying Heed

Mero's death devastated Tanner, although, characteristically, he carried on. It no doubt helped that both his daughters lived in Washington, where Ada still worked in the Treasury office, and Antoinette was a clerk in the War Department. In 1910 he and Ada were living in the Richmond, a hotel just a few blocks from the White House, but by 1920 all three were living at 1610 Nineteenth Street, in the DuPont Circle neighborhood, where mansions, embassies, and many three-story row houses like the one the Tanners occupied had been built in the 1880s and 1890s. It seems that Ada and Antoinette owned the house together; they would remain in it after Tanner's death.[40]

Tanner leaped into the news again when he became an ardent supporter of preparedness during the long lead-up to American entry into the First World War. As the debate raged about how the United States should respond to the European conflict between 1914 and 1917, Tanner spoke frequently on the war. Although he criticized the "blood drunk" nations of Europe, he supported the cause of military preparedness—the great issue in the election of 1916 was the United States' role in the war and the extent to which the military should prepare for potential conflict—as one of the most effective ways to ensure peace. He urged Americans "to pay some heed to the voice of the survivors of the battle days of the '60's," when the United States was caught by surprise and unnecessarily sacrificed thousands of men who might have lived if the military had been better prepared.[41]

But once the United States committed itself, Tanner was all in. The day before the United States declared war on Germany in April, after Germany had begun all-out submarine warfare on Allied and American shipping, the *Brooklyn Eagle* published a letter from Tanner in which he related a scene from his weeks in an army hospital when a dying Irishman asked to be turned toward the window to look at the American flag one last time. Tanner promoted the sale of Liberty Bonds to raise money for the war effort. When the GAR met in Oregon in 1918, Tanner, called by a local paper the "chief character of the GAR," and his daughters attended the launch of the supply ship USS *Lakota* at a local shipyard, where Antoinette would do the honors of christening the ship by breaking a bottle of champagne against its bow. The *Morning Oregonian* published a poem commemorating the occasion. It described the forty-eight-year-old Antoinette in an oddly sexual way, commenting on the "shapely arms" of the "lovely Antoinette" raising the bottle in her "fair hands." But, as always, the Corporal almost stole the show.

> The crowd sang patriotic songs
> And waved the starry banner.
> And then, as if with one accord,
> They called for Corporal Tanner.
>
> With rare and ready eloquence
> He swayed that mighty crowd.
> And they responded happily
> With cheering long and loud.[42]

The American entry into the war inspired the Corporal to bring out the red-meat rhetoric that he had sampled during the Spanish-American War. In a speech given at a reception (held, ironically, at the Pension Bureau Building) during the United Confederate Veterans' reunion in Washington in 1917, he suggested that "foes of the government should face the firing squad." He also compared "the modern pacifist and anti-conscription agitator" to the antiwar Democratic "Copperheads of the '60's." He supported banning German language classes in American schools, declaring that "any language that produces a people so lost to all sense of humanity . . . should be the only language spoken in hell." His fellow members of the GAR "cheered thunderously" when, at the national encampment in 1918, he wondered why "a righteous God [had] not consigned" the German kaiser "and his murderous cohorts to the most orthodox Hell that [was] known, and condemned them to everlasting damnation."[43]

Tanner also continued his and Mero's long association with the Red Cross, which had been completely reorganized early in the century. He had been appointed to the executive committee in 1906; had been one of three dozen politicians and celebrities (including former commanders in chief of the army, cabinet members, congressmen, senators, and Clara Barton) named in the "charter" and "reincorporation" passed by Congress in 1909; and was still on the board of incorporators as late as 1916.[44]

Tanner continued to make a case for the relevance of the Civil War when he performed perhaps his greatest service to the Red Cross: writing the most complete version of his gruesome experiences as a wounded soldier in a two-part article that appeared in the *American Red Cross Magazine* in the autumn of 1916. The editor's introduction declared, "Few living men have suffered from the combined effects of grievous wounds and unpardonable neglect" as Tanner ("the 'Corporal' . . . is as much a part of his name today as the 'Stonewall' in Stonewall Jackson's name"), who had been "pushed to the very brink of death by a miserably lax and meager war relief system." Tanner introduced his long account in hopes, he wrote, of bringing "to larger attention the horrible experience [he] underwent" and to "accentuate . . . the need of a Red Cross organization, scientifically and adequately 'equipped' for the handling of such tragedies" to anyone contemplating sending American soldiers into combat without first preparing to provide for their medical needs. Once the war began, Tanner helped Red Cross officials cut through some War Department red tape.[45]

Oddly, despite his extraordinary commitment to pensions for Civil War veterans, Tanner did not support the so-called bonuses passed for veterans of the Great War. Shortly after the armistice, he declared at the New York state GAR encampment that patriotism could not be measured in terms of dollars. Tanner urged Congress to direct funds only to wounded soldiers and the families of dead soldiers. And as someone who knew something about the power of the soldier vote, he suggested that many congressmen supported the bill "not because they want[ed] to do it, but [because] they [were] afraid of the influence back home."[46]

Today and Yesterday

Tanner appeared from time to time in short newspaper stories about minor celebrities. In April 1911 he was featured in a syndicated newspaper column called "This Is My Birthday" with a capsule biography published on his April 4 birthdate. The *Washington Times* included the Corporal in a series of "Today and Yesterday" photographs of prominent Washingtonians in 1918; it featured perhaps the only published version of the blurry image of

Tanner as a seventeen-year-old recruit alongside a current photograph of a white-haired, sad-eyed, rather sagging old man. In a 1920 Minnesota newspaper column called "Answers to Your Queries," a reader asked if Corporal Tanner still lived and how and where he was wounded.[47]

His health seemed to have faded slowly during this time, although no crisis was reported in the press. One of the few surviving comments by anyone who knew him appeared in the margins of a 1917 letter from Tanner to Eva Reckhard about her husband's pension. Tanner mentions looking forward to "the girls" and he driving to Boston for his forty-first national encampment of the GAR and describes a very painful attack of neuritis in his right arm, which made it hard for him to use the canes he needed to get around. Reckhard wrote in the margin, "Poor old man. I am afraid he will not go to [his] 42nd encampment." A few years later he was confined to a wheelchair, at least part of the time, according to a report from a GAR meeting.[48]

Yet he lived for another decade. A reporter described Tanner in 1923 as still having "the build of a powerful man. His great head, set on massive shoulders, [had] the lines that artists love to sketch." He continued to be the center of attention at national encampments. At the meeting held in Milwaukee that year, he sat with the current commander and staff, consulting on various GAR matters and accepting greetings and well wishes. An interview revealed that Tanner's vigorous patriotism had been unaffected by advancing age: "Corporal Tanner is a militarist—an apostle of Theodore Roosevelt. Bolsheviks, anarchists, socialists he classes with pacifists." He still had the energy to deliver an address to a thousand people at a Women's Relief Corps function and at the annual campfire (where, ironically, he appeared with Milwaukee's Socialist mayor, Daniel W. Hoan).[49]

By then Tanner had added to his list of undesirables the Ku Klux Klan, "the most dangerous, most infamous" of the groups he hated. This was a fairly recent development, no doubt spurred by the Klan's sudden revival in 1915 and its rise to prominence in the Democratic Party. A year later, hundreds of Klan members—many of them delegates—would rally at the party's national convention. Although a community made up of descendants of slaves occupied a hamlet less than a dozen miles from Cobleskill, Tanner had rarely mentioned race during his long public life. At the 1886 GAR encampment in San Francisco, he declared how proud he was that he and his fellow soldiers had helped end slavery—the only known time he specifically mentioned this particular outcome of the Civil War. Yet twenty years later, when he mentioned education in a speech at a GAR event in Dallas, he declared, "We have in Washington our neckful of the negro question. We have plenty of them and of the worst sort. But in the South I believe your people can take care of the negro question." The comment betrayed a fairly typical, if mild, version of early twentieth-century racism. Then he urged the nation's "rich men" to "give their wealth to the education of the mountain whites in the South and to the scum and scurf in the great cities like New York." And toward the end of his life, when he recalled his days as a new father in Cobleskill, he offered a story that could have come straight out of Uncle Remus about a friendly old "darkey," complete with an exaggerated "Negro dialect" playing with his baby daughter. Tanner's ideas about race may have been reflected in his rather unthinking approval of the brutal tactics used again Filipino "rebels" earlier in the century. But it is also entirely likely that Tanner did not think much about race, and that he held rather conventional, carelessly racist views.[50]

A Picturesque Character

Like all long-lived members of his generation, Tanner had witnessed extraordinary changes. He had always claimed that the first train he had ever seen was the one that took him to the army; he lived long enough to see his wife killed in an automobile accident and to have one of his last speeches to the GAR—at the national encampment in Boston in 1924—broadcast on the radio. "His vocabulary," reported one newspaper, "has lost none of its picturesque words and his voice is strong and vigorous as it was years ago."[51]

But it would not remain so for long. He attended his fiftieth encampment in Des Moines in 1926 (with both Ada and Antoinette accompanying him), where he told an Iowa newspaper that he had not missed a national encampment since 1876. It was his last one.[52]

As Tanner entered the last year of his life, the war was never far from his thoughts. Late in 1926, he wrote to a long-lost friend, James Jaycox, whom he had thought dead for more than two decades. Jaycox was a fellow Schoharie County native (from Jefferson, about fifteen miles from Cobleskill) who had served with Tanner in Company C of the Eighty-Seventh New York. Although Jaycox was never mentioned in any of the newspaper articles or in Tanner's account of his experiences at Second Bull Run, he was one of the five men who had carried Tanner to safety. Tanner's letter was chatty and cheerful, beginning with the comment that he had "had one of the surprises of [his] young life" when he heard from his nephew that Jaycox was still alive. The old Corporal recounted that hot day in Virginia, when five friends and comrades had made sure that Tanner was safe in the farmhouse-turned-hospital and had a full canteen when they fled just before the Confederates arrived. But something bothered him. Although Tanner remembered Jaycox and the Sproul brothers of Brooklyn, he could not remember the other two men. Isaac Lawrence had always taken credit for it—indeed, Tanner had given him a job in the collector's office as a result—but Tanner had been "doubtful" about Lawrence's claim all along. He wondered if Jaycox had any idea who the others might have been.[53]

There is no way of knowing if Jaycox ever responded, but Tanner went on to recount a trip he had taken earlier in the fall. "Well, Jim," he admitted, "it will sound rather strange to you, and it seemed strange to me when I did it." He and two carloads of "friends of modern times . . . some Confederates among them," had driven from Washington to Manassas, where they toured the battlefield. There, he "*walked* into that same room and sat down with [his] chair exactly on the spot where [they had] laid [him] down that night." He went on, "You can easily imagine that a great many thoughts surged up in my mind; it was a soul-stirring time to me." He promised to send Jaycox a copy of his *American Red Cross Magazine* article. "I had a horrible experience as you will easily imagine when you read it." He hoped that in the spring his old friend would come down to Washington so that they could make the same journey together "and live over the old days to a considerable extent," noting, "I can hardly believe that these things have come to pass myself."[54]

It is doubtful that they ever made the trip. In September 1927, when the GAR met in Grand Rapids, Michigan, a speaker announced "the absence and illness of [their] beloved comrade, James Tanner." He expressed the sentiments of the other old soldiers: "This encampment greatly misses the presence of a personage which for more than 50 years has unfailingly taken part in the councils of the Grand Army of the Republic. By his wisdom, his power of speech, his character, the appeal of his maimed body, he has always been a revered leader among us." However, "the overwhelming weakness of increasing years" had prevented him from taking "his accustomed place."[55]

The end seems to have come rather suddenly, although Tanner continued working as register of wills until a few weeks before his death. In the spring he had met in Washington with leaders of several other veterans' organizations to discuss national military preparedness. He felt well enough that day to deliver remarks at a dinner attended by the few remaining congressmen who had served in the Union and the Confederate armies. In what was probably his last public speech, he focused, of course, on reconciliation. The obituary published in the journal of the 1928 GAR encampment indicated that his condition had worsened during the summer. In addition to "the discomforts and often great pain in the remnants of limbs" that Tanner had endured for decades, the facial neuralgia—a painful nerve condition—that he had first experienced in 1888 (and for which he underwent at least two surgeries) worsened. "A slow and progressive loss of strength and emaciation" emerged, and by June he was too weak to attend the meeting of the New York GAR. His two daughters and son James were at his bedside in the DuPont Circle house when he died on October 2. Earl, by that time a colonel, had just been put in command of a reserve regiment in Utica, New York, less than fifty miles from Cobleskill, but he joined the family in Washington a day or two after Tanner's death.[56]

A few papers used the occasion to reflect on the transient nature of fame. One observed, "Corporal Tanner has not figured much in the news latterly but his death recalled in mind one of the picturesque characters who rose to fame in the aftermath of the Civil War." A New York paper published a wistful commentary on how most of the "restless and rather self-satisfied younger generation never heard of this man, whose name was once a 'household word,'" but who had "long outlived his fame." Appropriately enough, the *Brooklyn Eagle* published the most extensive obituary, which was mainly a narrative of his political career in Brooklyn.[57]

Tanner was buried with Mero in section 2, site 877 of Arlington National Cemetery.

Earl and James continued their careers in the military and the law, respectively, but Antoinette and Ada remained, in some ways, in the shadow of the famous father, to whom they had devoted their private lives. Both worked in government well into old age. The 1939 Washington City Directory listed Ada, then seventy, as an administrative assistant in the Treasury Department and Antoinette, sixty-three, as a clerk in the War Department (another source indicated that she worked in the surgeon general's office). In fact, President Franklin Roosevelt issued an executive order in 1938 allowing Ada to work past the compulsory retirement age. They appeared from time to time in newspapers as guests of friends in upstate New York and Florida; on at least one occasion, Antoinette gave

Ada Tanner at her desk in the Treasury Department in 1890. Prints and
Photographs Division, Library of Congress.

a talk at a special veterans meeting of the Rotary Club in Canandaigua,
New York. A decade after her father's death, she was still introduced as the
"daughter of the renowned Corporal Tanner." The sisters eventually purchased a winter home in Pass-a-Grille, near Saint Petersburg. Both died
there, Antoinette at the age of eight-three in 1950, and Ada nine years later
at the age of ninety. The Corporal loomed over them, even in death: her
obituary called Antoinette "a Washington resident for more than 60 years
and daughter of James Tanner, former Pension Commissioner and GAR
commander." They would join their parents at Arlington.[58]

Tanner's name came up several times at the national encampment of the
GAR, held in Denver—where he had been elected commander more than
two decades earlier—a year after his death. The official journal featured
a full-page photograph and a biography filling several pages. As did the
deaths of other old soldiers by the late 1920s, Tanner's demise caused at
least one past commander to reminisce about the old days, when thousands
of hearty old soldiers would attend encampments and literally take over the

host city. Those had passed, inevitably. From a high of nearly half a million members in 1890, the GAR had dwindled to less than thirty-three thousand at the time of Corporal Tanner's death, and over two hundred local posts had given up their charters during the previous year. "Now we are . . . just a mere handful of old men," lamented a veteran, who "have to be led around by boy scouts. They have to show us where to go, and to place this step here, or avoid this danger there. The story"—the story of Civil War veterans in American life—"is pretty near told."[59]

Epilogue and Conclusion

The Footless Ghost

James Tanner haunted Washington while he lived and, according to some witnesses, after he died. One night in 1972, a security guard making his rounds in the Superior Court of the District of Columbia (then housed in the old red-brick Pension Bureau Building on F Street) encountered a mysterious "man in a light-colored suit with a peculiar walk." The stranger opened his mouth to speak but instead emitted a "nightmarish yell." Later, the largely incoherent guard—who, the story goes, ended up in a mental hospital—claimed "that he had looked at a man with no eyes . . . and had seen the fires of hell and smelled the stench of the dead." An expert on ghosts in the district suggests that the specter's "strange gait," the location, and the legend that Abraham Lincoln's son Robert had hidden secret evidence about his father's assassination in the building's faux marble columns, all point to Tanner as the ghostly presence.[1]

Whether or not he became a restless spirit in the building he occupied for only a few months, James Tanner certainly remained a presence in his beloved Washington, where he was the most famous old soldier in America, known to many as, simply, "the Corporal." Yet when he died, a brief obituary, by turns bittersweet and dismissive, could say this about the long-lost life of this representative man of the Gilded Age:

> "Corporal" Tanner, who died Monday in his eighty-third year, long outlived his fame, for it is probable that our restless and rather self-satisfied younger generation never heard of this man, whose name was once a "household word." To the minds of the oldsters he will be represented by the appellation . . . "God-help-the-surplus" Tanner. This reminds one of the names which the Puritans of the seventeenth century were wont to take to themselves, such as "Praise-God-Barebones." . . . It was when Tanner was appointed commissioner of pensions by President Harrison that he said "God help the surplus," and he was not long in proving that there was need of divine protection for it.

Tanner did not last long as commissioner of pensions. For years there was no political campaign in which he was not prominent. Tanner served well in the Union army up to the second battle of Bull Run in August, 1862, in which he lost both legs. He was a lawyer by profession. When he died he was to most of his countrymen only a memory, and hardly that to many of them.[2]

At one level, Tanner was "airbrushed" out of American history as thoroughly as he was removed from scenes of Lincoln's deathbed. By the time of his death, he had become a relic of the previous century. The pension and soldiers' home issues with which he had been so closely associated had faded as Civil War veterans died off, and within a few years, the federal government had formed the Veterans Administration to take over the various issues associated with veterans—who were represented to most Americans by the millions of doughboys who had served during the Great War. New veterans' organizations like the American Legion and the Veterans of Foreign Wars had eclipsed the GAR. Civil service reform had eliminated the centrality of political patronage in the political process, and the Democratic and Republican Parties had taken sharp turns in principles and policies. Only the infamy Tanner had gained during his few months as commissioner of pensions outlived him. Like the trains he dreaded and the automobiles he detested, the twentieth century hurtled forward, while Tanner, the man with no feet, could only hobble into irrelevance.

Despite the anonymity in which he left this life, a generation earlier Tanner's ambition, drive, and opportunism had made him nearly a household name in Gilded Age America. His experiences as a Civil War soldier and veteran, as a politician and Republican insider, and as a self-made man despite his severe disability, make Tanner an emblematic figure for the period. The ghostly presence of the Corporal can be found almost everywhere we look during this formative period in American history.

At a superficial level, Tanner resembles the fictional Cyrus Trask, father of one of the main characters in John Steinbeck's *East of Eden*. Although the novel was published in 1952, it depicts the early twentieth century, and Steinbeck, born in 1902, may have heard of the aging Corporal. He certainly would have known veterans of the Civil War. Trask's story is eerily similar to Tanner's: he spends a few months in the Union army and half an hour on a battlefield, where a bullet shatters his leg. He returns home as a one-legged hero and parlays his brief service into a full-time job. He exaggerates his military service, writes letters to soldiers' newspapers, and touts his expertise on the war. He becomes active in the GAR, eventually becoming a general secretary traveling the country and advising the secretary of war and even the president on military affairs. He also becomes a behind-the-scenes politician by wielding the soldiers' vote like a sledgehammer. "I wonder if you know how much influence I really have," he brags to his estranged son. "I can throw the Grand Army at any candidate like a sock. . . . I can get senators defeated and I can pick [political] appointments like apples. I can make men and I can destroy men." There is no reason to think that Steinbeck based Trask on Tanner, and only his most bitter opponents would have characterized Tanner in this way, but the parallels are arresting.[3]

Tanner certainly believed his life had meant something. He wore his status as a celebrated veteran with unabashed pride. He was not a deep *thinker* about his service, but he did *feel* deeply that he and his fellow Union soldiers occupied a peculiar and paramount place in the nation's history. This conviction usually took the form of a fairly heartfelt, if generic, sense of patriotism, an increasingly strident support for U.S. foreign policy, and the belief that sectional reconciliation—to which he knew he had contributed mightily—had left the country stronger than ever.

Tanner's belief that his generation truly was the nineteenth century's "greatest generation" was best expressed just after the Great War ended, and eight years before his death, when he closed the campfire at the annual encampment of the GAR. As the comrade who introduced him said, "A camp fire would not be a camp fire without Corporal Tanner." It was already late in the evening, and his daughter—probably Ada—had urged him not to speak "a minute over" fifteen minutes. Tanner took a little longer than that, making his typical, for those years, comments about Bolsheviks, the kaiser, and other evildoers in the modern world and praising President Wilson's efforts at the peace talks in Paris. He went on to connect the veterans of the Civil War, the Spanish-American War, and the Great War as links in the chain of military might that had propelled the United States to its current glory. Not surprisingly, he highlighted the achievements of his generation of soldiers: "Where would this nation have been to-day and for the last few years, if we and our comrades had not done the work we did in the 60's?"[4]

Tanner closed his talk that night with the closest he ever came to the kind of elegiac tone achieved by another famous veteran, Oliver Wendell Holmes Jr., who had said on a Memorial Day a generation earlier,

"Through our great good fortune, in our youth our hearts were touched with fire. It was given to us to learn at the outset that life is a profound and passionate thing. While we are permitted to scorn nothing but indifference, and do not pretend to undervalue the worldly rewards of ambition, we have seen with our own eyes . . . the snowy heights of honor, and it is for us to bear the report to those who come after us."[5]

Tanner had been "bearing report" for over half a century. "We have had our day," he said.

> We have played our part. We have set an example for all the sons of America in the future. We have made every generation that follows us our debtor. Our boys have kept up the work; they have passed it along well. They have kept the chain taut, each link equally stood, and so when we come at last to lie down and quit these scenes, every individual among us who has lived to see and enjoy the progress and prosperity and power of the United States of America can exclaim with his last breath, "Mine eyes have seen the glory of the coming of the Lord."

This was, of course, what the old soldiers wanted to hear. They burst into applause, and the campfire ended with the band playing "The Star-Spangled Banner." Tanner had made similar comments previously; they were about as close to a philosophical approach to the meaning of his life as he got. But there was much more to him than that.[6]

As the preceding pages argue, Tanner's life reflected a number of the extraordinary currents of Gilded Age culture, society, and politics, and especially the ways in which the Civil War—the issues over which it was fought, the men who did the fighting—cast its long shadow over the rest of the century. He achieved too much fame and fortune, and achieved them in too unusual a way, to be considered a truly representative man. Yet he participated in the major events of the era. As a soldier, he took part in the most common experience of his generation; as a disabled veteran, he was a member of a large subgroup of old soldiers who endured the rest of their lives with disabilities large and small. And he cared about the same things that hundreds of thousands of men cared about: the moral and material responsibility of other Americans and the federal government to provide for the saviors of the Union, the fraternal comradeship of the GAR, the urgency of remembering the sacrifices of Union soldiers. His concerns were representative; the energy and personal resources he poured into them and the rewards he earned as a result were extraordinary.

Yet Tanner personifies several Gilded Age experiences and attitudes: First, Tanner's grueling ordeal in military hospitals and his struggle to cope as one of the many violently disabled men who survived the conflict provide case studies of the military experience and the state of medicine. Prior to the Civil War, disabilities of any kind were generally hidden from view—partly because of personal preference, partly because of the lack of resources and opportunities for disabled people to contribute to society. But becoming a disabled person led Corporal Jim Tanner to become "The Corporal": it not only forced him to dig deep into his personal fortitude and imagination but also led to the first of many sinecures reserved, first, for disabled veterans and, later, for active and loyal Republicans. Tanner's disability seems to have brought out the best in him, as it did for at least some grievously wounded men, inspiring in him a resolve not to become dependent on others.

Second, Tanner's career as a politician and government official offers a glimpse into the partisan, complicated, dirty politics of the Gilded Age. His patronage jobs gave him the opportunity to have a political career in Brooklyn and, eventually, the nation. Despite never holding elective office, Tanner was a central player in Gilded Age politics. He held a number of lucrative and locally important offices, campaigned for local and national candidates alike, and was often seen as the leading spokesman for veterans' interests. Indeed, despite his low rank, relatively brief experience, and lack of battlefield heroism, as one of the country's most famous Civil War veterans, Tanner would be expected to deliver the soldiers' vote to the Republican Party. As a speaker who popularized a soldier-centric view of the war, as a spokesman for sectional reconciliation, and as an advocate for soldiers' homes and pensions, he represented the most powerful special interest group in the United States at the time: former Union soldiers.

Third, his long career as an advocate of pensions and as a claims agent, his very short career as commissioner of pensions, and the often contentious politics that surrounded the pension issue made Tanner the symbol of both the benefits and the abuses of the massive and unprecedented system of federal aid to disabled men and their dependents. The constantly expanding and increasingly expensive pension system sparked a surprisingly virulent debate over the meanings of patriotism and the responsibility of government to its citizens. Tanner was the lightning rod for the sometimes shocking criticism of Union soldiers that complicated the ways in which the war was remembered, as well as the public debates over the appropriate role of government in its citizens' lives.

Finally, Tanner's unrelenting ambition and determination to overcome his disability show us something about the nature of Gilded Age culture. He was an entrepreneur who exploited several "modern" developments—the adoption of stenography in legal and business circles, the growth of government bureaucracy, the professionalization of the lobbying and claims industries, the rapidly improving transportation network—to gain afflu-ence, influence, and fame. And like other Gilded Age Americans who achieved notoriety, he was a popular subject for reporters and gossips.

Yet his celebrity failed to survive his death, which suggests something about the nature of fame but also about the kind of celebrity he was. News-papers and magazines could barely keep up with the public's demand for information about the various brands of eminence that flourished during the Gilded Age: the generals and statesmen, financial giants and inven-tors, sportsmen and women, humorists and actors, criminals and con men. These celebrities awed, inspired, titillated, and entertained. Tanner stood on many a platform, appeared in many a newspaper column, and was men-tioned in many of the same breaths as these other famous folk.

But two specific contemporaries of Tanner help locate the Corporal in his time and place. One was his good friend Capt. John "Jack" Crawford, the "poet scout"; the other was William "Buffalo Bill" Cody. As teenag-ers, all three had seen service in the Civil War—Crawford was wounded at Spotsylvania and Petersburg, Cody served as a teamster for a Kansas cavalry regiment. While Tanner rebuilt his life in the years immediately after the Civil War, Crawford and Cody worked as scouts and hunters in the West. And in the 1870s and 1880s (and beyond), both offered exciting narratives of their experiences in the West, Jack as a writer and stage per-former and Cody, most famously, as the subject of dime novels and leader of the most famous "Wild West show." Tanner may or may not have met Cody—they traveled in very different circles—but he and Crawford were connected by a forty-year friendship.

Crawford's fame was deeper and wider than Tanner's. He was a famous frontiersman and scout who had performed hard service in campaigns against Native Americans and working as a federal agent investigating corruption on Indian reservations. He published poems and articles con-stantly, appeared in plays, gave public readings, and delivered speeches. He even dabbled in movies late in his life. But, like Tanner, his memory faded for most Americans not long after he died in 1917.[7]

Not so, of course, Buffalo Bill Cody. He traveled the world with his Wild West shows, and even after his death a few months before Crawford's, extravaganzas like his drew large audiences. Although the shows were eventually eclipsed by movies, radio, and television, Cody—at least the mythic version of himself that he created—remained a cultural icon. He inspired many of the conventions of popular culture's romance with the West and appeared as a character in countless stories, books, and movies.

Why did Cody's resonance with the American public outlast Tanner's and even Crawford's? Crawford was a sometimes friend, more often competitor of Cody's. It seems that the latter simply outshone the former at his own game. Tanner's and Cody's public personae could hardly have been more different. One scholar has recently argued that Cody was a leading figure in the creation of a narrative of the recent American past—the aggressive, heroic, progressive opening of the frontier to civilization that, for many, personified some of Americans' best features. The experience of "the West"—the opening of the plains and the Southwest during the decades following the Civil War—became a bellwether of the American character, an adventure with which everyone could identify, however vicariously, and an exciting narrative that could thrill readers and viewers long after the history had passed.

The Civil War was, of course, just as thrilling. But Tanner's message from the 1870s through the 1890s asked—indeed, demanded—that Americans look backward to a tragic if glorious time; to dwell on obligations rather than opportunities; to acknowledge that they could never recognize or reward veterans enough. Even as he promoted American power and expansion in 1898 and 1917, he implied that no conflict could match the Civil War in the tremendous sacrifices it would claim or in the positive results that would ensue. Moreover, while Cody's narrative of the West floated free from politics, Tanner's personality, loyalty to the Republican Party, and love for politics led him almost gleefully to tether his narrative of the Civil War to political partisanship. Tanner must have seemed to Americans of the early twentieth century like a relic, stuck in an earlier time that no one wanted to think about. Cody, on the other hand, also offered a narrative of the past—but a more recent past, and one with which Americans, even those who had not fought Indians or persevered on a prairie homestead or built a railroad, could identify. The West became a metaphor for the American spirit, of which everyone had at least a little; the Civil War, at least the war narrated by Tanner, had become irrelevant to the lives of most Americans.[8]

In addition to the fact that his lifelong message lost its relevance, the fact that Tanner never held elective office, wrote a book, or produced a lasting record of his thoughts and deeds ensured that the public memory of his life would vanish as soon as he stopped making speeches and being interviewed by newspapers. As long as he was active and in the news, he was famous. As soon as he and his pet causes became unimportant to the American public, he fell out of view. Yet, despite his century-long anonymity, Corporal Tanner epitomized crucial aspects of the Gilded Age. He is worth getting to know, and in knowing him we can better understand this pivotal time in our history.

NOTES

Prologue

1. *Daily National Republican*, April 14, 1865; Ruth Painter, *Lincoln's Sons* (Boston: Little, Brown, 1955), 211.

2. Unless otherwise noted, the description of Tanner's role in events following Lincoln's assassination is taken from Tanner's letter to Walch, April 17, 1865, published as "The Assassination of President Lincoln, 1865," in the "Documents" section of the *American Historical Review* 29 (April 1924): 514–17. Tanner was still alive when the letter was published and confirmed its accuracy to the editors. Internal evidence suggests that although Tanner began and dated the letter in the days immediately after the events he describes, he added to it a couple of weeks later and sent it sometime after April 29. Another version, with a few added details, appears in Maxwell Whiteman's introduction to *While Lincoln Lay Dying: A Facsimile Reproduction of the First Testimony Taken in Connection with the Assassination of Abraham Lincoln as Recorded by Corporal James Tanner* (Philadelphia: Union League of Philadelphia, 1968).

3. Walt Whitman, *Memoranda during the War* (Camden, N.J.: by the author, 1876), 61.

4. "Assassination of President Lincoln," 516.

5. Thomas F. Schwartz, "Darwin, Lincoln, Stanton and Apes, Angels, and Ages," *For the People: Newsletter of the Abraham Lincoln Association* 11 (Fall 2009): 5–6.

6. *Frank Leslie's Illustrated Weekly*, April 29, 1865; diagram in Osborne Oldroyd, *The Assassination of Abraham Lincoln: Flight, Pursuit, Capture, and Punishment of the Conspirators* (Washington, D.C.: Osborne Oldroyd, 1901), 36, 30.

7. "Assassination of President Lincoln, 1865," 517.

Chapter One. The War Hit Me and Hit Me Hard

1. Dora L. Costa, *The Evolution of Retirement: An American Economic History, 1880–1990* (Chicago: University of Chicago Press, 1998), 198.

2. U.S. Census, 1860, schedule 1, Schoharie County, New York, http://go.fold3.com/1860census/.

3. J. H. French, *Gazetteer of the State of New York* (Syracuse: R. Pearsall Smith, 1860), 604, 606, 604; *Manual for the Use of the Legislature of the State of New York, 1869*

(Albany: Weed, Parsons, 1869), 102; William E. Roscoe, *History of Schoharie County, New York, with Illustrations of Biographical Sketches of Some of Its Prominent Men and Pioneers, 1713–1882* (Syracuse: D. Mason, 1882), 393–402.

4. James Tanner, *Glimpses of Cobleskill: Schoharie County, New York, 1852–1927* (Cobleskill: Cobleskill Times, [1927]), 2–3.

5. Roscoe, *History of Schoharie County,* 444–46; Capt. James E. Smith, *A Famous Battery and Its Campaigns, 1861–64* (Washington, D.C.: W. H. Lowdermilk, 1892), 180.

6. "New York State Education Department: Teacher Training and Certification, http://www.regents.nysed.gov/about/history-highered.html; Marion F. Noyes, ed., *A History of Schoharie County* (Richmondville, N.Y.: Richmondville Phoenix, 1964), 102; James Tanner Pension File, certificate 17405, National Archives and Records Administration, Washington, D.C.; Noyes, *History of Schoharie County,* 100.

7. "Military Affairs in New York," in *The Union Army: A History of Military Affairs in the Loyal States, 1861–65—Records of the Regiments in the Union Army—Cyclopedia of Battles—Memoirs of Commanders and Soldiers,* 8 vols.(Madison, Wis.: Federal Publishing, 1908), 2:18–49.

8. Smith, *Famous Battery,* 181.

9. Ibid., 181; Frederick Phisterer, *New York in the War of the Rebellion,* 3rd ed. (Albany: J. B. Lyon, 1912), 443–44, 479; http://dmna.ny.gov/historic/reghist/civil /rosters/Infantry/87th_Infantry_CW_Roster.pdf; *New York Times,* February 11, 1894; Noyes, *History of Schoharie County,* 38–39.

10. Tanner Pension File; Michael A. Flannery, *Civil War Pharmacy: A History of Drugs, Drug Supply and Provision, and Therapeutics for the Union and Confederacy* (New York: Haworth Press, 2004), 133, 115, 117; Ira M. Rutkow, *Bleeding Blue and Gray: Civil War Surgery and the Evolution of American Medicine* (New York: Random House, 2005), 126–27.

11. "Civil War Letters of the Shumway Bros. of Richmondville," originally published in *Worcester (N.Y.) Times,* Schoharie County NYGenWeb, http://rootsweb .ancestry.com/~hnyschoha/shumwayletters.html.

12. *Union Army,* 114.

13. Smith, *Famous Battery,* 182; *Brooklyn Eagle,* November 26, 1879.

14. "Civil War Letters of the Shumway Bros. of Richmondville."

15. *Annual Report of the Adjutant General of the State of New York for the Year 1901: Registers of New York Regiments in the War of the Rebellion,* ser. 29 (Albany: James B. Lyon, 1902), 1323–446. The most complete version of Tanner's military experience appears in Corp. James Tanner, "Before Red Cross Days; or, Second Bull Run and the End of the War for Me," *American Red Cross Magazine* 11 (September 1916): 306–13; (October 1916): 345–53. Unless otherwise noted, Tanner's personal recollections of his wounding come from this source. The same story was published a decade later as "Experience of a Wounded Soldier at the Second Battle of Bull Run," *Military Surgeon* 60 (February 1927): 121–39.

16. James Tanner Pension File.

17. *Brooklyn Eagle*, December 14, 1880, January 8 and December 1, 1881, and March 3, 13, and 21, 1882; *National Tribune*, June 9, 1887.

18. *Salt Lake Herald*, August 9, 1909.

19. Rutkow, *Bleeding Blue and Gray*, 186; Flannery, *Civil War Pharmacy*, 17.

20. Tanner, "Before Red Cross Days," 308; Smith, *Famous Battery*, 187.

21. Smith, *Famous Battery*, 187–88; Tanner "Before Red Cross Days," 308.

22. Rutkow, *Bleeding Blue and Gray*, 63–64; Alfred Jay Bollet, "Amputations in the Civil War," in *Years of Change and Suffering: Modern Perspectives on Civil War Medicine*, ed. James M. Schmidt and Guy R. Hasegawa (Roseville, Minn.: Edinborough Press, 2009), 58; Tanner, "Before Red Cross Days," 309.

23. Tanner, "Before Red Cross Days," 310.

24. Megan Kate Nelson, *Ruin Nation: Destruction and the American Civil War* (Athens: University of Georgia Press, 2012), 160–70.

25. Tanner, "Before Red Cross Days," 310.

26. "Civil War Letters of the Shumway Bros. of Richmondville"; Smith, *Famous Battery*, 183.

27. Smith, *Famous Battery*, 183–88; *Beaver (Okla.) Herald*, July 28, 1904; *Minneapolis Journal*, August 18, 1906.

Chapter Two. Living with Disability

1. Unless otherwise noted, all information about Tanner's wounding and treatment comes from James Tanner, "Before Red Cross Days; or, Second Bull Run and the End of the War for Me," *American Red Cross Magazine* 11 (September 1916): 306–13; (October 1916): 345–53; R. W. Jacklin, "Michigan in War," *Journal of the Association of Military Surgeons of the United States* 17 (1905): 414.

2. Elon G. Reynolds, ed., *Compendium of History and Biography of Hillsdale County, Michigan* (Chicago: A. W. Bowen, [1905]), 144–45; Thomas E. Sebrell II, "A Regimental History of the 5th Michigan Infantry Regiment From Its Formation through the Seven Days Campaign" (master's thesis, Virginia Tech, 2004).

3. W. W. Keen, "Surgical Reminiscences of the Civil War," *Transactions and Studies of the College of Physicians of Philadelphia*, 3rd ser., 27 (1905): 101.

4. Tanner's descriptions of his experiences in this and subsequent paragraphs come from James Tanner, "Before Red Cross Days; or, Second Bull Run and the End of the War for Me," *American Red Cross Magazine* 11 (October 1916): 345–53, quote on 310.

5. Alfred Jay Bollet, "Amputations in the Civil War," in *Years of Change and Suffering: Modern Perspectives on Civil War Medicine*, ed. James M. Schmidt and Guy R. Hasegawa (Roseville, Minn.: Edinborough Press, 2009), 64; Laurann Figg and Jane Farrell-Beck, "Amputation in the Civil War: Physical and Social Dimensions," *Journal of the History of Medicine and Allied Sciences* 48 (October 1993): 454, 459.

6. Tanner, "Before Red Cross Days," 311.

7. Ibid., 311, 312.

8. Ibid., 312.

9. "Civil War Letters of the Shumway Bros. of Richmondville," originally published in *Worcester (N.Y.) Times*, Schoharie County NYGenWeb, http://rootsweb.ancestry.com/~hnyschoha/shumwayletters.html.

10. Tanner, "Before Red Cross Days," 310.

11. Ira M. Rutkow, *Bleeding Blue and Gray: Civil War Surgery and the Evolution of American Medicine* (New York: Random House, 2005), 234–35; S. D. Gross, MD, *A Manual of Military Surgery* (Philadelphia: J. B. Lippincott, 1861), 93–94; William R. E. Smart, "On Hospital Gangrene," *The Half-Yearly Abstract of the Medical Sciences* (Philadelphia: Henry C. Lean, 1871), 178; Tanner, "Before Red Cross Days," 346.

12. Tanner, "Before Red Cross Days," 346.

13. Ibid.

14. Jane Stuart Woolsey, *Hospital Days: Reminiscence of a Civil War Nurse*, ed. Daniel John Hoisington (Roseville, Minn.: Edinborough Press, 1996), 19; Rutkow, *Bleeding Blue and Gray*, 154–55, 151 (for a map of the grounds, see p. 9).

15. Keen, "Surgical Reminiscences," 103–4.

16. Rutkow, *Bleeding Blue and Gray*, 44–48; Michael A. Flannery, *Civil War Pharmacy: A History of Drugs, Drug Supply and Provision, and Therapeutics for the Union and Confederacy* (New York: Haworth Press, 2004), 147–49.

17. Guy R. Hasegawa, *Mending Broken Soldiers: The Union and Confederate Programs to Supply Artificial Limbs* (Carbondale: Southern Illinois University Press, 2012), 2.

18. Rutkow, *Bleeding Blue and Gray*, 166–67; Woolsey, *Hospital Days*, 72–74; Keen, "Surgical Reminiscences," 103.

19. Woolsey, *Hospital Days*, 94.

20. Tanner, "Before Red Cross Days," 353.

21. *Altamont Enterprise*, July 1, 1955.

22. Frances M. Clarke, *War Stories: Suffering and Sacrifice in the Civil War North* (Chicago: University of Chicago Press, 2011), 74, 152.

23. Tanner, "Before Red Cross Days," 309; Stephen Smith, MD, *Hand-Book of Surgical Operations*, 4th ed. (New York: Baillière Bros., 1863), 149–53; Joseph K. Barnes et al., *The Medical and Surgical History of the War of the Rebellion*, part 2, vol. 2: *Surgical History* (Washington, D.C.: Government Printing Office, 1883), 462.

24. Tanner Pension File.

25. *Brooklyn Eagle*, February 6, 1894; *New York Tribune*, February 7, 1894; *New York Sun*, February 2, 1894; *New York Times*, February 14, 1894; *Brooklyn Eagle*, February 13, April 7, and July 2, 1894.

26. *Petition and Statements of U.S. Maimed Soldiers' League, for the Enactment of Senate Bill No. 833 (House Bill No. 3328)* (Philadelphia: n.p., 1890), 1–3.

27. "United States Soldiers Furnished with Artificial Limbs and Confederate Soldiers for Whom Orders for Artificial Limbs Were Given through the Association for the Relief of Maimed Soldiers," Supplement to Hasegawa, *Mending Broken Soldiers*, 107, http://www.siupress.com/downloads/excerpts/9780809331307_expt.pdf; Jennifer Davis McDaid, "'How a One-Legged Rebel Lives': Confederate Veterans and Artificial Limbs in Virginia," in *Artificial Parts, Practical Lives: Modern Histories of Prosthetics*, ed. Katherine Ott, David Serlin, and Stephen Mihm (New York: New York University Press, 2002), 122; *New York Times*, February 11 and April 11, 1894; *A Treatise on Marks' Patent Artificial Limbs* (New York: A. A. Marks, 1888), 23.

28. Stephen Mihm, "'A Limb Which Shall Be Presentable in Polite Society': Prosthetic Technologies in the Nineteenth Century," in Ott, Serlin, and Mihm, *Artificial Parts, Practical Lives*, 284–86; Figg and Farrell-Beck, "Amputation in the Civil War," 461–62; *A Treatise on Marks' Patent Artificial Limbs* (New York: A. A. Marks, 1888), 7.

29. *Treatise on Marks' Patent Artificial Limbs*, 37–39.

30. Col. John A. Joyce, *Jewels of Memory* (Washington, D.C.: Gibson Brothers, 1895), 124; *Abstract of General Orders and Proceedings of the Forty-Fifth Annual Encampment, Department of New York G. A. R.* (Albany: J. B. Lyon, 1911), 447; copied in *Mohave County (Ariz.) Miner*, July 6, 1889; *Zion's Herald*, September 18, 1889; *Brooklyn Eagle*, August 31, 1889.

31. Letter from James Tanner to Capt. Jack Crawford, May 10 and 21 and June 28, 1890, folder 21, box 2, John W. Crawford Papers, McCracken Research Library, Buffalo Bill Historical Center, Cody, Wyoming; Judith Anderson, "'Haunted Minds': The Impact of Combat Exposure on the Mental and Physical Health of Civil War Veterans," in Schmidt and Hasegawa, *Years of Change and Suffering*, 151–52.

32. *Sacramento Daily Record-Union*, September 23, 1889; *Omaha Daily Bee*, August 13, 1906.

33. Quoted in Cameron C. Nickels, *Civil War Humor* (Jackson: University Press of Mississippi, 2010), 88; *Society of the Army of the Cumberland, Twelfth Reunion* (Cincinnati: Robert Clarke, 1881), 146; *New York Times*, February 9, 1894; *Saline County (Kans.) Journal*, July 4, 1889; *Brooklyn Eagle*, May 23, 1889; *Oswego Times and Express*, April, 17, 1885; "For Blue Monday," *Homeletic Review* 50 (November 1905): 402; "In the Procession," *Advance* 50 (October 19, 1905): 437.

34. *Washington Critic*, March 27, 1889.

35. Frances M. Clarke, *War Stories: Suffering and Sacrifice in the Civil War North* (Chicago: University of Chicago Press, 2011), 51–83; *Pittsburgh Dispatch*, March 24, 1889; *St. Paul Globe*, September 6, 1896; *Western Kansas World*, July 6, 1889; *Rochester Democrat and Chronicle*, September 10, 1890; *Neighbor's Home Mail* 6 (December 1879): 180.

36. Larry M. Logue, *To Appomattox and Beyond: The Civil War Soldier in War and Peace* (Chicago: Ivan R. Dee, 1996), 86–89.

37. Tanner Pension File.

38. *Soldier's Friend*, June 1865; Brian Matthew Jordan, "'Living Monuments': Union Veteran Amputees and the Embodied Memory of the Civil War," *Civil War History* 57 (June 2011): 121–52.

39. *Circulars of Information of the Bureau of Education*, no. 2 (Washington, D.C.: Government Printing Office, 1884), 48, 54.

40. Benn Pitman, *History of Shorthand* (Cincinnati: Phonographic Institute, 1856), n.p.; "Discoveries and Research Finds," *Books & Friends* 22 (2007): 10–11.

41. Isaac Pitman, *Exercises in Phonography; Designed to Conduct the Pupil to a Practical Acquaintance with the Art* (London: Fred Pitman, Phonetic Depot on Paternoster Row, 1850), 9, 10. The Rare Books Collection at the University of North Texas received a copy of this book from the same collector who donated another Pitman book that was labeled with Tanner's personal bookplate.

42. Daniel T. Ames, *Ames' Guide to Self-Instruction in Practical and Artistic Penmanship* (New York: Daniel T. Ames, 1884), n.p.

43. *Syracuse Journal*, June 20, 1910; L. E. Stacy, *The Blue Book: Containing Photographs and Sketches of a Few Commercial Teachers* (Meadville, Pa.: n.p., 1907), 76; Hamilton Child, comp., *Gazetteer and Business Directory of Wayne County, N.Y., for 1867–8* (Syracuse: Journal Office, 1867), 101, 224; Chris Lee, ed., "Memoirs of Willard Littlefield Cook, 1899," n.p., www.http://rockislandlighthouse.org/wlcmemoirs .doc.

44. Benn Pittman, *Manners: Extracted (by Permission) from Illustrated Manner Book* (Cincinnati: Benn Pittman, ca. 1857).

45. Samuel Smiles, *Duty: With Illustrations of Courage, Patience, and Endurance* (New York: Harper & Brothers, 1881), 191; H. A. Lewis, *Why Some Succeed While Others Fail* (Cleveland: Wright, Moses & Lewis, 1887), 481.

46. John F. Chase, *Inventor and Temperance Lecturer* (Augusta, Maine: n.p., ca. 1886); *New York Times*, June 18, 1886; Jim Weeks, *Gettysburg: Memory, Market, and an American Shrine* (Princeton, N.J.: Princeton University Press, 2003), 78.

47. *Schoharie Republican*, September 25 and October 30, 1862, in "Schoharie County Miscellany," comp. Joseph Brown, Schoharie County NYGenWeb Site, http://www .rootsweb.ancestry.com/~nyschoha/miscel13.html.

48. *Schoharie Republican*, February 11, 1864, January 19, 1865, January 11, 1866, January 10, 1867, and January 21, 1869, in Brown, "Schoharie County Miscellany."

49. James Marten, *Sing Not War: The Lives of Union and Confederate Veterans in Gilded Age America* (Chapel Hill: University of North Carolina Press, 2011), 236–40; United States Civil Service Commission, *History of Veterans Preference in Federal Employment, 1865–1955* (Washington, D.C.: United States Civil Service Commission, 1955), 1–3.

50. James Tanner, *Glimpses of Cobleskill: Schoharie County, New York, 1852–1927* (Cobleskill: Cobleskill Times, [1927]), 19–20.

51. Kim E. Nielsen, *A Disability History of the United States* (Boston: Beacon Press, 2012), 78–99, quote on 89.

52. *New York Times*, October 24, 1885; Tanner Pension File.

53. For a discussion this problem, see, for example, Megan Kate Nelson, *Ruin Nation: Destruction and the American Civil War* (Athens: University of Georgia Press, 2012), 179–200.

54. *New York Sun*, March 17, 1887; Mark Aldrich, *Death Rode the Rails: American Railroad Accidents and Safety, 1828–1965* (Baltimore: Johns Hopkins University Press, 2006), 2, 79; *Brooklyn Eagle*, March 14, 1887.

55. Soldiers and Sailors Home Fair, *Great Fair! Academy of Music, Philadelphia* (Philadelphia: King & Baird, [1865]).

56. *Soldier's Friend*, June 1865, and September 19, 1868; Henry Bellows to Stephen G. Perkins, August 15, 1862, document 49, in USSC, *Documents of the United States Sanitary Commission* (New York, 1866), 2.

57. Tanner Pension File; Tanner, *Glimpses of Cobleskill*, 19–20.

58. Brian Craig Miller, "Confederate Amputees and the Women Who Loved (or Tried to Love) Them," in *Weirding the War: Stories from the Civil War's Ragged Edges*, ed. Stephen Berry (Athens: University of Georgia Press, 2011), 301–20; *Ancestral Chronological Record of the William White Family, from 1607–8 to 1895* (Concord [N.H.?]: Republican Press Association, 1895), 120–21.

59. Tanner, *Glimpses of Cobleskill*, 19–20.

60. Tanner Pension File; *Documents of the Assembly of the State of New York*, vol. 10 (Albany: C. Van Benthuysen & Sons, 1867), 670; "Cobleskill," in *Topographical Atlas of Schoharie Co., New York, from Actual Surveys by S. N. & D. G. Beers and Assistants* (Philadelphia: Stone & Stewart, 1866), Schoharie County NYGenWeb Site, http://www.rootsweb.andestry.com/~nyschoharie/mapvilco.html.

61. Lawrence M. Friedman, *A History of American Law*, 3rd ed. (New York: Simon and Schuster, 2005), 263; William E. Roscoe, *History of Schoharie County, New York, with Illustrations and Biographical Sketches of Some of Its Prominent Men and Pioneers* (Syracuse: D. Mason, 1882), 116; William P. LaPiana, *Logic and Experience: The Origin of Modern American Legal Education* (New York: Oxford University Press, 1994), 83–85; Robert Stevens, *Law School: Legal Education in America from the 1850s to the 1980s* (Chapel Hill: University of North Carolina Press, 1983), 6–10, 21–22.

62. Tanner, *Glimpses of Cobleskill*, 6.

63. Ibid., 6.

64. Ibid., 14–15.

65. Ibid., 10.

66. *New York Times*, February 11, 1894; Tanner, *Glimpses of Cobleskill*, 17–19.

67. Tanner, *Glimpses of Cobleskill*, 2; Thomas Raynesford Lounsbury, *Yale Book of American Verse* (New Haven, Conn.: Yale University Press, 1912), 395.

68. *Schoharie Republican*, June 10, 1869, and August 3, 1871.

Chapter Three. Brooklyn Days

1. Stephen M. Ostrander, *A History of the City of Brooklyn and Kings County*, ed. Alexander Black, 2 vols. (Brooklyn: n.p., 1894), 2:133–35.

2. Ira Rosenwaike, *Population History of New York City* (Syracuse: Syracuse University Press, 1972), 59; Harold Coffin Syrett, *The City of Brooklyn, 1865–1898: A Political History* (New York: Columbia University Press, 1944; New York: AMS Press, 1968), 140.

3. Ostrander, *History of the City of Brooklyn*, 134–63; Syrett, *City of Brooklyn*, 12–24.

4. Sergeant Fred C. Floyd, *History of the Fortieth (Mozart) Regiment, New York Volunteers* (Boston: F. H. Gilson, 1909), 440; Ostrander, *History of the City of Brooklyn*, 127; James Tanner to James Jaycox, December 15, 1926, collection of Sabrina Ramoth; "Kings County GAR Posts," http://localhistory.morrisville.edu/sites/gar_post/kings_gar.html.

5. *1874 Brooklyn City Directory*, U.S. City Directories, 1821–1989, ancestry.com; Timothy J. O'Hanlon, "Neighborhood Change in New York City: A Case Study of Park Slope, 1850–1980 (PhD diss., City University of New York, 1982), 137–49.

6. Capt. James E. Smith, *A Famous Battery and Its Campaigns, 1861–64* (Washington, D.C.: W. H. Lowdermilk, 1892), 192; Brian Lusky, *On the Make: Clerks and the Quest for Capital in Nineteenth-Century New York* (New York: New York University Press, 2010), 2, 23.

7. Carl E. Prince and Mollie Keller, *The U.S. Customs Service: A Bicentennial History* (Washington, D.C.: Department of the Treasury, 1989), 146–53.

8. Quoted in Prince and Keller, *U.S. Customs Service*, 152.

9. Smith, *Famous Battery and Its Campaigns*, 195; *New York Daily Tribune*, November 4, 1876.

10. Syrett, *City of Brooklyn*, 25–69, 91–137, 180–193; *New York Sun*, June 25, 1878.

11. Mark Wahlgren Summers, *The Gilded Age: or, The Hazard of New Functions* (Upper Saddle River, N.J.: Prentice Hall, 1997), 205.

12. Charles W. Calhoun, *From Bloody Shirt to Full Dinner Pail: The Transformation of Politics and Governance in the Gilded Age* (New York: Hill & Wang, 2010), 3–10; Summers, *The Gilded Age*, 50–55.

13. *Brooklyn Eagle*, May 5, 1871, August 30, 1872, and December 13 and October 16 and 30, 1873; *New York Times*, November 4, 1877; *New York Sun*, October 19 and November 15, 1879.

14. *Syracuse Sunday Herald*, July 14, 1895; *Brooklyn Eagle*, May 23, 1889.

15. *New York Times*, August 24, 1873; *Harper's Weekly*, May 8, 1875.

16. *Brooklyn Eagle*, June 11, 1873.

17. Ibid., July 15, 1873.

18. Ibid., July 15, 1873; *Zion's Herald*, September 18, 1889; *Brooklyn Eagle*, July 15, 1873, and January 10, 1880.

19. Raymond A. Schroth, *The Eagle and Brooklyn: A Community Newspaper, 1841–1955* (Westport, Conn.: Greenwood Press, 1974), 70–90.

20. *Brooklyn Eagle*, March 18, 1878, and January 29, 1882.

21. Ibid., April 5, 1884.

22. Ibid., July 9, 1889, and September 29, 1892.

23. Ibid., July 7, 1895.

24. Syrett, *The City of Brooklyn*, 120–123.

25. *Brooklyn Eagle*, January 9 and June 18, 1880, and March 30, 1902.

26. Smith, *A Famous Battery and Its Campaigns*, 192.

27. *Brooklyn Eagle*, October 22, 1884.

28. Ibid., May 13, 1878, and November 3, 1884.

29. Ibid., November 4, 1879.

30. Ibid., July 11 and September 12, 1884.

31. Ibid., October 30, 1884, and January 29, 1882.

32. Ibid., October 24, 1884.

33. Syrett, *The City of Brooklyn*, 181.

34. *National Tribune*, October 30, 1884.

35. *New Haven Daily Register*, September 12, 1884; http://www.measuringworth
.com/uscompare/relativevalue.php.

36. Larry M. Logue, *To Appomattox and Beyond: The Civil War Soldier in War and Peace* (Chicago: Ivan R. Dee, 1996), 94–95.

37. "Kings County GAR Posts," http://localhistory.morrisville.edu/sites/gar_post
/kings_gar.html, accessed April 5, 2012.

38. *Remarks Explanatory of the Beneficent Workings of the Grand Army of the Republic* (Brooklyn: Bureau of Employment and Emergency Fund, 1884), 4, 6.; *New York Times*, February 20, 1880; *Brooklyn Eagle*, April 6, 1877.

39. Stuart McConnell, *Glorious Contentment: The Grand Army of the Republic, 1865–1900* (Chapel Hill: University of North Carolina Press, 1992), 166–85.

40. Sherwood Anderson quoted in Gerald F. Linderman, *Embattled Courage: The Experience of Combat in the American Civil War* (New York: Free Press, 1987), 280.

41. *Brooklyn Eagle*, December 30, 1875.

42. *New York Times*, May 31, 1882.

43. James De Mandeville, comp., *History of the 13th Regiment, N. G. S. N. Y.* (New York: James De Mandeville, [1894]), 47; *New York Times*, May 20, 1902.

44. *Brooklyn Eagle*, May 29 and 30, 1873.

45. Ibid., May 6, 1876.

46. Henry Whittemore, *History of U. S. Grant Post No. 327, Brooklyn, N.Y., including Biographical Sketches of Its Members* (Detroit: Detroit Free Press, 1885), 152–54.

47. James Marten, *Sing Not War: The Lives of Union and Confederate Veterans in Gilded Age America* (Chapel Hill: University of North Carolina Press, 2011), 13–14.

48. Smith, *Famous Battery and Its Campaigns*, 193; "A Soldiers' Home," *Christian Union* 15 (June 20, 1877): 550.

49. Robert E. Yott, *From Soldiers' Home to Medical Center: A Glance at the 125 Year History of the Bath Soldiers' Home* (Bath: Robert Yott, 2006).

50. *Proceedings of the Semi-Annual Encampment of the Department of New York, Grand Army of the Republic, held at Yonkers, New York* (New York: Grand Army of the Republic, 1876), 5, 6–17, 19–21.

51. Ibid., 36–37.

52. Ibid.

53. Ibid., 36–37, 42–43.

54. *New York Tribune,* March 23, 1877; Smith, *Famous Battery and Its Campaigns,* 193

55. Quoted in Yott, *From Soldiers' Home to Medical Center,* 12.

56. *Brooklyn Eagle,* April 25, 1878. For the investigation into the Bath home, see Marten, *Sing Not War,* 158–63.

57. David W. Blight, *Race and Reunion: The Civil War in American Memory* (Cambridge, Mass.: Harvard University Press, 2001). For important interpretations of how reconciliation occurred in the North and the South, respectively, see Nina Silber, *The Romance of Reunion: Northerners and the South, 1865–1900* (Chapel Hill: University of North Carolina Press, 1993); and Gaines M. Foster, *Ghosts of the Confederacy: Defeat, the Lost Cause, and the Emergence of the New South* (New York: Oxford University Press, 1987).

58. Caroline E. Janney, *Remembering the Civil War: Reunion and the Limits of Reconciliation* (Chapel Hill: University of North Carolina Press, 2013).

59. *Macon Telegraph,* April 10, 1906; *Brooklyn Eagle,* June 16, 1887; *Dallas Morning News,* April 26, 1906.

60. *Confederate Veteran,* April 1895.

61. Ibid., August 1896.

62. *Birmingham State Herald,* July 2, 1896; *Confederate Veteran,* August 1896.

63. *Confederate Veteran,* December 1912.

64. *Richmond Times Dispatch,* June 19, 1909.

65. *Minutes of the Twenty-First Annual Convention of the United Daughters of the Confederacy, Held in Savannah, Ga., November 11–14, 1914* (Raleigh: Edwards & Broughton Printing, 1915), 8.

66. *Oswego Palladium,* December 23, 1889.

67. N. P. Chipman, *The Tragedy of Andersonville: Trial of Captain Henry Wirz the Prison Keeper,* 2nd ed. (Sacramento: N. P. Chipman, 1911), 15–16; J. R. Gibbons, "The Monument to Captain Henry Wirz," *Southern Historical Society Papers,* vol. 36 (Richmond: Southern Historical Society, 1908), 226.

68. John B. Gordon, *Reminiscences of the Civil War* (New York: Charles Scribner's Sons, 1904), 130.

69. Darlis A. Miller, *Captain Jack Crawford: Buckskin Poet, Scout, and Showman* (Albuquerque: University of New Mexico Press, 1993), 126, 137, 176.

70. *Brooklyn Eagle,* June 16, 1887, April 30, 1888, and September 29, 1892.

71. *American Tribune,* November 16. 1888; *Grand Army Advocate,* April 18, 1889; *Ohio Soldier,* August 8, 1888.

72. "Complete Bibliography," Ulysses S. Grant Association, Mississippi State University, http://library.msstate.edu/usgrant/combined_bibliography.asp#h-books; "'Agents Wanted': Subscription Publishing in America," Exhibitions and Events of the Rare Book and Manuscript Library: Spring 2012, University of Pennsylvania Libraries, http://www.library.upenn.edu/exhibits/rbm/agents/index.html.

73. *Brooklyn Eagle*, December 18, 1886; Smith, *Famous Battery and Its Campaigns*, 199; *San Francisco Daily Evening Bulletin*, October 29, 1886; *Daily Morning Astorian* (Astoria, Ore.), May 30, 1888.

74. *Stark County Democrat* (Canton, Ohio), October 22, 1896; *Wichita Daily Eagle*, September 15, 1896; *Oswego Daily Palladium*, October 8, 1896.

75. *Brooklyn Eagle*, October 13, 1883; *New York Sun*, January 17, 1879; *Brooklyn Eagle*, May 9, 1881; *New York Times*, September 19, 1883; *Brooklyn Eagle*, March 26, 1884; December 18, 1886; and July 3, 1887.

76. Smith, *Famous Battery and Its Campaigns*, 199, 197–98; Elsie M. Wilbor, ed., *Werner's Directory of Elocutionists, Readers, Lecturers and Other Public Instructors and Entertainers* (New York: Edgar S. Werner, 1887), 381.

77. *The Civil War from Sumter to Appomattox: The Stirring Scenes of the Civil War Magnificently Illustrated* (New York: Star Lyceum Bureau, ca. 1890), n.p.

78. *National Tribune*, August 2, 1883; *New York Tribune*, July 25, 1886; *Hillsboro (Ohio) News-Herald*, February 23, 1888.

79. *Hillsboro (Ohio) News-Herald*, February 23, 1888; *Ninth Annual Reunion of the Buffalo 21st Veteran Association Held at Sheenwater, Grand Island* (Buffalo: Buffalo Democrat, 1888), 19; *Journals of the Encampment Proceedings of the Department of Massachusetts G. A. R. from 1881 to 1887 Inclusive* (Boston: E. B. Stillings, 1902), 316; *Albuquerque Morning Democrat*, August 21, 1886; *Washington Times*, August 14, 1904.

80. *National Tribune*, August 18, 1887; February 16–August 2, 1888; February 16, 1888.

81. *Vermont Phoenix*, November 4, 1887.

82. Wilbor, *Werner's Directory*, 317, 319, 322, 315, 329, 328.

83. Angela G. Ray, *The Lyceum and Public Culture in the Nineteenth-Century United States* (East Lansing: Michigan State University Press, 2005), esp. 173–89.

84. Letter from Tanner to Capt. Jack Crawford, September 7, 1890, folder 21, box 2, John W. Crawford Papers, McCracken Research Library, Buffalo Bill Historical Center, Cody, Wyoming; J. Matthew Gallman, *America's Joan of Arc: The Life of Anna Elizabeth Dickinson* (New York: Oxford, 2006), 66–67; *Zion's Herald*, September 4, 1889.

85. The information provided in this and several subsequent paragraphs is drawn from the *Brooklyn Eagle*, October 15, 1885.

86. *Lowell Daily Courier*, January 28, 1890.

87. *Sacramento Daily Record-Union*, December 4, 1886; *St. Paul Daily Globe*, November 12, 1890; Annie Wentworth Baer, "Visits of Famous Men to Dover," *Granite Monthly* 47 (July 1915): 332.

88. *Brooklyn Eagle*, April 23, 1883.

89. Ibid., August 11, 1924.

Chapter Four. God Help the Surplus

1. "Union Veterans and Their Pensions," *Century Magazine* 38 (August 1889): 636–37; Claudia Linares, "The Civil War Pension Law," CPE *Working Paper Series* (Center for Population Economics, University of Chicago, 2001), 8–13, 16, 26–30; Chen Song, "Filing for the Union Army Pension: A Summary from Historical Evidence" (unpublished paper, Center for Population Economics, University of Chicago, 2000), 3–4. http://www.cpe.uchicago.edu/publication/lib/pension_sum.pdf.

2. Clarence D. Long, *Wages and Earnings in the United States, 1860–1890* (Princeton, N.J.: Princeton University Press, 1960), 41; Alexander Klein, "Personal Income of U.S. States: Estimates for the Period 1880–1910," Warwick Economic Research Papers, no. 916 Department of Economics, University of Warwick, http://ideas.repec.org/p/wrk/warwec/916.html.

3. W. R. Brock, *The United States, 1789–1890* (Ithaca, N.Y.: Cornell University Press, 1975), 62; United States Census Bureau, *2012 Statistical Abstract*, http://www.census.gov/compendia/statab/cats/federal_govt_finances_employment/federal_civilian_employment.html); Morton Keller, *Affairs of State: Public Life in Late Nineteenth Century America* (Cambridge, Mass.: Harvard University Press, 1977), 310–11.

4. Linda Brody Lyons, *A Handbook to the Pension Building: Home of the National Building Museum* (Washington, D.C.: National Building Museum, 1989); Laura Burd Schiavo, *National Building Museum* (London: Scala, 2007).

5. *Report of the Secretary of the Interior for the Fiscal Year Ending June 30, 1889*, vol. 1 (Washington, D.C.: Government Printing Office, 1890), 421–22.

6. Keller, *Affairs of State*, 311.

7. Wallace Evan Davies, *Patriotism on Parade: The Story of Veterans' and Hereditary Organizations in American, 1783–1900* (Cambridge, Mass.: Harvard University Press, 1955), 166–69.

8. Claire Prechtel-Kluskens, "'A Reasonable Degree of Promptitude': Civil War Pension Application Processing, 1861–1885," *Prologue* 42 (Spring 2010): 1–26.

9. *Ohio Soldier*, October 27, 1888; *Home Bulletin*, January 15, 1887; *Soldiers' Tribune*, May 10, 1888.

10. *Ohio Soldier*, October 24, 1888; *American Tribune*, September 7, 1888.

11. *Ohio Soldier*, July 28, 1888; *American Tribune*, October 25, 1888.

12. *Ohio Soldier*, January 14, 1888; *Soldiers Tribune*, June 14, 1888.

13. John William Oliver, *History of the Civil War Military Pensions, 1861–1885*, Bulletin of the University of Wisconsin, History Series, 4 (Madison: University of Wisconsin, 1917), 91–95; *New Orleans Times Picayune*, October 10, 1887.

14. *Grand Army Advocate*, May 16, 1888.

15. *Campaign Text Book of the Democratic Party of the United States for the Presidential Election of 1888* (New York: Brentano's, 1888), 5, 10.

16. George Francis Dawson, *The Republican Campaign Text-Book for 1888* (New York: Brentano's, 1888), 187–94.

17. Quoted in *Ohio Soldier*, October 7, 1888.

18. *Washington Critic*, January 17, 1889; *Brooklyn Eagle*, January 22, 1889.

19. *New York Evening Telegram*, March 8, 1889.

20. *National Tribune*, May 9, 1889.

21. *Life*, April 18, 1889.

22. George A. Armes, *Ups and Downs of an Army Officer* (Washington, D.C.: n.p., 1900), 700; *Oswego Palladium*, March 23, 1889.

23. *Annual Report of the Commissioner of Pensions to the Secretary of the Interior for the Fiscal Year Ended June 30, 1901* (Washington, D.C.: Government Printing Office, 1901), 142; *Report of the Secretary of the Interior for the Fiscal Year Ending June 30, 1889*, vol. 1 (Washington, D.C.: Government Printing Office, 1890), 411; Keller, *Affairs of State*, 311.

24. *Report of the Secretary of the Interior*, 420.

25. "The Pension Investigation," *Illustrated American* 10 (March 19, 1892): 216.

26. Henry O. Wills, *Twice Born; or, the Two Lives of Henry O. Wills, Evangelist* (Cincinnati: Western Methodist Book Concern, 1890), 171–72.

27. Mark Wahlgren Summers, *The Gilded Age: or, The Hazard of New Functions* (Upper Saddle River, N.J.: Prentice Hall, 1997), 184–85; *Sacramento Daily Record-Union*, April 9, 1889; *Brooklyn Eagle*, April 1 and 5, 1889; *Fitchburg (Mass.) Sentinel*, June 15, 1889; Sam M. Clapp, *Elsie Ripley Clapp (1879–1965): Her Life and the Community School* (New York: Peter Lang, 2004), 28–31; *St. Paul Daily Globe*, August 14, 1889; *New York Sun*, June 18, 1889; Darlis A. Miller, *Captain Jack Crawford: Buckskin Poet, Scout, and Showman* (Albuquerque: University of New Mexico Press, 1993), 132.

28. *St. Paul Daily Globe*, August 14, 1889; *New York Sun*, June 18, 1889; *Ohio Democrat*, June 29, 1889.

29. Reproduced in *Kellogg (Iowa) Enterprise*, July 2[6], 1889.

30. *Lancaster Daily Intelligencer*, April 5, 1889; "Pension Investigation," 216; *National Tribune*, April 25, 1889; *Brooklyn Eagle*, September 9, 1889.

31. *Brooklyn Eagle*, July 3, 1889; *Deseret Weekly*, July 6, 1889.

32. Donald McMurry, "Civil War Pensions, 1885–1897" (master's thesis, University of Wisconsin, 1921), 203–12.

33. *Ohio Democrat*, July 13, 1889; *Omaha Daily Bee*, July 3, 1889.

34. Quoted in McMurry, "Civil War Pensions," 202; *Brooklyn Eagle*, June 26, 1889.

35. *New York Times*, July 13, 1889.

36. *Brooklyn Eagle*, August 3, 1889.

37. *Brooklyn Eagle*, September 10, 1889; *Oswego Record* [ca. September 10, 1889]; Davies, *Patriotism on Parade*, 170–71.

38. *Brooklyn Eagle*, September 27, 1889.

39. *New York Times*, September 13, 1889; *Watertown (N.Y.) Daily Times*, September 12, 1889; Capt. James E. Smith, *A Famous Battery and Its Campaigns, 1861–64* (Washington, D.C.: W. H. Lowdermilk, 1892), 209–10.

40. *New York Times*, December 13, 1889.

41. *Belmont (Ohio) Chronicle*, May 30, 1889; *Ste. Genevieve (Mo.) Fair Play*, September 28, 1889; Summers, *Gilded Age*, 213.

42. *Brooklyn Eagle*, June 26, 1889.

43. *St. Paul Globe*, September 17, 1889; quoted in *Brooklyn Eagle*, September 12, 1889.

44. *Puck*, May 29 and June 19, 1889.

45. *Puck*, August 28 and September 25, 1889. See also Bert Hansen, "New Images of a New Medicine: Visual Evidence for the Widespread Popularity of Therapeutic Discoveries in America after 1885," *Bulletin of the History of Medicine* 73 (1999): 652–53.

46. *Life*, August 29, September 19, October 3, and November 14, 1889.

47. *Ohio Democrat*, October 12, 1889.

48. *Ibid.*; "Sweet, Alexander Edwin," The Handbook of Texas Online, http://www.tshaonline.org/handbook/online/articles/fsw09.

49. Ambrose Bierce, *The Collected Works of Ambrose Bierce*, vol. 4 (New York: Neale, 1910), 350.

50. *New York Times*, September 27, 1889.

51. Davies, *Patriotism on Parade*, 172–73.

52. *New York Times*, June 13, July 10, August 19, and May 25, 1890; Leonard Woolsey Bacon, "A Raid upon the Treasury," *Forum* 6 (January 1889): 540–48; Edward H. Hall, *An Indignity to Our Citizen Soldiers* (Cambridge, Mass.: John Wilson & Son, 1890), 5; William M. Sloane, "Pensions and Socialism," *Century* 42 (June 1891): 180.

53. *Puck*, September 20, 1893.

54. Milwaukee *Sunday Telegraph*, October 18, 1885.

55. *Report of the Commissioner of Pensions to the Secretary of the Interior for the Year Ended June 30, 1892* (Washington, D.C.: Government Printing Office, 1892), 5–6.

56. *National Tribune*, July 25, 1890.

57. *Report of the Commissioner of Pensions to the Secretary of the Interior for the Year Ended June 30, 1892*, 30; J. A. Bentley, *Address of Hon. J. A. Bentley, Commissioner of Pension: Delivered under the Auspices of Army and Navy, Veteran Club of Boston, at Tremont Temple, Tuesday, October 19th, 1880* (Boston: n.p., 1880), 13.

58. *American Tribune*, September 7, 1888, and May 30, 1890.

59. Oliver, *History of the Civil War Military Pensions*, 100; *Grand Army Advocate*, March 24, 1892.

60. Peter Blanck, "Civil War Pensions and Disability," *Ohio State Law Journal* 62, no. 1 (2001): 123; "The Pension Sharks," *Nation* 48 (March 28, 1889): 258; *New York Times*, December 16, 1897; *Brooklyn Eagle*, December 31, 1897; *New York Times*, October 20, 1898.

61. Song, "Filing for the Union Army Pension," 9.

62. *Puck*, December 20, 1882.

63. *Puck*, December 20, 1882, and September 18, 1889.

64. *Brooklyn Eagle*, September 13, 1889.

65. *Pittsburgh Dispatch*, January 18, 1890; *Brooklyn Eagle*, July 9 and April 5, 1890.

66. *New York Times*, July 8, 1890.

67. *Sedalia Weekly Bazoo*, June 17, 1890; *Knoxville Journal*, November 13, 1892; *Evening Bulletin* (Maysville, Ky.), June 6, 1890; *New York Times*, November 26, 1892; *Forest, Stream, and Farm*, June 17, 1890.

68. Letters from Tanner to Capt. Jack Crawford, May 10, June 18, May 21, and June 28, 1890; May 12 and 24, 1891; September 7, 1890, folder 21, box 2, John W. Crawford Papers, McCracken Research Library, Buffalo Bill Historical Center, Cody, Wyoming.

69. Letter from Tanner to Harry Crawford, May 9, 1890, folder 21, box 2, Crawford Papers.

70. Quoted in *Louisiana Democrat*, October 16, 1889.

71. Letters from Tanner to Harry Crawford, September 7 and November 6, 1890, folder 21, box 2, Crawford Papers.

72. *Minneapolis Journal*, November 9, 1896.

73. *Pittsburgh Dispatch*, January 18, 1890; James Tanner Pension File, Certificate 17405, National Archives and Records Administration, Washington, D.C.

74. Tanner to Barrett, August 21, 1864, James Tanner Pension File, National Archives and Records Administration, Washington, D.C.

Chapter Five. The Most Celebrated GAR Man in the World

1. *Niagara Falls Gazette*, June 17, 1904.

2. *Life*, August 22, 1889; *New York Times*, July 28, 1889.

3. George A. Lofton, *Character Sketches; or, The Blackboard Mirror* (Nashville: Southwestern, 1898), 352; *Akron Daily Democrat*, August 9, 1901; *Columbia (S.C.) The State*, October 4, 1910; William Bayard Hale, "The Pension Carnival, Third Article," *World's Work* 21 (December 1910): 13734–35; "Tariff Reform and Extravagance," *Century Magazine* 83 (May 1912): 788.

4. Frederic L. Paxson, *The New Nation* (Boston: Houghton Mifflin, 1915), 172; William Dudley Foulke, *Politics and People: The Ordeal of Self-Government in America* (New York: Putnam, 1919), 51; "Observations on the Insane," *Quarterly: Representing the Minnesota Educational, Philanthropic, Correctional and Penal Institutions under the State Board of Control* (Minneapolis: State Board of Control, 1916), 84; Allan Nevins, *The Evening Post: A Century of Journalism* (New York: Boni & Liveright, 1922), 536; *Lehi (Utah) Sun*, March 2, 1922; *New York Times*, May 26, 1924, and November 2, 1927.

5. D. W. Brogan, *The American Political System* (London: H. Hamilton, 1933), 208–9; Robert A. Horn, *Groups and the Constitution* (Stanford, Calif.: Stanford University

Press, 1956), 162; Willard Walker, *The Veteran Comes Back* (New York: Dryden Press, 1944), 199.

6. *Houston Post*, August 1, 1899.

7. *Anaconda (Mont.) Standard*, September 15, 1891.

8. Eugene Field, "Peace Hath Its Victories," *Pocket Magazine* 1 (February 1896): 57–74.

9. Capt. James E. Smith, *A Famous Battery and Its Campaigns, 1861–64* (Washington, D.C.: W. H. Lowdermilk, 1892); *A Night with the 'Poet Scout': A Plain Talk* (New York: Funk & Wagnalls, 1886); Captain Jack Crawford, *The Poet Scout: A Book of Song and Story* (New York: Burr Printing House, 1889), 153.

10. *Ohio Poland-China Record*, vol. 12 (Dayton: Journal Book & Job Rooms, 1890), 152; *Standard Poland-China Record* (Maryville, Mo.: Standard Poland-China Record Association, 1890), 177; *American Hereford Record and Hereford Herd Book*, vol. 11 (Columbia, Mo.: American Hereford Cattle Breeders' Association, 1891); *Forty-Fourth Annual Report of the Ohio State Board of Agriculture* (Columbus, Ohio: Westbote, 1890), 159; Dave Wells, *History of the NE G. A. R. Posts*, http://www.civilwarmu seumnc.org/history%20GAR.html.

11. *Washington City Directory, 1899*, ancestry.com.

12. *Brooklyn Eagle*, October 4, 1891.

13. *Milwaukee Journal*, September 12, 1896; "Presidential Canvass of 1896," *Appleton's Annual Cyclopaedia and Register of Important Events of the Year, 1896*, 3rd ser., vol. 1 (New York: D. Appleton, 1896), 670.

14. *Kansas City Daily Journal*, October 6, 1896.

15. *Omaha World Herald*, September 29 and 30 and October 1, 1896.

16. *New York Sun*, October 31, 1896; *National Tribune*, September 20, 1900; *Washington Times*, July 22, 1904.

17. *New York Times*, March 16, 1904; Jacob Riis, *The Making of an American* (New York: Macmillan, 1922), 279.

18. *New York Sun*, January 10, 1904; *Philadelphia Inquirer*, September 11, 1905. This basic description of the register's position was published in the *Washington Evening Times*, April 4, 1900.

19. *New York Times*, November 1, 1895, April 1, 1896, and October 24, 1897.

20. *Rochester Democrat and Chronicle*, May 30, 1898.

21. *Watchman and Southron* (Sumter, S.C.), May 14, 1902; *Independent*, May 1, 1902.

22. *Brooklyn Eagle*, October 19, 1895; *Records of Members of the Grand Army of the Republic with a Complete Account of the Twentieth National Encampment* (San Francisco: H. S. Crocker, 1886), 136–37; *Rochester Democrat and Chronicle*, July 19, 1886.

23. *Brooklyn Eagle*, August 14, 1889; *Omaha World-Herald*, September 9, 1905.

24. *Kansas City Star*, September 12, 1905; *Duluth (Minn.) News Tribune*, September 13, 1905; John E. Gilman & William M. Olin, *Events at American House, Algonquin Club, Faneuil Hall, Mechanics Hall* (n.p., ca. 1906), William Olin Papers, Massachusetts

Historical Society (to see Groucho Marx singing "Everybody Works but Father," visit http://www.youtube.com/watch?v=0FeyAGn6690); letter from Capt. Jack Crawford to Tanner, September 8, 1905, folder 21, box 2, John W. Crawford Papers, McCracken Research Library, Buffalo Bill Historical Center, Cody, Wyoming.

25. *Charlotte Observer*, July 22, 1906.

26. *Charlotte Observer*, March 14, 1906.

27. *Roll of the 40th National Encampment of the Grand Army of the Republic* (Philadelphia: Town Printing, 1906), quote on 69.

28. *Minneapolis Journal*, August 15, 1906.

29. James Tanner, *Glimpses of Cobleskill: Schoharie County, New York, 1852–1927* (Cobleskill: Cobleskill Times, [1927]), 19; *Omaha Daily Bee*, September 11, 1887.

30. Mrs. Corporal Tanner, "Heroic Service, or Civil Service," *Acme Haversack* 3 (September 1889): 61.

31. *Brooklyn Eagle*, August 11, 1889, June 10 and November 11, 1887, December 31 and June 8, 1883, June 13, 1889.

32. *American Tribune*, December 1, 1887; *Brooklyn Eagle*, May 7, 1887, and March 24, 1888.

33. Clara Barton, *The Red Cross in Peace and War* (Washington, D.C.: American Historical Press, 1898), 398, 403.

34. *Brooklyn Eagle*, March 27, 1886.

35. *National Tribune*, April 18, 1889.

36. *Washington Sunday Herald and Weekly National Intelligencer*, April 26, 1891; *Brooklyn Eagle*, March 27, 1886; *Wilkes-Barre (Pa.) Times*, August 28, 1906; *Saint Paul Globe*, September 9, 1896; *Rochester Democrat and Chronicle*, January 7, 1904; *New York Times*, March 10, 1913; *Washington Herald*, April 14, 1913.

37. Tanner, *Glimpses of Cobleskill*, 21–22; *Minneapolis Journal*, June 30, 1906; *Salem (Ore.) Capital Journal*, July 4, 1906; *Washington Times*, July 1, 1906; James Tanner [to GAR post commanders], July 21, 1906, folder 21, box 2, John W. Crawford Papers.

38. *Confederate Veteran*, July 1906.

39. *Roll of the 40th National Encampment of the Grand Army of the Republic*, 99–101.

40. 1905 Washington City Directory; 1910 Census, Washington, District of Columbia, roll T624_150, p. 12B; 1920 Census, Washington, District of Columbia, roll T625_210, p. 2B; 1930 Census, Washington, District of Columbia, roll 293, p. 16B; all from Ancestry.com; *Washington Post*, June 24, 1913, and July 15, 1915.

41. *Philadelphia Inquirer*, November 28, 1915.

42. *Brooklyn Eagle*, April 5, 1917; *Washington Times*, October 1, 1918; *Morning Oregonian*, October 20, 1918.

43. *Washington Times*, June 6, 1917; *Morning Oregonian*, August 21, 1918.

44. *New York Times*, December 5, 1906; William M. McKinney, ed., *Federal Statutes, Annotated Supplement, 1909* (Northport, N.Y.: Edward Thompson, 1909), 57; "A Stellar Red Cross Meeting," *American Red Cross Magazine* 11 (January 1916): 15.

45. Corporal James Tanner, "Before Red Cross Days; or, Second Bull Run and the End of the War for Me," *American Red Cross Magazine* 11 (September 1916): 307; Grace Hathaway, *Fate Rides a Tortoise: A Biography of Ellen Spencer Mussey* (Chicago: John C. Winston, 1937), 116.

46. *Utica Morning Telegram*, June 25, 1921; *Schenectady Gazette*, June 25, 1921.

47. *Macon Telegraph*, April 4, 1911; *Washington Times*, May 3, 1918; *Duluth (Minn.) News Tribune*, July 12, 1920.

48. Tanner to Eva Reckhard, August 6, 1917, Buffalo Bill Online Archive, Buffalo Bill Historical Center, Cody, Wyoming, http://library.bbhc.org/cdm/printview /collection/BBOA/id/2119/type/singleitem; *Milwaukee Sentinel*, September 3, 1923.

49. *Milwaukee Sentinel*, September 3, 1923.

50. Ibid.; Marion F. Noyes, ed., *A History of Schoharie County* (Richmondville, N.Y.: Richmondville Phoenix, 1964), 111; *Los Angeles Daily Herald*, August 6, 1886; *Dallas Morning News*, April 26, 1906; Tanner, *Glimpses of Cobleskill*, 13–14.

51. *Brooklyn Eagle*, August 20, 1924.

52. *Iowa City Press-Citizen*, September 22, 1926.

53. Sergeant Fred C. Floyd, *History of the Fortieth (Mozart) Regiment, New York Volunteers* (Boston: F. H. Gilson, 1909), 362; James Tanner to James Jaycox, December 15, 1926, personal collection of Sabrina Ramoth.

54. Tanner to Jaycox, December 15, 1926.

55. *Journal of the Sixty-First National Encampment, Grand Army of the Republic, Grand Rapids, Michigan: House Document No. 67, Seventieth Congress, First Session* (Washington, D.C.: Government Printing Office, 1928), 78.

56. *Brooklyn Eagle*, April 26, 1888, and October 3, 1927; *Journal of the Sixty-Second National Encampment, Grand Army of the Republic, Denver, Colo., House Document No. 389, Seventieth Congress, Second Session* (Washington, D.C.: Government Printing Office, 1929), 279–81; *Utica Daily Press*, October 13, 1921.

57. *Rochester Democrat and Chronicle*, October 6, 1927; *Niagara Falls Gazette*, October 7, 1927; *Brooklyn Eagle*, October 3, 1927.

58. *Washington City Directory, 1939*, ancestry.com; *Washington Times*, September 3, 1904; *Code of Federal Regulations, Title 23—The President, 1936–1965: Consolidated Tables* (Washington, D.C.: Government Printing Office, 1970), 81; *Canandaigua New York Daily Messenger*, May 23, 1936; Michael Robert Patterson, "James Tanner, Corporal, United States Army," Arlington National Cemetery website, http://www .arlingtoncemetery.net/jtanner.htm; *Washington Post*, March 14, 1953.

59. *Journal of the Sixty-Second National Encampment*, 140, 218.

Epilogue and Conclusion

1. John Alexander, *Ghosts: Washington's Most Famous Ghost Stories* (Arlington, Va.: Washington Book Trading, 1988), 105–7.

2. *Niagara Falls Gazette*, October 6, 1927.

3. John Steinbeck, *East of Eden* (New York: Viking, 1952), 52.

4. *Abstract of General Orders and Proceedings of the Fifty-Third Annual Encampment, Department of New York, G. A. R.* (Albany: J. B. Lyon, 1919), 264.

5. Mark DeWolfe Howe, comp., *The Occasional Speeches of Justice Oliver Wendell Holmes* (Cambridge, Mass.: Harvard University Press, 1962), 15.

6. *Abstract of General Orders and Proceedings of the Fifty-Third Annual Encampment*, 270.

7. For a brisk, thorough biography of Captain Jack, see Darlis A. Miller, *Captain Jack Crawford: Buckskin Poet, Scout, and Showman* (Albuquerque: University of New Mexico Press, 1993).

8. For Buffalo Bill's place in American culture, see Joy S. Kasson, *Buffalo Bill's Wild West: Celebrity, Memory, and Popular History* (New York: Hill & Wang, 2000).

REFLECTION ON SOURCES AND
SELECTED BIBLIOGRAPHY

Every book poses its own research challenges. In this case, the first challenge was actually learning about James Tanner. I had "discovered" him while writing a very different book about veterans, *Sing Not War: The Lives of Union and Confederate Veterans in Gilded Age America*, but even then I knew little about him. Like most readers, and every historian I asked, I had little to go on. Inevitably, given what I came to know as Tanner's passions and experiences, the more I found out, the more I thought Tanner's life could illustrate a number of issues related not only to Civil War soldiers and veterans but also to the dramatic changes in the United States that took place in the decades following the Civil War.

My interest piqued, I encountered another obstacle: aside from a dozen or so letters written between 1889 and 1891 to his good friend Capt. John "Jack" Crawford and a single letter that found its way into a New Jersey attic, Tanner left virtually no papers—diaries, letters, or other personal documents—at least none in public archives. Such documents usually form the core of the evidence in the biography of a historical figure. So I had to look elsewhere.

Fortunately, Tanner's voice is not entirely absent from the public record, for the Corporal produced three personal narratives covering crucial phases of his life. He told of his childhood and early adulthood in *Glimpses of Cobleskill: Schoharie County, New York, 1852–1927* (Cobleskill, N.Y.: Cobleskill Times, [1927]). The most detailed description of his military service and treatment after his wounding was published in two parts: "Before Red Cross Days; or, Second Bull Run and the End of the War for Me," in the *American Red Cross Magazine* 11 (September 1916): 306–13, and (October 1916): 345–53. And the earliest known document produced by Tanner is the letter in which he described the long night he spent in the Petersen House on April 14, 1865: "The Assassination of President Lincoln, 1865," in the *American Historical Review* 29 (April 1924): 514–17. Also hints of Tanner's voice and condition appear in his thick pension file, which includes letters written and forms completed by Tanner in the 1860s and 1870s as well as testimony about his injuries from friends and officers (see James Tanner Pension File, certificate 17405, National Archives and Records Administration, Washington, D.C.).

A third obstacle is the fact that, aside from Tanner's brief appearances in various books and articles as described in the text, very little has been written about him. Despite his decades-long prominence, the only biography of Tanner is the admiring but fact-filled "The Career of Corporal James Tanner in War and Peace," which appears in *A Famous Battery and Its Campaigns, 1861–64*, by Capt. James E. Smith (Washington, D.C.: W. H. Lowdermilk, 1892). This curious compilation also includes an account of *Early Days in the Black Hills by Capt. Jack Crawford, the Poet Scout,* Tanner's good friend.

Due to the relative paucity of personal records and other sources, I had to rely on the emerging availability of primary-source websites hosted by historical societies, newspapers, government agencies, personal websites, and for-profit websites normally used by genealogists. Indeed, without the Internet, *America's Corporal* might have been an article but would never have been a book. Perhaps the most remarkable find was the letters from Tanner's hometown friend and army buddy Silas Shumway, which are available as the "Civil War Letters of the Shumway Bros. of Richmondville" on the genealogy website "Schoharie County NYGenWeb" (http://rootsweb.ancestry.com/~hnyschoha/shumwayletters.html). Other online resources helped bring the Corporal to life. Tanner made countless speeches at Grand Army of the Republic and other veterans' gatherings, which were frequently published in proceedings distributed to local chapters, state legislatures, and libraries. Today the surviving copies are scattered in libraries and archives, but many have been digitized and can be downloaded from Google Books, which also provided electronic versions of rare and unusual documents ranging from livestock registries to memoirs by forgotten Americans to obscure journals and magazines. Ancestry.com, a commercial website favored by genealogists, provided images of pages from the manuscript census and of city directories.

Newspapers probably appear in more citations in the notes to this book than any other kind of source. Veterans' newspapers provided context for much of Tanner's "veteranizing," but newspapers covered Tanner's every move. He loved talking to reporters, who in turn loved to provide long quotes from his informal comments and formal remarks. Until recently, getting access to this rich resource would have meant scrolling through hundreds of reels of microfilm, which, for someone like Tanner, would have been like searching for a needle in a haystack. A number of vast online archives of newspapers became a treasure-trove of information and opinion about this very public man. The most far-reaching is the "Chronicling America: Historic American Newspapers" site (http://chroniclingamerica.loc.gov/) at the Library of Congress, a still-expanding archive of images of millions of pages of newspapers from all over the United States. Gilded Age newspapers frequently copied (often without acknowledgment) articles from other papers, so it was not unusual for a Tanner speech or comment in New York to be reported in a paper from far-off Oregon. The subscription-only "American Periodicals Series Online" offers digitized issues of hundreds of magazines, some quite obscure, while the quirky "Old Fulton, NY, Postcards" genealogical website (http://www.fultonhistory.com/Fulton.html), although rather difficult to use, claims to contain over twenty million page images from New

York newspapers. A search for "Corporal Tanner" yields over five thousand hits. Finally, the newspaper that spent more column inches than any other on the Corporal, the *Brooklyn Eagle*, has found a web-based home created by the Brooklyn Public Library (http://www.brooklynpubliclibrary.org/); easy to use and reliable, it is an indispensable source for studying Tanner's two decades in Brooklyn—and beyond.

Selected Bibliography

Tanner came from a long-settled but still very rural area of New York that, like Tanner, has had very little written about it. Conversely, his adopted home of Brooklyn has a long and rich historiography. I relied on several books to provide geographical contexts for the places most identified with Tanner:

Noyes, Marion F., ed. *A History of Schoharie County*. Richmondville, N.Y.: Richmondville Phoenix, 1964.

Ostrander, Stephen M. *A History of the City of Brooklyn and Kings County*. Edited by Alexander Black. 2 vols. Brooklyn: n.p., 1894.

Roscoe, William E. *History of Schoharie County, New York, with Illustrations and Biographical Sketches of Some of Its Prominent Men and Pioneers*. Syracuse: D. Mason, 1882.

Rosenwaike, Ira. *Population History of New York City*. Syracuse: Syracuse University Press, 1972.

Schroth, Raymond A. *The Eagle and Brooklyn: A Community Newspaper, 1841–1955*. Westport, Conn.: Greenwood Press, 1974.

Syrett, Harold Coffin. *The City of Brooklyn, 1865–1898: A Political History*. New York: Columbia University Press, 1944; New York: AMS Press, 1968.

The military side of the Civil War is obviously the most written-about subject in American history. Among the most useful books on the lives of Civil War soldiers and the campaigns in which Tanner participated are the following:

Barton, Michael, and Larry M. Logue, eds. *The Civil War Soldier: A Historical Reader*. New York: New York University Press, 2002.

Brasher, Glenn David. *The Peninsula Campaign and the Necessity of Emancipation: African Americans and the Fight for Freedom*. Chapel Hill: University of North Carolina Press, 2012.

Gallagher, Gary, ed. *The Richmond Campaign of 1862: The Peninsula and the Seven Days*. Chapel Hill: University of North Carolina Press, 2000.

Hennessy, John. *Return to Bull Run: The Campaign and Battle of Second Manassas*. New York: Simon & Schuster, 1993.

Linderman, Gerald. *Embattled Courage: The Experience of Combat in the Civil War*. New York: Free Press, 1987.

Martin, David G. *The Second Bull Run Campaign: July–August 1862*. New York: Da Capo Press, 1997.

Mitchell, Reid. *Civil War Soldiers: Their Expectations and Their Experiences*. New York: Viking, 1988.

Patchan, Scott C. *Second Manassas: Longstreet's Attack and the Struggle for Chinn Ridge*. Washington, D.C.: Potomac Books, 2011.

Tanner was very much a product of the Gilded Age, a period that has inspired a vast literature on topics ranging from industrialization to geographic expansion, from political corruption to social reform, from clashes over cultural values to the gradually shifting roles of men and women during the era, and, finally, the ways in which Americans remembered and forgot the Civil War. Tanner's life was touched by a number of these issues; the most important books for my efforts to fit the Corporal into his times are the following:

Blight, David W. *Race and Reunion: The Civil War in American Memory*. Cambridge, Mass.: Harvard University Press, 2001.

Calhoun, Charles W. *From Bloody Shirt to Full Dinner Pail: The Transformation of Politics and Governance in the Gilded Age*. New York: Hill & Wang, 2010.

Carnes, Mark C. "Middle-Class Men and the Solace of Fraternal Ritual." In *Meanings for Manhood: Constructions of Masculinity in Victorian America*, edited by Mark C. Carnes and Clyde Griffen, 37–66. Chicago: University of Chicago Press, 1990.

Edwards, Rebecca. *New Spirits: Americans in the Gilded Age, 1865–1905*. New York: Oxford University Press, 2006.

Foster, Gaines M. *Ghosts of the Confederacy: Defeat, the Lost Cause, and the Emergence of the New South, 1865 to 1913*. New York: Oxford University Press, 1987.

Hilkey, Judy. *Character Is Capital: Success Manuals and Manhood in Gilded Age America*. Chapel Hill: University of North Carolina Press, 1997.

Janney, Caroline E. *Remembering the Civil War: Reunion and the Limits of Reconciliation*. Chapel Hill: University of North Carolina Press, 2013.

Kasson, Joy S. *Buffalo Bill's Wild West: Celebrity, Memory, and Popular History*. New York: Hill & Wang, 2000.

Lusky, Brian. *On the Make: Clerks and the Quest for Capital in Nineteenth-Century New York*. New York: New York University Press, 2010.

Silber, Nina. *The Romance of Reunion: Northerners and the South, 1865–1900*. Chapel Hill: University of North Carolina Press, 1993.

Simpson, John A. *S. A. Cunningham and the Confederate Heritage*. Athens: University of Georgia Press, 1994.

Skocpol, Theda. *Protecting Soldiers and Mothers: The Political Origins of Social Policy in the United States*. Cambridge, Mass.: Harvard University Press, 1992.

Stott, Richard. *Jolly Fellows: Male Milieus in Nineteenth-Century America*. Baltimore: Johns Hopkins University Press, 2009.

Summers, Mark Wahlgren. *The Gilded Age: or, The Hazard of New Functions.* Upper Saddle River, N.J.: Prentice Hall, 1997.
Wilson, Charles Reagan. *Baptized in Blood: The Religion of the Lost Cause, 1865–1920.* Athens: University of Georgia Press, 1980.

The most important sources for my description of the medical circumstances in which Tanner found himself include two primary works—by a doctor who also experienced Second Bull Run and by a nurse who began working at Tanner's hospital not long after he left—and several books and articles by historians, economists, and other scholars on the physical and psychological effects of wounds and war service. The primary sources are the following:

Keen, W. W. "Surgical Reminiscences of the Civil War." *Transactions and Studies of the College of Physicians of Philadelphia,* 3rd ser., 27 (1905): 96–101.
Woolsey, Jane Stuart. *Hospital Days: Reminiscence of a Civil War Nurse.* Edited by Daniel John Hoisington. Roseville, Minn.: Edinborough Press, 1996.

The secondary sources include the following:

Anderson, Judith. "'Haunted Minds': The Impact of Combat Exposure on the Mental and Physical Health of Civil War Veterans." In Schmidt and Hasegawa, *Years of Change and Suffering,* 151–52.
Dean, Eric. *Shook over Hell: Post-Traumatic Stress, Vietnam, and the Civil War.* Cambridge, Mass.: Harvard University Press, 1999.
Figg, Laurann, and Jane Farrell-Beck. "Amputation in the Civil War: Physical and Social Dimensions." *Journal of the History of Medicine and Allied Sciences* 48 (October 1993): 454–75.
Flannery, Michael A. *Civil War Pharmacy: A History of Drugs, Drug Supply and Provision, and Therapeutics for the Union and Confederacy.* New York: Haworth Press, 2004.
Gerber, David A., ed. *Disabled Veterans in History.* Ann Arbor: University of Michigan Press, 2000.
Hasegawa, Guy R. *Mending Broken Soldiers: The Union and Confederate Programs to Supply Artificial Limbs.* Carbondale: Southern Illinois University Press, 2012.
Jordan, Brian Matthew. "'Living Monuments': Union Veteran Amputees and the Embodied Memory of the Civil War." *Civil War History* 57 (June 2011): 121–52.
Lee, Chulhee. "Health, Information, and Migration: Geographic Mobility of Union Army Veterans, 1860–1880." *Journal of Economic History* 68 (September 2008): 862–99.
———. "Wealth Accumulation and the Health of Union Army Veterans, 1860–1870." *Journal of Economic History* 65 (June 2005): 352–85.
Mihm, Stephen. "'A Limb Which Shall Be Presentable in Polite Society': Prosthetic Technologies in the Nineteenth Century." In *Artificial Parts, Practical Lives:*

Modern Histories of Prosthetics, edited by Katherine Ott, David Serlin, and Stephen Mihm, 282–98. New York: New York University Press, 2002.

Nelson, Megan Kate. *Ruin Nation: Destruction and the American Civil War.* Athens: University of Georgia Press, 2012.

Nielsen, Kim E. *A Disability History of the United States.* Boston: Beacon Press, 2012.

Rutkow, Ira M. *Bleeding Blue and Gray: Civil War Surgery and the Evolution of American Medicine.* New York: Random House, 2005.

Schmidt, James M., and Guy R. Hasegawa, eds. *Years of Change and Suffering: Modern Perspectives on Civil War Medicine.* Roseville, Minn.: Edinborough Press, 2009.

Wegner, Ansley Herring. "Phantom Pain: Civil War Amputation and North Carolina's Maimed Veterans." *North Carolina Historical Review* 75 (July 1998): 286–96.

Williams-Searle, John. "Cold Charity." In *The New Disability History: American Perspectives*, edited by Paul K. Longmore and Lauri Umansky, 157–86. New York: New York University Press, 2001.

Finally, although historians have covered virtually every aspect of the experiences of Civil War soldiers as *soldiers* in great detail, much less has been written about them as *veterans*. Perhaps inspired by the presence of hundreds of thousands of veterans of the Iraq and Afghanistan wars—many disabled or suffering from posttraumatic stress—historians and economists have begun to fill this historiographical gap. Among the most important secondary sources that provided context for Tanner's experiences as a veteran are the following:

Blanck, Peter. "Civil War Pensions and Disability," *Ohio State Law Journal* 62 (2001): 109–238.

Blanck, Peter, and Chen Song. "Civil War Pension Attorneys and Disability Politics." *University of Michigan Journal of Law Reform* 35 (Fall 2001–Winter 2002): 137–216.

———. "'Never Forget What They Did Here': Civil War Pensions for Gettysburg Union Army Veterans and Disability in Nineteenth-Century America." *William and Mary Law Review* 44 (February 2003): 1109–71.

Cimbala, Paul A., and Randall M. Miller, eds. *Union Soldiers and the Northern Homefront.* New York: Fordham University Press, 2002.

Clarke, Frances M. *War Stories: Suffering and Sacrifice in the Civil War North.* Chicago: University of Chicago Press, 2011.

Grant, Susan-Mary. "Reimagined Communities: Union Veterans and the Reconstruction of American Nationalism." *Nations and Nationalism* 14 (2008): 498–519.

Hess, Earl J. *The Union Soldier in Battle: Enduring the Ordeal of Combat.* Lawrence: University Press of Kansas, 1997.

Johnson, Russell L. *Warriors into Workers: The Civil War and the Formation of Urban-Industrial Society in a Northern City.* New York: Fordham University Press, 2003.

Kelly, Patrick J. *Creating a National Home: Building the Veterans' Welfare State, 1860–1900.* Cambridge, Mass.: Harvard University Press, 1997.

Linderman, Gerald F. *Embattled Courage: The Experience of Combat in the American Civil War.* New York: Free Press, 1987.

Logue, Larry M. *To Appomattox and Beyond: The Civil War Soldier in War and Peace.* Chicago: Ivan R. Dee, 1996.

Logue, Larry M., and Michael Barton, eds. *The Civil War Veteran: A Historical Reader.* New York: New York University Press, 2007.

Marten, James. *Sing Not War: The Lives of Union and Confederate Veterans in Gilded Age America.* Chapel Hill: University of North Carolina Press, 2011.

McClintock, Megan J. "Civil War Pensions and the Reconstruction of Union Families." *Journal of American History* 83 (September 1996): 456–80.

McConnell, Stuart. *Glorious Contentment: The Grand Army of the Republic, 1865–1900.* Chapel Hill: University of North Carolina Press, 1992.

Neff, John R. *Honoring the Civil War Dead: Commemoration and the Problem of Reconciliation.* Lawrence: University Press of Kansas, 2005.

Oliver, John William. *History of the Civil War Military Pensions, 1861–1885.* Bulletin of the University of Wisconsin, History Series, vol. 4. Madison: University of Wisconsin, 1917.

Shaffer, Donald R. *After the Glory: The Struggles of Black Civil War Veterans.* Lawrence: University Press of Kansas, 2004.

Sinisi, Kyle S. "Veterans as Political Activists: The Kansas Grand Army of the Republic, 1880–1893." *Kansas History* 14 (Summer 1991): 89–99.

United States Civil Service Commission. *History of Veterans Preference in Federal Employment, 1865–1955.* Washington, D.C.: United States Civil Service Commission, 1955.

Wylie, Alexander. *Veteran and Affiliated Organizations Arising from the Civil War.* Mendota, Ill.: Mendota Reporter, 1966.

Yott, Robert E. *From Soldiers' Home to Medical Center: A Glance at the 125 Year History of the Bath Soldiers' Home.* Bath, N.Y.: Robert Yott, 2006.

INDEX

UnCivil Wars

Weirding the War: Tales from the Civil War's Ragged Edges
edited by Stephen Berry

Ruin Nation: Destruction and the American Civil War
by Megan Kate Nelson

America's Corporal: James Tanner in War and Peace
by James Marten